seasonings

FLAVOURS OF THE SOUTHERN GULF ISLANDS

seasonings

FLAVOURS OF THE SOUTHERN GULF ISLANDS

Andrea & David Spalding

Harbour Publishing

Dedication

For Georgina Montgomery, a dear friend and collaborator,
who so generously passed this project to us

Harbour Publishing Co. Ltd.
P.O. Box 219, Madeira Park, BC V0N 2H0
www.harbourpublishing.com

Cover photograph and food photography by Christina Symons
Edited by Sarah Weber
Indexed by Ellen Hawman
Cover design by Anna Comfort O'Keeffe
Text design by Roger Handling, Terra Firma Digital Arts
Printed on FSC-certified, chlorine-free paper made with 10% post-consumer
    fibres
Printed and bound in Canada

Canada Council   Conseil des Arts
for the Arts   du Canada

BRITISH COLUMBIA
ARTS COUNCIL
An agency of the Province of British Columbia

Harbour Publishing acknowledges financial support from the Government of
Canada through the Canada Book Fund and the Canada Council for the Arts,
and from the Province of British Columbia through the BC Arts Council and the
Book Publishing Tax Credit.

Library and Archives Canada Cataloguing in Publication

Spalding, Andrea   Seasonings : flavours of the southern Gulf Islands / Andrea
and David A.E. Spalding.

Includes index. ISBN 978-1-55017-569-1

    1. Cooking—British Columbia—Gulf Islands. 2. Cooking, Canadian—
British Columbia style. I. Spalding, David A. E., 1937–   II. Title.

TX715.6.S62 2012   641.59711'28   C2012-904294-3

Additional photo credits:

All Canada Photos—Romain Bale, 208;
    Chris Cheadle, 2–3, 9, 22, 67, 178, 203;
    Boomer Jerritt, 12; Dean van't Schip,
    125; Michael Wheatley, 14, 126, 177

Teresa Carle-Sanders—17, 46

Anna Comfort O'Keeffe—11, 72 (top),
    81, 131, 136 (left)

David Dossor and Cherie Thiessen—134

Galiano Inn—60, 61 (bottom, Kent
    Kallberg photo), 66

Gulf Islands Brewing—78, 118 (bottom)

Hastings House—221

iStockphoto—7 (middle; bottom), 19
    (bottom), 27 (top), 41, 57, 92, 117, 146,
    162, 170, 209, 222

Kikuchi family—152, back cover (kids)

Charles Mardres—31

Jan Mangan (jmangan@got.net)—72
    (bottom), 88, 109 (top), 136 (right),
    160, 164 (top), 165, 214, 229

Poets Cove Resort—171, 172

Salt Spring Apple Festival—164 (bottom)

Salt Spring Vineyards—118 (top left)

Christina Symons—5, 6, 7 (top), 8 (top;
    middle) 28, 34, 38, 52, 64, 71, 82, 90,
    98, 104, 106, 130, 144, 150, 180, 192,
    204

Howard White—47, 69 (top), 70 (top;
    middle left; bottom row), 80 (top), 107,
    184

Contents

SUMMER

Summer Beautiful Beginnings

Summer Interesting Entrées

Summer Simply Sides

Summer Fabulous Finishes

Exploring Southern Gulf Island Wines

Celebrating Summer

FALL

Fall Beautiful Beginnings

Fall Interesting Entrées

Fall Simply Sides

Fall Fabulous Finishes

Celebrating Fall

WINTER

Winter Beautiful Beginnings

Winter Interesting Entrées

Winter Simply Sides

Winter Fabulous Finishes

Celebrating Winter

APPENDICES

Acknowledgements

Many people were involved in the making of this book. Those whose stories we have shared are named in the text, but some went out of their way to help with this project.

Special thanks to the four chefs who generously made time to plan and share a seasonal menu with us:

Steve Boudreau of Poets Cove Resort, Pender Island
Theresa Carle-Sanders of islandvittles.com
Dean Hillier of Galiano Inn, Galiano Island
Bruce Wood of Bruce's Kitchen, Salt Spring Island
Also Richard Massey of Galiano Inn for his insights on Gulf Island wines

Our daughter, chef Penny Spalding, tirelessly helped testing recipes and was always at the end of the phone for advice

BC Ferries generously supported our food-related travels

The following provided delightful accommodation, delicious meals, abundant information, and assistance in networking in their communities:

Conny Norden of Galiano Inn
Ed Andrusiak and Sher O'Hara, Galiano
John and Helen O'Brian, Mayne
Joanne and Dev McIntyre, Salt Spring Vineyards B&B
Margriet Ruurs, Between the Covers B&B Salt Spring

Last but not least, major thanks to our fearless editor, Sarah Weber, who tackled complex recipes with humour and patience, and Harbour's delightfully supportive Anna Comfort O'Keeffe, without whom none of this would have happened.

Foreword

Sit among the poppies on Saturna Island.

We never knew you could smell and taste the seasons until we came to live on Pender, one of the Southern Gulf Islands. In our previous life in the city, the pervading smell was the same year-round—exhaust fumes. Here, the air is like wine and titillates our senses a little differently each day. Today, winter's crisp smell of salt and cedar is tempered with a tinge of woodsmoke. We write on our laptops, within reach of the radiance from the woodstove, and the aroma of the lamb stew simmering on top gradually pervades the room. Despite revelling in this comfort, we passionately long for the warmth of a summer sun.

This cookbook is filled with passion. Passion about small islands, passion about island food and the passion Gulf Islanders apply to growing, cooking and sharing it no matter the season.

Previous page: Browning Harbour, Pender Island.

Western Canada's Southern Gulf Islands are small emerald gems scattered across the Salish Sea between British Columbia's mainland and Vancouver Island. Salt Spring, Pender, Mayne, Galiano and Saturna Islands are a small group connected by BC Ferries' main Tsawwassen to Swartz Bay routes. They are our own beloved community, and we invite you to explore them with us.

Passion is needed when living on a small island, for one must embrace and honour Mother Nature while dealing with human needs for food and water, shelter and waste management. (This means no cursing when a tree falls and there is a power outage. Like today!)

All five islands have some version of the general store where people can purchase food supplies, but island diets are augmented by small farms, acreages and individual garden plots, lovingly carved out of the forest. They increasingly produce a dazzling variety of organic produce, from fields of humble potatoes to exotic olive groves.

Growing food has caught on. Even the most urban islander grows a few herbs on the deck, out of reach of marauding deer. Island acreages are peppered with tiny, creatively fenced vegetable plots where staples such as zucchinis and tomatoes flourish in sunny corners. Many gardeners add to both their food supplies and incomes by selling surplus herbs and veggies, as well as flowers, at roadside stands. More serious growers attend weekly farmers' markets.

A grande coffee cup, Gulf Island style.

Each island has its own distinct flavour, but all share a passionate, and often vocal, interest in food and its production in what some islanders laughingly refer to as "our 100-foot diet." Visitors are also becoming aware of the amazing varieties of homegrown, organic, sustainable food and wine produced here. Farmers' market veggies sell out early, and there are lineups for the crab boat. The Slow Food/Slow Island movement is gaining popularity. Since food is produced here all year, not just in the summer months, we have rediscovered the joys of roasted winter root vegetables and the warm comfort of Gulf Island lamb stew.

Individual islands manifest their interest in food in unique ways. Saturna, the island with the smallest population, throws the biggest public party once a year with its famous Saturna Island Lamb Barbeque. Salt Spring, the largest island, has two weekly markets, the Saturday market and the Tuesday market. Galiano Island has a vibrant year-round community food program and community greenhouse. Mayne Island has an award-winning community garden and is the home of a cheese maker of international repute, who travels around teaching the art of homemade cheeses. As for Pender, where we live, an online chef shares wonderful recipes for island food through her blog. And that's just to whet your appetite!

On the Southern Gulf Islands you can dine on local delights at high-end resorts, shop at farmers' markets or roadside "honesty stands," visit coffee roasters in the woods, sip local wines at the vineyards or forage in hedges to glean delicious unsprayed blackberries.

So join us in celebrating Southern Gulf Island food through these stories and recipes. They are only a sampling of the food available here, for unfortunately there isn't room in this book to include every producer or favourite dish. This means you can visit the islands and make wonderful foodie discoveries for yourself. Explore our local products; they are fresh, organic, sustainable and delicious. Your support of island farmers helps

Merlot
05/97

them produce more and keeps prices reasonable. Growing organic is expensive and the local market is small, but if every islander and visitor alike vowed to spend ten to twenty dollars a week, throughout the year, on local organic food, the prices would tumble, the varieties increase and our island farming economy blossom.

Your support of island organic products keeps our environment clean and safe and maintains your health. The pleasure gained in exploring the delights of local food is life enhancing. Then, when your basket is full, use these recipes to treat your taste buds to a passionate explosion of seasonal flavour.

Bon appétit,

Andrea and David

Pender Island, 2012

Opposite: Merlot grapes await harvest on Saturna Island.

Spring

The Delight of Foraging and Planting

While most of Canada is gripped by snow and ice, a wet spring creeps over the Southern Gulf Islands, and it starts early, as January snowdrops carpet dormant orchards. February brings salmonberry blossoms, eagerly sought out by rufous hummingbirds in March. In April, eagles line Active Pass, the narrow passage between Mayne and Galiano Islands. These raptors watch for fish, food for their nesting mates and young. The islands' human inhabitants also wait for the fish runs, while optimistically using garden forks to poke and prod the sodden earth. We gather in the remaining winter root vegetables, and crop kale and chard in between attacking rose bushes with pruning shears. Despite the cold, watery sun and damp air, we delight in our cool weather, loving the salad greens already sprouting in a sheltered tub on the deck.

The coming of spring brings a bustle of activity. Organic "winter cooked" compost and leaf mould are spread on the newly dug vegetable beds, and buds are anxiously checked on the orchard branches. Our pantry shelves, down to a few jars of canned pears and peaches made last fall, are spring cleaned. The bottom can be glimpsed in the freezer, once full of frozen blackberries, strawberries, applesauce and Gulf Island beef, pork and world-famous lamb. It's time to defrost and take stock.

We welcome the sight of tiny lambs gamboling in the fields. They are beautiful and we always photograph them. But let's be realistic: we hope the spring rains produce rich grassy pastures. We can still enjoy the lambs' beauty while understanding that these creatures will be next winter's rosemary-flavoured dinner. Still dreaming of future food, we plant our seeds and gather in the islands' first spring crop—nettles!

Victor Reece's Bear Mother poles welcome visitors to Pender's Community Hall.

Middens: Remains of Ancient Feasts

For over 6,000 years the Southern Gulf Islands have been home to several Pacific Northwest First Nations. Extensive evidence of their early habitation can be seen at the heads of coves and on beaches in the form of middens.

Middens are layered mounds of discarded shells, fire ashes and fish bones, and sometimes include skeletal remains and artifacts such as fishing spears and net weights. Today most look like ordinary banks, as they are overgrown with grasses and other vegetation. But where waves have cut into a bank and revealed layer upon layer of different shells, a midden is easy to identify.

These mounds are treasured and protected. They are important sites telling of ancient feasts, built up after thousands of years of fishing and feasting, for "when the tide is out the table is set," say the Elders.

All middens are protected archeological sites, so don't dig into them. But do enjoy the site, knowing you walk in the footsteps of the ancestors who like you enjoyed the shellfish and salmon caught in this beautiful area.

Two of the best places to see middens are Montague Harbour on Galiano Island and Medicine Beach on Pender Island.

Steamed Shellfish

Shellfish from these waters have been feasted on for thousands of years. Steaming them is one of the easiest and most traditional ways to cook them. The only things that have changed are our stoves and cook pots. Serve this dish with warm artisan bread to mop up the juices.

Makes 4 appetizer servings, 2 main servings

> 2 lbs (900 gr) assorted clams and mussels, and swimming scallops
> 1 Tbsp (15 mL) oil
> 4 shallots, quartered
> 2 large cloves garlic, chopped
> 1 bay leaf
> 1 bottle dry white Gulf Island wine
> Handful chopped fresh cilantro, parsley or dill
> Salt and pepper

Scrub the outsides of the shellfish. Pull the beard off the mussels and discard.

Heat oil gently in a wok (or Dutch oven). Sauté the shallots and garlic over low heat until the shallots are soft and translucent, taking care not to let the garlic burn.

Add bay leaf, wine, cilantro, and salt and pepper, and bring mixture to a boil.

Add the shellfish. Cover wok, adjust heat to medium and steam approximately 10 minutes, until shells open. Discard any that don't open.

Spoon shellfish into bowls, and divide the broth between them.

Safety Tip: Watch for Open Shells

Before you scrub the shellfish, check them carefully and discard any that do not close when tapped with finger—as it means that they are dead. Cook only tightly closed shellfish, and discard any that do not open during cooking.

Safety Tip: Red Tide Warnings

Sadly, gone are the days when one could simply pick oysters, mussels and clams off the beach. Now pollution and red tide are hazards. Despite its name, red tide, a toxic algal bloom, is not always visible. So be safe, heed the warnings that Fisheries and Oceans Canada posts, and buy your shellfish from fishing boats or stores.

Wild and Free: Stinging Nettles

Don't panic, we're not crazy. Nettles taste like spinach. In fact, most people cannot tell the difference!

It all comes down to how you view things. Nettles, which to many people are noxious weeds, are considered a gourmet treat on the Southern Gulf Islands. There is even a festival to honour them.

Nettles are the first free food of spring. The tender green leaves are full of vitamins and minerals. Don't worry about the sting; cooking neutralizes it. The only problem with nettles is collecting them.

Each ragged-edged leaf is covered in fine stinging hairs. Brushing bare skin against them causes a burning itch, so dress for the job—wear rubber boots, long pants, a long-sleeved shirt and sturdy gardening gloves.

Take several bags or large baskets, and scissors, when you go foraging. Clip only the top three to four inches (7.6–10 cm) from the new growth. Old nettles are tough and stringy, so use them only for nettle tea.

Wear protective clothing and sturdy gloves when harvesting nettles.

Collect lots because, like spinach, nettles cook down. Don't worry about picking them—they are a renewable resource.

At home, use rubber gloves to strip the leaves from the stems. Wilt the leaves as you would spinach. Discard the stems in your compost where they will help break it down.

Once wilted, the leaves can be handled normally. Squeeze out excess water and use the wilted leaves in any recipe calling for spinach or chard. They also freeze well.

Nettlefest

Thought we were teasing about a festival to honour the nettle? Here is the invitation we received for Galiano Island's spring 2011 Nettlefest celebration:

> Let's begin the day gathering in a wooded area lush with nettles. There we will fill bags and baskets and return to cook, community kitchen style, nettle soup, nettle buns and nettle spanakopita. A full-on island potluck follows with all manner of song and story built around our guest of honour, The Nettle. Young and old will find a place in this day of celebrating community and nature.

Who could resist?

Forager's Soup

This easy, super-nutritious and delicious spring soup has nettles as its base but also incorporates other woodland greens, such as sorrel, wild onion and lamb's quarters. Versions of it are made at Galiano's Nettlefest, found in Galiano's community cookbook and referenced in pioneer histories from the other islands. It's fun to forage in the woodlands, but if you are hesitant about identifying wild edibles (other than the obvious nettle), take a knowledgeable friend with you. Alternatively, forage in your garden and use a selection of chard, parsley, kale, chickweed and chives. You can also make this soup using only nettles.

Makes 4 to 6 servings

2 Tbsp (30 mL) butter
1 onion, chopped
½ lb (227 gr) fresh foraged mixed greens—sorrel, wild onion, chickweed, lamb's quarters, etc. (or garden greens)
6 cups (1.4 L) rich chicken or vegetable broth (add extra if needed)
1 large clove garlic, minced
1 lb (454 gr) potatoes, peeled, diced and cooked
2 cups (475 mL) wilted stinging nettle leaves
1 cup (250 mL) heavy cream
Salt and pepper
Dash hot sauce (optional)
1 cup (250 mL) grated sharp cheddar cheese
Freshly grated nutmeg

In a large pot, melt the butter. Add onion and sauté until soft and translucent.

Wash and chop mixed greens. Add them to the pot, and stir gently until wilted.

Add the stock, garlic, potato and nettles. Combine gently.

Bring mixture to a boil. Reduce heat and simmer for 20 minutes until greens are soft and tender. Remove from heat and cool 5 minutes.

Purée soup with an immersion blender, or in small batches in a blender or food processer. Add extra stock if needed to thin.

Return soup to pot, reheat (do not boil) and stir in cream. Season with salt and pepper, and stir in hot sauce if using.

Ladle into bowls, and garnish with grated cheese and a sprinkle of grated nutmeg.

Cheese Please

The attendees in the cheese-making class are spellbound as guerrilla cheese maker David Rotsztain upends the simple yogurt tub he'd earlier poked holes in and holds up a fledgling Camembert cheese.

And therein lies the magic. Cheese making is done quietly, without fanfare or special equipment, and the message is simple—you too can make cheese.

David (pronounced "Daveed") is a cheese maker with a mission—to bring the long lost art of cheese making back into the home kitchen.

As a cheese maker, David has access to raw milk, particularly during springtime lambing and calving. Most home cooks in Canada don't, however, so when teaching he works with what's available. All the cheeses demonstrated in his class were made from store-bought organic milk and yogurt. The utensils were simple: heavy-based cooking pots, sieves and muslin, and homemade moulds, such as coffee filters and yogurt containers. David brings a lot of love and respect for the milk to the process; as he talks, his hands never stop caressing the sides of the pots to check the temperature or gently jiggling them to check for set.

David lives on Mayne Island in a small cob house. He supports his cheese-making habit by teaching the techniques across North America and farming in his spare time. He lives what he teaches, constantly experimenting with small batches of cheese and ageing them in his own version of a "cheese cave"—a converted fridge. He shares his products with family, friends and neighbours. The cheese artist is not allowed to sell his art; Canadian regulations regarding cheese making allow sales only from commercial operations.

So why does he do it? David's passion is living a healthy sustainable lifestyle and teaching others how to do the same. He does this by demonstrating the simple act of making cheese, a basic food for which recipes are thousands of years old, the techniques employed belonging to everyone. How could we forget this life skill? How wonderful to rediscover it!

Top: David Rotsztain demonstrates the curd stage of cheese making.

Above: Cream cheese can be flavoured with a variety of ingredients, such as garlic and chopped jalapeño.

David Rotsztain's Simple Cream Cheese Ball

Safety Tip: Cleanliness Is Next to Cheesiness

Cleanliness is always important when handling food, but especially important in cheese making. Organic or raw milk may contain bacteria because it hasn't been overly processed. Before making cheese, sterilize countertops, any equipment you use and your hands.

As I watched David demonstrating this, I was flooded with memories. I knew how to do it. I had stood on a stool as a child and watched my mother make what she called "cream cheese" from sour milk. In postwar inner-city Manchester, England, no one threw food away, especially milk. Since we had no fridge, Mum regularly made cream cheese. Salt and pepper were all that flavoured ours. My mouth watered at the memory. I couldn't believe I had forgotten it.

To make this cheese, you'll need a square of fine muslin—part of a worn pillowcase or sheet works well. Do not use store-bought cheesecloth, as the weave is too open.

Instead of making one cheese ball, as described below, you can also make many small ones and store them in flavoured olive oil.

Makes a 5 inch (12 cm) cheese ball

> 1 quart (1 L) organic full-cream thick Greek-style yogurt
> Salt
> Flavouring of your choice—finely chopped garlic, hot peppers, dried tomato, olives, etc.
> Dried *fines herbes** and edible flowers

Pour the yogurt onto the square of muslin, gather the corners together without squeezing the yogurt, twist the ends of the cloth and tie them over the handle of a wooden spoon.

Rest the wooden spoon across the rim of a deep pot so the bag of yogurt is suspended and hangs down inside. It should not touch the liquid draining into the pot.

Leave it on the counter for 1 or 2 days to drip. The longer you allow the cheese to drain, the longer it will keep.

Unwrap the cheese, mix in salt to taste and add any flavouring you fancy. Rewrap and hang again for a few more hours. The salt will extract more whey from the cheese and also improve its flavour.

Unwrap the cheese ball and roll it in herbs and edible flowers.

Store, wrapped in plastic, in the fridge. Consume within 4 to 10 days.

Tip: Cheese making produces whey. Do not throw this out. Use it as the liquid when baking scones or bread, or in soups and stews. If you are not doing any baking, water your garden veggies with whey, which is full of nutrients.

* A mix of finely chopped fresh herbs, often including chervil, chives, parsley and tarragon.

Wild West Coast Salmon and Halibut

Canada's west coast has been prized for its abundant fish for thousands of years. First Nations people of the area were known as "the People of the Salmon."

Today, due to the rising human population and poor fishing practices, most wild fish stocks are not as plentiful as they once were. In an effort to protect fish, rules and regulations are in place, fishing licences are required and fishing is allowed only in certain seasons.

There are several distinct species of West Coast salmon, which vary in colour, from pale pink to deep red, as well as flavour. All are delicious. The fishing season for each species also varies:

Spring (chinook) salmon, can be caught year-round.

Coho season is June to October.

Chum season is late June to October.

Pink season is early July to the end of September.

Sockeye season is May to the end of August.

In recent years, farms for raising Atlantic salmon have been set up along the BC coast. Unfortunately, fish farms have increased risks for native salmon species, as disease is rife among farmed salmon because large numbers are kept in a small enclosure. Evidence suggests that parasites and diseases from fish farms are spreading to wild salmon populations.

Halibut, the largest flatfish in the world, is currently fished year-round along the west coast of Canada. This fishery is considered sustainable. It employs a hook and line method, and therefore has a minimal impact on the sea bottom. Halibut is a highly prized, firm-fleshed white fish that needs little seasoning. It is delicious steamed, grilled or fried, but does not smoke well as it has very little fat content.

Gulf Islanders generally are very concerned about the origin of the fish they eat. If they have not caught it themselves, they prefer wild fish and often consult the SeaChoice seafood guide for information about the sustainability of their choices. Some chefs like to be able to trace the source of individual tagged fish and so purchase from PASCO Seafood Enterprises' Coastal Waters product line (see "Sources" section, page 234).

Harriet's Gravlax with Mustard Sauce

Opposite: Fishing from a skiff between Salt Spring and Portland Islands.

The run of spring salmon is eagerly awaited on the West Coast. Springs—also known as chinook salmon—make their way to our waters as early as March. A favourite West Coast way to serve this salmon is in the form of gravlax, and it is found on many restaurant menus. However, it is rarely prepared at home, except by British Columbians of Scandinavian descent who have grown up familiar with the process.

We hope that this recipe will demystify gravlax so this moist and succulent dish is available to everyone.

The recipe is very easy, but it takes time—three days—so plan ahead. Don't panic, though, as for most of the time the salmon sits in the fridge and you ignore it! Gravlax is "cooked" in brine and the juices it generates. Served in very thin slices, gravlax is delicious as a dinner appetizer. It can also be served at breakfast, with a poached egg, buttered toast and a topping of Mustard Dill Sauce.

Our Pender friend Harriet Stribley, originally from Sweden, gave Andrea this recipe many years ago. As is the way of recipes, adaptations crept in. Now we don't know what Harriet's original recipe was, but this one is an easy, terrific way to impress guests with a West Coast staple food.

Makes 10 servings

Gravlax

    1 spring salmon fillet, approximately 2.2 lb (1 kg)
    ¹/₃ cup (80 mL) aquavit*
    Sprigs fresh dill (lots—Harriet said you cannot have too much!)
    4 Tbsp (60 mL) sea salt
    4 Tbsp (60 mL) sugar
    2 Tbsp (30 mL) lemon zest
    1 Tbsp (15 mL) freshly ground pepper

Three days before you plan to serve the gravlax, rinse salmon fillet in cold water. Pat dry and carefully remove bones. Score skin side in four places, and freeze fillet, laid flat, overnight, for at least 24 hours (freezing will reduce the risk of illness caused by parasites).

The next day, defrost fillet. Pour aquavit into a glass or ceramic baking dish large enough to accommodate the fillet. Place some dill sprigs in the dish and lay the fillet, skin-side up, on top. Cover and marinate in the refrigerator for at least 6 hours, basting the top side with the juices every couple of hours.

Continued on next page

*A Scandinavian liquor available in liquor and wine stores.

Turn fillet skin-side down and sprinkle the remaining ingredients evenly on top. Baste with the juices. Cover tightly and marinate another 24 hours in the refrigerator. (This "cold cooks" the fish.)

On the third day, drain the fish and lay it skin-side down on a serving platter. Slice as thinly as possible through the flesh at an angle, down towards the skin. Start slicing from the tail end, letting the knife curve away at the skin so you don't cut through it.

Mustard Sauce
4 Tbsp (60 mL) Dijon mustard
4 Tbsp (60 mL) sweet mustard
4 Tbsp (60 mL) sugar
4 Tbsp (60 mL) vinegar
2 Tbsp (30 mL) aquavit
2 Tbsp (30 mL) lemon juice
½ cup (125 mL) olive oil
2 Tbsp (30 mL) chopped fresh dill
Salt and pepper

Place all sauce ingredients in a blender and process to combine.

Assembly
Chopped fresh dill
Twists of lemon

Garnish the gravlax slices with chopped fresh dill, drizzle with the sauce and top with twists of lemon.

Springtime Quiche à la Figaro

One of the first real indications of spring are the "EGGS" signs that go up on numerous honesty stands around the Southern Gulf Islands. As the daylight lengthens, the chickens start to lay regularly and there are plenty of eggs to share. There is nothing like a fresh free-range organic egg. The white isn't watery, the yolk is a brilliant orange and the shells are strong. These eggs are also low in cholesterol, because organic free-range chickens eat what chickens are supposed to eat—greens and grains.

Figaro's beautiful eggs are carefully colour coordinated from cream, blues and browns to one glorious brick red.

The prettiest eggs are found at Figaro's honesty stand on Bluff Road, Galiano Island, so this recipe is named after them. After the winter, sweet young spears of asparagus supply much-needed vitamins in this crust-less quiche. The recipe can be varied by using fish instead of meat, or made for vegetarians by substituting precooked veggies. It will also work with whatever cheese you have in the fridge.

Makes 6 servings

Butter
1½ Tbsp (22.5 mL) fine dry bread crumbs
1 clove garlic, minced
½ cup (125 mL) chopped onion
1 cup (250 mL) diced cooked ham (or flaked fish, or blanched spring vegetables)
1 cup (250 mL) chopped fresh asparagus
1 cup (250 mL) wilted nettles or spinach
2 cups (475 mL) grated Swiss cheese
4 large eggs
1 cup (250 mL) heavy cream
1 cup (250 mL) whole milk
½ cup (125 mL) all-purpose flour
1 tsp (15 mL) dried dill or 1 Tbsp (15 mL) chopped fresh dill*
Salt and pepper

Place rack in middle of oven and preheat oven to 350F (175C).

Butter 10 inch (25 cm) quiche dish, and sprinkle base and sides with bread crumbs.

Continued on next page

* Dried herbs are much stronger than fresh herbs. Use only one-third to one-half as much dried herb as fresh. Taste testing is important because even this smaller amount of dried herb might be overwhelming. It is always best to start with less and add more bit by bit if the taste is not strong enough.

In a heavy skillet, sauté garlic, onion and ham in butter for about 5 minutes. Stir until onion is pale and slightly golden.

Spread onion mixture in the quiche dish. When cool, top with even layers of asparagus and nettles. Sprinkle on the grated cheese.

Whisk together eggs, cream, milk, flour, dill, and salt and pepper. Pour mixture over cheese.

Bake quiche until top is golden and slightly puffed, and custard is set in centre, approximately 35 to 45 minutes. Before serving, cool slightly to firm up.

Honesty Stands

"What a pity so many people have been killed on your roads," said a guest as we served breakfast. We looked blank: in 25 years we knew of only two fatalities. "But the memorial shrines are a nice idea," she continued.

We chuckled. "Those aren't shrines. They're honesty stands."

Fruit, vegetables and jam are all available at roadside stands.

Now it was her turn to look blank. Her city knowledge of traffic accidents made more sense to her than islands so crime-free that people regularly display produce on a roadside stand, allowing passersby to help themselves and drop their money in an old coffee can or cookie tin—an "honesty box."

Flowers dominate some stands, creating that shrine-like look, but fruit, vegetables, herbs and jams also abound. Many free-range organic eggs are also sold this way. Watch for coolers beside the road. If you see one, stop. There will be a sign stuck to the top telling you the price of eggs; lift the lid, deposit your money in a box inside and take your eggs, making sure to close the cooler firmly afterwards.

This is a system in which everybody wins: buyers get organic produce picked fresh that morning; sellers enjoy a means of sharing their extra bounty and earn a little cash to help support their gardening habit.

Sometimes, while driving to get the mail, we cruise a few honesty stands to see what possibilities present themselves for lunch or dinner. Tangy tomatoes from here, basil from there, crisp lettuce from a shaded cooler at the corner. Resisting a fragrant bunch of flowers for the table centre is impossible. This is serendipitous shopping at its best.

Sustainably fished, trap-caught, wild BC spot prawns are a springtime delight not to be missed. Spot prawns—sometimes called spot shrimp—have a short season of maybe 12 weeks if it is a good year. "Have you seen the prawn sign yet?" is often heard as we pick up mail or call in at the grocery store, for islanders start watching the docks for the first prawn boat in early May. Spot prawns have a delicate flavour, easily lost by overcooking. Simple recipes work best; don't shell prawns before cooking or they lose flavour.

Allot 10 spot prawns per person.

Spot Prawns 101

Place prawns in a single layer in the bottom of a large grill pan.

Pour boiling water over until prawns are covered. Wait 5 minutes. Drain prawns and serve in a large bowl so everyone can peel their own and enjoy.

Spot prawns.

Sautéed Spot Prawns—Master's Level!

Melt 2 Tbsp (30 mL) butter or olive oil in a large frying pan. Add 2 finely chopped cloves garlic, and sauté for 30 seconds. Add the spot prawns, sprinkle with sea salt and pepper, and sauté 2 minutes a side, until they have just changed colour. Longer cooking toughens them. Peel and enjoy.

Tip: Save the prawn shells. Cover with water, bring to a boil and simmer for 30 minutes. Strain the broth and refrigerate to use later as a soup base or stock. Covered, it will keep in the fridge for 4 days. Alternatively, freeze for up to a month.

Crab Dancer sells fish at Galiano Island's Sturdies Bay dock.

Saturna Cioppino—Hubertus' Fish Stew

If this delicious local fish stew is on the specials board at the Saturna Café, we don't bother to check the menu. The stew shows to advantage the spring seafood available locally. Chef Hubertus Surm says this is a particularly easy recipe to prepare at home, as the base can be made the day before and stored in the fridge. This makes it the perfect Gulf Island dinner party dish, as it takes only minutes to cook and assemble after your guests have arrived.

Chef Hubertus suggests pairing cioppino with a bottle of Blanc de Noir from Garry Oaks Winery on Salt Spring.

Makes 4 servings

Stew Base

3 Tbsp (45 mL) olive oil
2 cups (475 mL) sliced leek (white portion only)
2 tsp (10 mL) salt
Few pinches ground pepper
1 large yellow pepper, halved, seeded and diced
1 small fennel bulb, halved, cored and sliced lengthwise
1½ cups (350 mL) sliced carrot
1 tsp (5 mL) chopped fresh oregano
1 tsp (5 mL) ground fennel
½ tsp (2.5 mL) ground coriander
1 cup (250 mL) good white wine (plus another glass for the cook)
2½ cups (600 mL) chopped canned tomato
4–5 cups (1–1.2 L) chicken or fish stock
2 tsp (10 mL) chili paste with soy bean oil*

Heat olive oil in a large saucepan. Add leek, salt and ground pepper, and sauté over medium heat for 3 to 4 minutes.

Add yellow pepper, fresh fennel, carrot, oregano, ground fennel and coriander. Simmer for 5 minutes, and then add wine to saucepan (give the cook the other glass of wine). Cook, stirring occasionally, until most of the liquid has disappeared.

Add tomato and cook another 5 minutes.

Add stock and chili paste, cover and simmer until vegetables are tender.

At this point, the stew base can be chilled and stored in the refrigerator for 24 hours.

Continued on next page

* This Thai sauce, Chef Hubertus' seasoning of choice, can be found in Asian grocery stores. A common brand is Pantainorasingh. Sambal, another kind of chili sauce, can be substituted.

To Assemble

1 lb (454 gr) fresh local fish fillets (ling cod, wild salmon or halibut)
12 local fresh mussels (scrubbed and beard removed)
12 local spot prawns (preferably with head on)
Fresh fennel sprigs, or chopped fresh parsley or cilantro
Sambuca (optional)

If the stew base was stored in the refrigerator, return to stove and bring to a boil, and then lower heat to medium.

Cut fish fillets into 8 relatively equal pieces (2 per person). Add fish to hot stew base, ensuring that the fish is covered by liquid; reduce heat and simmer slowly for 3 minutes.

Add mussels and simmer for another 2 minutes.

Add prawns and simmer another 2 to 3 minutes, turning prawns once (do not overcook!). Discard any mussels that have not opened.

Remove fish, prawns and mussels and set aside.

Ladle stew into pre-warmed, large soup or pasta bowls. Evenly divide the fish and shellfish among the bowls, placing them in the middle of the stew.

Garnish with fennel sprigs and parsley. Drizzle with a little sambuca if using.

Chef Hubertus Surm

Saturna Island is the most remote of all the Southern Gulf Islands and has the fewest facilities, so the local joke is that Hubertus couldn't cook if his restaurant wasn't part of the grocery store. Patrons of the café often spot him sauntering from the kitchen to peruse the store shelves. He'll pick out a spice here or a bunch of fresh vegetables from the display and saunter back, smiling shyly at anyone he knows. The store is his pantry, and why not? Much of its produce is both local and organic.

We teased him.

"I couldn't work on a 'real' island," he said with a grin.

Hubertus came to Saturna from Isadora's Restaurant in Vancouver but slipped easily into island style and the delights of using local food. "I don't have a standard menu," he said. "It changes every day and I love to cook fish ... and that's always fresh." He paused. "I can identify the fishermen." We both raised our eyebrows, and he explained how he is a part of an Ecofish Canada initiative, in which chefs adhere to a code and can trace the origins of their fish.

The day we visited Saturna Café the menu featured salad items and vegetables just brought in from Breezy Bay Farm (10 minutes away). The spot prawns were straight from the boat, and the glowing spring strawberries dazzling us from the counter were picked that morning from a neighbour's garden. Hubertus' beef and lamb are both raised and humanely slaughtered at the Campbell farm on the other side of Saturna. The meat is organic and very tender.

We were interviewing Hubertus over lunch, and between orders he was preparing. The place was packed. He asked if we'd like a dessert (made by his wife, Peggy Warren), and we asked for crème caramel. He shook his head. "Sorry, they're gone." Four people at the table beside us groaned.

Hubertus has a reputation, not only locally but across Canada—particularly on the live music circuit. When visiting musicians give a show on Saturna, Hubertus caters for them. They often rave about the food, and quite a number of well-known songwriters have written songs about him and his table.

If you are visiting Saturna in the summer, you can have lunch at the café every day, but it is not open every evening. Watch for posters when you arrive on the island; you might be lucky enough to catch one of his special dinner events. Reserve your table immediately, as the dinners are always fully booked.

Seafood at The Fishery

In Salt Spring Island's main centre, Ganges, there is a brown wooden hut with a white and blue sign: The Fishery. The modest exterior hides what has been dubbed "the best little fishery in BC." The Fishery sells not only fresh fish, but also a line of canned and smoked fish from local waters, and its policy is "wild fish only." Ganges is also home dock for Fishery Afloat, a boat-based store that brings fresh, frozen, canned and smoked seafood to several Gulf Islands during the warmer months. Arnie Hengstler and his wife, Julia, are the owners of this booming business. Arnie is from a fishing family. He started selling his fresh catch in the Ganges Saturday market in 1972. They opened the store in 1992 and branched out into their own gourmet line of wild-only seafood products soon after. Watch for the Fishery Afloat boat *Crab Dancer* when visiting other Southern Gulf Islands. Its times of arrival are usually posted on the dock, but you will be able to guess when it's expected because of the basket-carrying queue.

Salt Spring's Fishery is not much bigger than a boat.

Halibut à la Morning Bay

Barbara Reid of Pender's Morning Bay Vineyard & Estate Winery (see "Sources" section page 234) loves cooking—especially with the wine produced in the estate vineyard she created with partner Keith Watt. "It's such a pleasure to open a wine bottle and look out of the kitchen window and see the vines that produced it," she said with a smile.

"Yes, everything tastes better with a little wine," agreed Keith, holding out his glass.

Barbara gave us her favourite recipe featuring locally caught halibut, complemented by Morning Bay Bianco, and Keith provided the pairing and tasting notes below.

Makes 4 servings

Morning Bay's Keith Watt recommends Bianco with fish.

> Four 6 to 7 ounce (170–200 gr) halibut fillets
> Salt and pepper
> All-purpose flour
> 4 Tbsp (60 mL) olive oil
> 2 large shallots, chopped
> ¼ tsp (1 mL) dried crushed red chili pepper
> 4 plum tomatoes, seeded and chopped
> ½ cup (125 mL) chopped pitted kalamata olives
> ½ cup (125 mL) chopped fresh basil
> 1 Tbsp (15 mL) drained capers
> 1/3 cup (80 mL) bottled clam juice
> ¼ cup (60 mL) dry white wine, such as Morning Bay Bianco

Sprinkle fish fillets with salt and pepper and lightly dredge in flour.

Heat 2 Tbsp of the oil in a large heavy skillet over medium-high heat. Add fish and sauté until lightly browned and just opaque in the centre (approximately 4 minutes per side). Transfer fish to serving platter and keep warm.

Heat remaining oil in same skillet. Add shallots and chili pepper and sauté for 1 minute.

Mix in tomato, olives, ¼ cup of the basil and capers. Add clam juice and wine. Boil, stirring occasionally, until sauce thickens slightly, about 4 minutes.

Mix in remaining basil. Season sauce with more salt and pepper to taste. Spoon sauce over fish and serve immediately.

Keith Watt's Pairing: Morning Bay Vineyard's Bianco

Bianco is Morning Bay's house white, a blend of five aromatic whites grown at our estate vineyard on Pender Island. It is the quintessential seafood wine. Dry, crisp and fresh, with a delightful hint of citrus, Bianco refreshes the palate between bites of the delicious halibut.

Pair Morning Bay Bianco with any seafood, but especially that from the waters around Pender Island—Dungeness crab, spot prawns, salmon and oysters. It's proof, once again, that the wines grown in a region pair best with the foods that come from that region. Cheers!

Michael and Juliet show off their young olive trees.

Mediterranean Dreaming, Saturna Style

"Wouldn't it be lovely," mused Juliet Kershaw, of Saturna Island, to her partner, Michael Pierce, "to own an olive grove!" This idea became practical when shared with friends who have a greenhouse and experience growing a Mediterranean garden. They formed a consortium and, in spring 2009, imported 100 tiny bare-rooted olive trees to Saturna from the United States. They sold out in no time, so the following spring the consortium imported another 500 trees. The result—several budding olive groves are now scattered across the Southern Gulf Islands. The most established is on Pender, where owner Andrew Butt hopes to start oil production in a few more years.

"Gulf Island olive groves have become practical because of climate change," explained Michael. "But harvesting the fruit depends on a warm sunny spring and early flowers."

Locally grown olives give island dishes a Mediterranean flavour.

Juliet chuckled and chanted, "Flowers in April, a bushel in November. Flowers in May, a pan in November. Flowers in June, a handful in November." We all turned our faces hopefully towards the spring sun.

Contact the Saturna Olive Consortium through its website (see "Sources" section, page 234).

Saturna Olive Consortium's Moroccan-Style Chicken with Olives and Lemon

Saturna chef Hubertus Surm helped the Saturna Olive Consortium celebrate its first successful season. He made his version of a dish featuring olives that the group found in *Mediterranean Street Food*, by Anissa Helou (William Morrow Cookbooks, 2002). Hubertus used local organic chicken and preserved lemons. We've tweaked the recipe further, since most people do not preserve their own lemons. If you do, however, for a more authentic flavour use your own preserved lemons instead of the lemon zest.

Serve this dish with thick hunks of bread for mopping up the juice—a loaf from Saturna Island Haggis Farm Bakery is perfect.

Makes 4 to 6 servings

2 Tbsp (30 mL) extra-virgin olive oil
1½ Tbsp (22.5 mL) unsalted butter
2 medium onions, thinly sliced
1 clove garlic, finely chopped
1 tsp (5 mL) ground ginger
½ tsp (2.5 mL) ground cumin
½ tsp (2.5 mL) paprika
¼ tsp (1 mL) finely ground white pepper
Pinch saffron threads
Sea salt
12 organic chicken thighs, skin removed
1 cup (250 mL) chopped fresh cilantro
1 cup (250 mL) chopped fresh parsley
1 cinnamon stick
2 to 3 cups (475–700 mL) water
Juice of ½ lemon
Zest of 2 lemons
1½ cups (350 mL) pitted mixed green and purple olives
Salt and pepper

Place oil and butter in a Dutch oven over medium heat, and melt butter. Add onion and sauté gently until translucent and fragrant.

Put the garlic, ginger, cumin, paprika, white pepper, saffron and a pinch of sea salt in a large plastic bag and shake to combine.

Add the chicken thighs to the bag. Shake well to cover with the spice mixture and, through the bag, rub the mixture thoroughly all over the chicken. Place chicken and any loose spice mixture in Dutch oven. Sauté briefly on all sides to seal in the juices.

Continued on next page

Add cilantro, parsley and cinnamon stick, and half cover with water. Bring mixture to a boil over medium-high heat. Cover, reduce heat and simmer for 45 minutes, or until the chicken is tender and the broth has become very concentrated. If the sauce is still quite thin, remove the lid, turn up the heat and boil to reduce.

Discard the cinnamon stick, and stir in the lemon juice, lemon zest and olives. Reduce heat to medium-low and simmer for another 10 to 15 minutes.

Using a slotted spoon, transfer the chicken pieces to a warmed casserole dish. Taste the sauce, adjust seasoning if necessary and pour sauce over chicken.

Ladle into bowls and serve.

Mayne Island's Farm Gate Store

A dream that Shanti and Don McDougall (of Deacon Vale Farm) had finally came true in 2010 with the opening of the first designated Farm Gate Store on the Southern Gulf Islands, at the Fernhill Centre on Mayne Island.

For 17 years this innovative couple have farmed on Mayne and sold their produce in a variety of places, including the Mayne Island farmers' market, which they started. No one was more aware that the small growers on the island needed a permanent outlet, one that would operate year-round and specialize in local seasonal products.

Mayne's Farm Gate store specializes in local produce.

It took guts, cash, perseverance, political lobbying and sheer hard work, but the Farm Gate Store is now up and running and open throughout the year. This is a flagship business venture for all the islands, and a definite must-see for visitors who wish to buy locally produced fresh organic products.

The store sells Mayne Island produce whenever possible, plus stock from the other Gulf Islands. Any gaps are filled with products from farms in the Saanich and Victoria areas. Produce is mainly organic, though a few clearly labelled non-organic and imported goods are carried, because there is a demand for them.

This is the place to buy not only local fruit and vegetables, such as Varalaya Farm's mixed greens and apples from Starry Night Meadows, but also Mayne Island organic grass-fed beef, lamb and chicken, as well as eggs. Deacon Vale Farm's impressive variety of jams and chutneys competes for shelf space with freshly baked bread and muffins, and Mile Zero coffee, and the deli counter is brimming with Salt Spring cheeses and our favourite find, Don's homemade sausages.

Don, a chef who trained at the Dorchester Hotel in London, England, makes his sausages from scratch. When did you last cook a sausage that didn't shrink to half its size? These don't! Packed full of interesting flavours, made with lean meat organically raised on Deacon Vale Farm and flavoured with herbs grown by Shanti in the couple's extensive vegetable garden, they are delicious.

Dan is willing to share. He gave us his recipe for lamb and fennel sausages. Obviously, home kitchens don't usually have sausage casings on hand, but this sausage mix makes wonderful lamb burgers or meatballs.

Deacon Vale Lamb Sausage or Burgers with Fennel Seed

Made into lamb burgers, this sausage mix is delicious. We also found it a wonderful sausage wrap for Dave's favourite picnic food, Scotch eggs.. Making this recipe as sausages requires standard hog casings, which are not readily available in supermarkets, but you could try talking nicely to a butcher who makes sausage in house—you might even get some expert advice on filling the sausage.

Serve these sausages or burgers with a mixed green salad and Deacon Vale Farm Fresh Minted Relish.

Makes 10 sausage links or 6 burgers

>   4 cloves garlic, minced
>   2 lbs (900 gr) ground lamb
>   ½ cup (125 mL) finely chopped onion
>   ¼ cup (60 mL) chopped fresh mint
>   1 Tbsp (15 mL) fennel seed, crushed
>   1 tsp (5 mL) chili flakes
>   1 tsp (5 mL) lemon pepper
>   1 tsp (5 mL) salt
>   1 cup (250 mL) water
>   12 feet (3.6 m) standard hog casings (optional), soaked overnight in water

Mix everything but the casings together and knead the mixture to distribute spices evenly.

Either stuff mixture into casings (if using) and form into links of desired length, or form mixture into six patties.

Grill sausages or patties until juices run clear, turning once halfway through cooking.

Asparagus, Orange and Walnut Salad

Nothing announces spring more than the appearance of tender spears of asparagus. Unfortunately, the season is short, and it's hard to find local asparagus at honesty stands. Growing asparagus takes space, time and patience, so most people eat what they grow. However, Foxglove Farm grows amazing asparagus, and occasionally Mayne Island's Farm Gate Store and Galiano's Daystar Market carry some from local farms. If the harvest is particularly abundant, you may be lucky enough to find asparagus at the farmers' market—if you are there at opening time!

Never overcook asparagus. This recipe keeps the crispness, pairs it with the crunch of walnuts and brightens it with a touch of orange.

Makes 6 servings

Salad
    2 lbs (900 gr) asparagus, trimmed
    1 orange (zest removed first), peeled and segmented

Dressing
    Zest of half orange
    ½ cup (125 mL) vegetable oil
    ¼ cup (60 mL) walnut oil
    ¼ cup (60 mL) white wine vinegar
    1 Tbsp (15 mL) minced shallot
    2 tsp (10 mL) Dijon mustard
    ¾ tsp (4 mL) salt
    ½ tsp (2.5 mL) freshly ground black pepper
    Salt and freshly ground black pepper

Garnish
    ⅓ cup (80 mL) chopped toasted walnuts
    1 Tbsp (15 mL) chopped fresh parsley
    Zest of half orange

Quickly steam the asparagus until bright green and barely tender, and then plunge into ice-water to stop cooking. Drain and pat dry. Place spears on a shallow platter.

Arrange orange segments on top of asparagus. Chill.

Whisk together half the orange zest with the rest of the dressing ingredients. Taste, and adjust seasoning if necessary.

Pour desired amount of dressing over asparagus and orange.

Garnish with the walnuts and parsley, and sprinkle with remaining orange zest. Serve immediately.

Grilled Baby Fingerling Potatoes with Yogurt Sauce

Watch for the tender new potatoes of the season and try them grilled instead of boiled. The first warm spring weekend is often when Gulf Islanders spring clean and test out their barbecues, and this is the recipe to use. Both Daystar Market on Galiano and the Farm Gate Store on Mayne regularly carry locally grown fingerlings. Grill these "tater treats" in a foil packet and serve with yogurt sauce.

Makes 4 servings

> 1 lb (454 gr) new fingerling potatoes
> ½ onion, thinly sliced
> 1 Tbsp (15 mL) chopped fresh rosemary
> Salt and pepper
> 2 tsp (10 mL) melted butter or olive oil

Wash the potatoes and remove any brown spots or eyes. Dry. Cut larger ones in half so pieces are of uniform size. Prick the skins.

Place a 12 by 24 inch (30 by 60 cm) double layer of aluminum foil on counter. Grease foil and arrange potatoes in a single layer on half of the foil.

Spread onion and rosemary over potatoes, season with salt and pepper, and dot with butter (or sprinkle with oil).

Fold foil over and double crimp the edges firmly to seal packet. Place it on a medium-hot grill and cook for 20 to 30 minutes or until potatoes are cooked through, turning packet once halfway through cooking time. Meanwhile, prepare the sauce.

Yogurt Sauce

> ½ cup (125 mL) plain Greek yogurt
> 1 green onion, chopped
> Dash hot pepper sauce
> Sea salt

In a small bowl, mix yogurt with green onion, hot pepper sauce and salt.

When potatoes are cooked, remove from foil and serve immediately with yogurt sauce.

Roger Pettit—The Potato Man

Take a clearcut hillside, a supportive wife, a passion for heritage potatoes, an equally passionate distrust for chemical companies and what do you get? Roger and Lisa Pettit's Sunshine Farm.

Roger is volubly anti-chemicals, and he knows what he's talking about. He worked for a chemical company for some years, becoming their "field man," consulting on 19,770 acres (8,000 hectares) of potatoes grown in the Niagara area of Ontario.

After becoming totally disillusioned with chemical-based farming practices, Roger decided to return to his roots, for he was raised on a small farm. At a time of life when most people retire, the couple bought a clearcut on Galiano and proceeded to transform it using sustainable organic techniques and crop rotation. The results are Sunshine Farm, Roger's nickname "The Potato Man" and a full-time job for them both.

They grow dwarf fruit trees, year-round crops such as kale, chard and garlic, plus melons in fabric tunnels, tomatillos for Lisa's salsa, zucchini, squash and potatoes. Lots of potatoes—over 20 different varieties. Tiny fingerlings, red and purple ovals, knobbly Irish cobblers. They are all totally different in looks and taste and are Roger's passion.

"Those Peruvians know what they are doing," said Roger. "For eight thousand years Peruvians have grown between 16 and 37 different varieties and colours of potatoes in poor soil without chemicals. They understand farming and variety is key. The only way our monoculture farming survives is by using fertilizers, sprays and insecticides to stop bugs and blights. Heritage varieties don't need this. If one fails the other thrives. So support your local organic grower of several kinds of wonderful and unusual kinds of potatoes; they're good for your health."

Sunshine Farm currently supplies produce to some local island restaurants and stores, as well as the Galiano farmers' market. Roger and Lisa are there every Saturday over the summer months. It's a great place to drop in and buy some purple-flesh potatoes or yellow-flesh fingerlings and try a taste test.

Fingerling potatoes are sometimes available at Daystar Market on Galiano Island.

Nettle Pudding

We couldn't resist this recipe, as it's been declared "the oldest recipe in the world" and dates back 6,000 years. Archeologists discovered it was a staple of Stone Age people, who made it by mixing nettles and other herbs, such as dandelion and sorrel, with flour, salt (if available) and water. "Pudding" is actually the old term for dumpling. On our islands, pioneers from many backgrounds commonly cooked dumplings similar to this in the stew pot.

One day when you have a delicious pot of stew on hand, mix up this dumpling and cook it right in the stew.

Makes 6 to 8 servings

> 2 bunches young nettle leaves, wilted
> Handful each chives, sorrel, watercress and young dandelion leaves*
> 1 cup (250 mL) flour (any type)
> 1 tsp (5 mL) salt
> Water or stock

Finely chop wilted nettles.

Wash, pat dry and finely chop the other greens. Add to the nettles and toss together.

Place flour in a bowl, stir in salt and then mix in the greens.

Add just enough water to bind ingredients together into a ball of dough.

Place dough in the centre of a square linen or muslin cloth. Knot the corners of the cloth securely. Using the knot as a handle, place the dumpling in the centre of a pot of simmering stew. (Venison stew would be most authentic, but any red meat stew will do.)

Leave dumpling to cook in the pot until the meat is tender (a minimum of 1 hour, but as long as it takes).

Remove dumpling from the stew, unwrap and slice.

Half submerge a steaming slice of dumpling in each bowl of stew and serve.

* This dumpling can also be made with the equivalent amount of spinach, chard, chives and your preferred herbs .

Haggis Farm's Nettle Pasta

Homemade pasta has made a much-deserved comeback—it really does taste different than commercial pasta. This is no surprise to Jon Guy, of Saturna Island's Haggis Farm, whose homemade nettle pasta has been carried by the Saturna Grocery Store for years. It sells out as fast as he can make it. Not only do you have to be quick to catch a batch, you also have to go in the spring when it's made. Since old nettles are tough, this delight is available for only a few short weeks. Jon has kindly shared his recipe.

You'll need a pasta machine to make this pasta, and an electric mixer is a big help too. The noodles will stay fresh for 24 hours. They also freeze well in bags from which the air is removed.

Makes 8 servings

Preparation

If you haven't stored any batches of wilted nettles in the freezer, go and forage for some. Take gloves and a bag with you, and collect two or three large handfuls of the top 3 inches (7.6 cm) of tender young nettles. This will give you approximately 1 cup (250 mL) cooked nettle leaves—enough for a batch of Jon's pasta.

Boil a large pot of salted water, drop in the nettles straight from the bag. Stir around and cook for 1 to 2 minutes.

Drain nettles in a colander and immediately dunk both into a big bowl of ice water. Once nettles are cool, allow them to drain thoroughly.

Tip nettles onto a clean tea towel. Roll and wrap the nettles in the towel, and then twist the ends of the roll to squeeze out as much moisture as you can. Now the nettles are stingless and ready to use.

Pasta

> About 1 cup (250 mL) wilted nettles or spinach (a little less works fine)
> 1½ cups (350 mL) all-purpose flour
> Pinch salt
> 2 eggs
> Olive oil

Chop the nettles finely—don't use a food processor or you will get mush. The finer you chop, the smoother your pasta. Remove any tough stems.

In a bowl, whisk together flour and salt to combine. Make a well in the centre and drop in eggs and nettles.

Using a fork, whisk together eggs and nettles in the centre, gradually working outward to incorporate flour, until mixture is a shaggy mass.

Continued on next page

Scrape the dough into the bowl of an electric mixer fitted with a dough hook, and knead dough for 4 to 6 minutes. (You can do this by hand, but it will take longer—up to 8 minutes.)

Cover the dough with a thin film of olive oil and wrap in plastic. Let it rest for 1 hour at room temperature.

Cut off a small piece of the dough and roll it out in a pasta machine according to the manufacturer's instructions, until the dough is about ⅛ inch (0.3 cm) thick.

Once you have a sheet of pasta, you can use it as is for lasagna, or cut it into ¼ inch (0.6 cm) noodles using your pasta cutter.

When cutting nettle noodles, dust with flour whenever necessary, because all green pastas made with fresh ingredients will have some fibres running through that make the strands stick together. Lay the noodles on the counter. Gently separate by hand, dusting with flour when needed.

Hang noodles to dry on a clean broom handle resting between two chairs.

Repeat with remainder of nettle dough. After every little batch, pick up the previous one that has been drying and give it a slight twist, making it into a loose nest. Store in a resealable plastic bag.

To use, boil the noodles in lots of salty water until they float, and then for another minute or two. Serve at once.

Haggis Farm

If you move to a Gulf Island, you don't mind the ferries separating you from the mainland or Vancouver Island. If you move to Saturna, you don't care if the ferries are even running. "Saturna Islanders are the only islanders that lobby for fewer ferries rather than more," said Jon Guy with a chuckle. "We are true islanders."

Jon and partner Priscilla Ewbank live on Haggis Farm, a name synonymous with food throughout the Gulf Islands. For years, Priscilla has written a column about life on the farm and on Saturna for the local paper, the *Island Tides*. We have followed the comings and goings on Saturna, the raising of food and her children, the activities of her friends and neighbours, all through snippets in her bi-weekly column. The Haggis Farm name also became known across the island as a trademark, for Jon was a baker and his Haggis Farm Organic Breads were delivered to the other islands twice a week by boat, to be sold in island stores. Sadly the Haggis Farm bakery is no more; John has retired, though he can be persuaded to make Haggis Farm cookies or Haggis Farm Pasta for special Saturna occasions.

Theresa's Rhubarb Barbecue Sauce

If the spring sun is warming the air, out come the barbecues. There is nothing like standing on the deck admiring a newly furled blossom with a glass of wine in your hand—an island vintage of course—and smelling that distinctive smoky fragrance wafting through the air. If it's not from your own barbecue, it makes you change supper plans really quickly.

The barbecue can be used most months on the islands—in between rainstorms. We have a friend who uses hers to cook her Christmas turkey every year. A barbecue is also very useful during our occasional winter power outages, especially if the barbecue is sheltered!

But here's the quandary: to sauce or not to sauce? Not being fans of store-bought barbecue sauces, we were delighted to discover this tangy alternative, featuring local rhubarb, on the Island Vittles food blog (see "Sources" section, page 234) of Theresa Carle-Sanders, Pender's creative online chef.

Use this delicious concoction as a basting sauce for grilled meat or poultry. It will keep for one week in the refrigerator.

Makes about 2½ cups (600 mL)

    1 cup (250 mL) chopped fresh or frozen rhubarb
    ⅔ cup (160 mL) water
    1 medium onion, finely chopped
    1 tsp (5 mL) olive oil
    1 clove garlic, minced
    ⅔ cup (160 mL) packed brown sugar
    1 cup (250 mL) ketchup
    ½ cup (125 mL) corn syrup
    2 Tbsp (30 mL) cider vinegar
    2 Tbsp (30 mL) Worcestershire sauce
    1 Tbsp (15 mL) Dijon mustard
    1 tsp (5 mL) grated lemon zest
    1 tsp (5 mL) *herbes de Provence**
    1 tsp (5 mL) hot pepper sauce
    ½ tsp (2.5 mL) crushed dried red pepper
    ¼ tsp (1 mL) salt

In a medium saucepan, bring rhubarb and water to a boil. Reduce heat; simmer, uncovered, for 5 to 6 minutes or until rhubarb is tender. Remove from heat and cool.

Place cooled rhubarb in a blender or food processor; cover and process until smooth. Set aside.

Continued on next page

*A mixture of dried herbs—typically basil, fennel seed, lavender, marjoram, rosemary, sage, summer savory and thyme — commonly used in southern France.

Sauté onion in oil until tender. Add garlic; sauté for 1 minute. Add the remaining ingredients and cooled rhubarb, and stir well.

Bring mixture to a boil. Reduce heat immediately and simmer, uncovered, for 5 minutes till reduced a little.

Cool sauce and store in a covered jar in the fridge.

What Is an Online Chef?

Theresa Carle-Sanders is a new breed of chef. Instead of working in a restaurant, she works from her Pender home, creating new recipes, and writing and talking about food. The results can be accessed by signing up for her two online blogs: Island Vittles, where Theresa explores the wonderful variety of local food and the realities of island living, and Outlander Kitchen (see "Sources" section, page 234), where she recreates the food mentioned in author Diana Gabaldon's Outlander series of historical fantasy adventures.

"I love talking about food," said Theresa. "When I came to Pender, I decided being an online chef made most sense and would give me more freedom than working in a restaurant. It took me three days to come up with the right blog name—Island Vittles. I write about discovering local seasonal foods and island life (one person moved here because of my blog), and I alternate between recipes for restaurant-style fare that is more intricate and easy-to-make fresh meals and baking. Told you I love talking about food—I am now on the radio once a month with Patty Mack of Talk Radio Victoria 1070, so listen in."

Theresa cooks as well as she writes, so check out her celebrating Solstice menu on page 227.

Teresa Carle-Sanders is both a chef and an enthusiastic brewer.

Raven Rock's Glazed Baby Beets in a Nest

Most people are familiar with beets, the large burgundy red globes that many stores carry. But organic island farmers are increasingly experimenting in varieties you might not recognize as beets at first glance. Raven Rock Farm on Pender Island grows large, small, oval and round beets in a variety of colours, including striped and golden—if you've never tried golden beets, you don't know what you've missed. Local beets are sold in both spring and fall, as there are two planting seasons. They are a "two-for-one" vegetable: the fresh tops can be sautéed and served too. Raven Rock's sweet spring beets are a delight. They are not only tasty but time saving, as you don't have to peel the skins. In this recipe, the natural sweetness of the beets is highlighted with the glaze made from farm-pressed apple juice and given a tang with the hint of balsamic.

Makes 4 to 6 servings

> **24 Raven Rock baby beets, washed, trimmed, and tops chopped and reserved**
> **2 cups (475 mL) organic apple juice (use fresh pressed if available)**
> **3 Tbsp (45 mL) balsamic vinegar**
> **2 Tbsp (30 mL) honey**
> **1 Tbsp (15 mL) olive oil**
> **1 clove garlic, minced**
> **Sea salt and pepper**

A delicious assortment of multi-hued beets for sale at the Salt Spring Farmers' Market.

Place the beets (reserve beet tops) and the apple juice in a large sauté pan. Cover and cook on medium-high heat for 10 minutes.

Add the vinegar and honey and cook for another 10 minutes. Check and shake pan occasionally to be sure the liquid hasn't evaporated entirely. If it has, adjust heat and add a tablespoon more juice.

If the glaze isn't thick enough to coat beets, remove lid, increase heat and gently stir beets until glaze has evaporated to your liking.

Remove pan from heat and keep covered while you cook the beet tops.

In a second sauté pan, heat olive oil to a shimmer, add garlic and cook for 30 seconds.

Add the reserved beet tops, season with salt and pepper to taste, and sauté until tops are wilted, 2 to 4 minutes.

Using a slotted spoon, remove the wilted beet tops from pan and mound them in the middle of a warm serving plate, using the spoon to make a large hollow in the middle so the tops make an even "nest" around the perimeter of the dish.

Nestle the glazed beets in the hollow. Drizzle any leftover glaze on the edges of the nest and serve immediately.

Leftover beets? Dice the cold beets and serve them topped with crumbled feta cheese, chopped fresh dill, the juice of one lemon and a sprinkle of lemon zest as a garnish. Delicious!

Raven Rock Farm—from Land to Mouth

"It's not possible to make a living farming. It costs two dollars to produce each dollar of product." So spoke the former CEO of a large agrifood company, in his best boardroom manner. George Leroux looked at me sternly from under his eyebrows, then a smile broke out on his face. His wife, Kelly, joined in the laughter. "But we have a wonderful lifestyle, feeding ourselves," they said together.

We were sitting in George and Kelly's living room, looking out over one of the most productive small farms on Pender Island. The land swept away below us into a shallow valley. A row of old heritage fruit trees edged an orchard of modern espaliered trees and vigorous berry bushes. Rows of hardy vegetables surrounded fabric tunnels sheltering tender plants. Ponds for irrigation, kiwi vines, a potato field, garlic, a corn patch and winter greens filled the available space. This is mixed farming at its best.

Raven Rock's stunning new greenhouse.

"I move the earth, Kelly plants the crops," said George. Kelly shook her head. "Not really, you do lots with the plants, especially the greenhouse tomatoes." The greenhouse soared serenely on a ridge over the farm; it was one of the most beautiful greenhouses we've ever seen. Almost two stories high, the curved hand-hewn beams arced to support the glass and gave a churchlike feeling to the interior. "We needed it to extend the seasons," said Kelly as we entered. "But Jude designed it to feed the spirit." She was referring to Jude Farmer, designer extraordinaire, who has designed and built several outstanding Gulf Island greenhouses.

The Lerouxs not only feed themselves, but also sell surplus product at their farm gate and are regulars at the Pender farmers' market. You cannot miss them: just look for George's tractor. It pulls the nifty folding produce stand he designed down the road and into place at the market every Saturday.

Despite spending many hours on the farm, George still shares his expertise in the food business, helping a new generation of managers to be successful in an ever-changing, and challenging, food market. Before we left he pulled out a sample of his latest venture—a bag of parsnip chips. He's interested in promoting different types of vegetable chips as snack foods. We can attest that the parsnip chips are totally addictive!

Rhubarb Cranberry Sorbet

Rhubarb is abundant in spring and easy to freeze for use year-round—simply wipe, chop and bag. Rhubarb pies, crumble, muffins and fool, not to mention Dave's annual favourite, rhubarb jam—the list is endless. But this refreshing spring sorbet also makes use of that bag of frozen BC cranberries left over from Christmas, and newly sprouted mint. Mint is a staple herb in many Southern Gulf Island gardens but is often overlooked for use in desserts. This sorbet can also be used as a tiny palate cleanser between the courses of a special dinner party.

Makes 6 to 8 servings

Syrup

> 1 cup (250 mL) water
> ¾ cup (180 mL) sugar
> 2 sprigs fresh mint, crushed

Combine the syrup ingredients in saucepan, bring to a boil, reduce heat and simmer for 5 minutes.

Remove from heat, strain syrup and discard mint. Set syrup aside to cool while preparing fruit mix.

Fruit Mix

> 5 cups (1.2 L) chopped rhubarb
> 2 cups (475 mL) frozen cranberries
> ¾ cup (180 mL) water
> Pinch salt
> 1 envelope unflavoured gelatin
> 1 egg white
> Fresh mint leaves, for garnish

Combine rhubarb, cranberries, ½ cup (125 mL) of the water and salt in a large pan, bring to a boil, reduce heat and simmer for 7 minutes, or until cranberries begin to pop and rhubarb is soft. Remove fruit mixture from heat. Transfer mixture to a bowl.

Stir reserved syrup into fruit. When well combined, cool quickly by placing bowl in an ice-water bath.

Sprinkle gelatin over remaining water. Let stand 1 minute.

Remove bowl containing fruit mixture from ice-water bath. Stir gelatin, and then mix into the cool fruit mixture.

Continued on next page

In a separate bowl, whip egg white until frothy and stiff. Fold egg white into fruit mixture and chill in fridge until thickened.

Freeze fruit mixture using an ice cream maker, following the manufacturer's instructions. Store sorbet in freezer until almost serving time.

Remove sorbet from freezer and allow to soften for a few minutes at room temperature. Serve in individual bowls and garnish with fresh mint leaves.

Mint—Not Just a Garnish

Probably the most popular culinary herb after parsley, mint is found in many Southern Gulf Island gardens. Since our islands are known as the "Friendly Islands," this is fitting, for mint symbolizes hospitality.

Mints grow wild in Asia and the Mediterranean region, where it is customary to offer mint tea to arriving guests. Many varieties of mint have now been developed—you can grow chocolate mint, and orange, grapefruit, apple, lemon and even 'Eau de Cologne' mint. The last I find too overpowering for most purposes except scenting my bath water with crushed sprigs! Mint grows very vigorously in this climate, so plant it only in containers, unless you want it to spread through your entire garden.

Here are 10 of our favourite ways to add a mint zing to life:

Chopped apple mint sprinkled on salad

Chopped chocolate mint with fresh strawberries

Mint sauce with lamb

Tea made with any variety of mint

Crystallized mint leaves on cakes

A bed of mint sprigs under grilled lamb chops

Chopped mint, lemon zest and salt stirred into yogurt for an instant sauce

Chopped mint added to tabbouleh, couscous, Greek salad or hummus

Minty marinades

Chopped mint stirred into rice, curries or bean dishes

All-Seasons Crunchy Toffee Crumble—Rhubarb and Ginger

This is a new take on crumble—the quintessential all-season, all-purpose, feed-unexpected-guests, adaptable dessert. It's a lifesaver on the islands, where the visitors you've so fondly waved off may unexpectedly return for another night, because the ferry isn't running or they missed it. So we make double the quantity of crumble topping and keep it in the freezer to pull out when needed.

This topping is decadent. The high ratio of butter to sugar makes a crunchy toffee topping once it has cooled and set, so it is at its best when served at room temperature. Serve it with cream, ice cream or custard.

Makes 6 servings

Crumble Topping

- ⅓ cup (80 mL) all-purpose or whole-wheat flour
- ⅓ cup (80 mL) old-fashioned rolled oats or quick-cooking oats
- ⅓ cup (80 mL) packed dark brown sugar
- ⅓ cup (80 mL) sugar
- ½ cup (125 mL) butter
- ½ tsp (2.5 mL) ground ginger
- Zest of 1 lemon or orange, finely chopped

Preheat oven to 375F (190C). Butter an 8 cup (2 L) casserole dish.

Place all crumble ingredients in a food processor and briefly pulse a few times until the mixture consists of crumbs. Do not overprocess. Set aside.

Continued on next page

Spring Fruit Combo

1½ lbs (680 gr) fresh or frozen rhubarb,* chopped into small pieces
1 cup (250 mL) sugar
¼ cup (60 mL) chopped crystallized ginger
1½ Tbsp (22.5 mL) cornstarch
Zest of 1 orange
½ cup (125 mL) orange juice
1 tsp (5 mL) butter

Place rhubarb, sugar, ginger, cornstarch and orange zest in a separate bowl and toss using a fork. Pour in the orange juice and stir. Spread fruit mixture on bottom of dish. Dot fruit with butter, divided into four portions.

Cover fruit evenly with reserved crumble mixture to desired thickness. (Freeze any leftover crumble.)

Bake for 45 to 60 minutes, until top is golden and fruit is bubbling. Remove from oven.

Turn on oven grill. Place crumble under grill to add more crunch. Watch carefully so topping browns and caramelizes but does not burn.

Let stand for 20 minutes to allow toffee topping to harden to a crunch.

Serve at room temperature.

*If using frozen rhubarb, defrost in a colander first and reserve the liquid that drains from fruit. Make the liquid into a sauce or save for another use.

Seasonal Crumble

Ring the changes to make this crumble a truly seasonal dessert. Here are some suggestions.

Summer
Use pitted cherries for the fruit.

Omit the ground ginger and oatmeal from the topping.

Substitute ⅓ cup (80 mL) crumbled amaretto cookies for the oatmeal and sprinkle some flaked almonds over the crumble topping.

Fall
Use a mix of plums and pears stewed with 1 tsp (5 mL) vanilla. Add a handful of toasted chopped hazelnuts to the topping.

Winter
Use apples and cranberries stewed with lemon and lemon zest instead of the orange. For the topping, substitute cinnamon for the ground ginger and add ⅓ cup (80 mL) dark chocolate chips.

Dan Jason and Salt Spring Seeds

Dan Jason's life is a political act. He is not a politician and is never seen in Parliament. He is found in the fields of his Salt Spring Island farm tending ancient grains, his beloved legumes, lettuces and fruit trees, and sharing his knowledge with a steady stream of visitors. So what is political about that? He is single-handedly mounting an attack on the major petrochemical and pharmaceutical giants that have become the worldwide masters of food production and seed distribution.

Dan challenges their use of monocultures, monopolies, patents and genetic modification, and their growers' reliance on the fertilizers and pesticides these companies produce. He talks quietly about caring for the soil, crop rotation and diversification. He grows and sells heritage seeds, ones that can be planted and grown, and then their seeds saved, shared and planted again (many seeds sold now are genetically modified so that the plants they produce will be infertile, and you will need to buy new seeds the following year).

Dan believes we need to take control of our food and he demonstrates how to do it. It was Dan Jason who introduced Canadians to amaranth and quinoa, two ancient grains that are garnering a growing number of fans. They are easy to grow, naturally disease resistant, high in protein, easy to cook and a viable option for people who have a wheat intolerance.

Growing food in a sustainable way is Dan's pleasure and passion. His gardens are food and seed sanctuaries, as well as places for renewal of the spirit. His farms always have a meditation area. His current one has a labyrinth and seats surrounded by different varieties and colours of thyme.

A prolific author, Dan works tirelessly to raise the public awareness needed to protect our food and its sources. He coordinates a network of equally passionate organic growers who produce seeds for Salt Spring Seeds. Check out his Salt Spring Seeds website (see "Sources" section, page 234) for the seeds he sells, as well as mind-blowing information about the food you eat and food you too can grow.

Dan's Quinoa (or Amaranth) Pudding

Thanks to Dan Jason's efforts, many people are now familiar with quinoa (pronounced "keen wah") and amaranth. This quick and surprisingly light dessert is an unusual cross between a porridge and a rice pudding. You can use either grain. It also makes a good breakfast dish as both amaranth and quinoa are high in protein.

Amaranth and quinoa cook quickly: Simply bring to a boil 1 cup (250 mL) of the grain with 1 cup (250 mL) water and a pinch of salt. Reduce heat and simmer for 15 minutes. This makes 2 cups of precooked grains, the amount needed for this recipe.

Makes 6 servings

> 2 cups (475 mL) precooked amaranth or quinoa
> 1 cup (250 mL) apple juice
> ½ cup (125 mL) finely chopped almonds
> ½ cup (125 mL) raisins or chopped dates
> ½ tsp (2.5 mL) vanilla
> Grated zest of 1 lemon
> Juice of ½ lemon
> Pinch cinnamon
> Fresh fruit for topping, such as grapes, blueberries, strawberries, raspberries or kiwi
> Optional: 1 cup (250 mL) whipping cream

Combine amaranth, apple juice, almonds, raisins, vanilla, lemon zest, lemon juice and cinnamon in a saucepan. Cover and bring mixture to a boil. Reduce heat and simmer for 15 minutes.

Pour pudding into individual dessert bowls, cover with plastic wrap and chill overnight to allow flavours to develop. Serve topped with fresh fruit.

To make this dessert richer and similar in style to the festive rice pudding served in Scandinavia, chill the entire pudding mixture overnight in a large covered bowl. Whip cream until thick, and fold it into the chilled pudding. Mound it into dessert bowls. Top with fresh fruit and drizzle with maple syrup.

Panna Cotta with Peaches and Blackberry Port Drizzle

Panna cotta (cooked cream) is a simple Italian dessert—the perfect one for us since we love dessert and love dinner parties that end with something showy. This easy-to-make, pretty dessert can be prepared ahead and is easily adapted throughout the year to showcase local fresh fruit. In spring, fruit (other than rhubarb) is in short supply, so now is the time to use the last of your home-canned delights (peaches or other fruits). The smoothness of the ivory *panna cotta* paired with the sunny colour of the peaches reflects the spring daffodils and narcissus that settlers planted to dance along the island roadsides. We use the blackberry port drizzle for an interesting contrast colour, and to add depth to the taste of the peaches and the tang of the buttermilk. This is the perfect visual ending to a spring dinner, especially if you've continued the spring theme with a vase of daffodils as a table centrepiece.

Makes 8 servings

Panna Cotta
2½ cups (600 mL) buttermilk
1 envelope unflavoured gelatin
½ cup (125 mL) whipping cream
½ cup (125 mL) sugar
1 vanilla bean

Place 1½ cups (350 mL) of the buttermilk in a small bowl and sprinkle gelatin evenly on top. Let stand 10 minutes to allow gelatin to soften slightly.

Place the whipping cream in a medium saucepan on medium heat, stir in the sugar, add the vanilla bean and bring mixture to a boil. Immediately reduce heat to low.

Whisk in gelatin mixture. Cook for 1 to 3 minutes, stirring continually, to allow gelatin to dissolve.

Remove saucepan from heat, remove vanilla bean and stir in remaining buttermilk.

Divide buttermilk mixture between eight ½ cup (125 mL) ramekins and place them on a cookie sheet. Cover with plastic wrap and refrigerate *panna cotta* for at least 4 hours or overnight, until well chilled.

Blackberry Port Drizzle
½ cup (125 mL) Salt Spring Vineyard's Blackberry Port
3 Tbsp (45 mL) sugar

Place port and sugar in a non-reactive skillet and cook until bubbles look thick and syrup is reduced to half its original quantity. Remove from heat, scrape into a small bowl and allow to cool completely before using.

Assembly

8 peach halves (home-canned if available)

Drain peaches (reserving juice for another purpose) and slice each peach half into 3 or 4 pieces, depending on size. Set aside.

To unmould *panna cotta*, run a small knife around the side of each ramekin, invert it onto a small plate and give ramekin a sharp tap and a little jiggle. If necessary, place ramekin briefly in hot water and tap again.

Garnish *panna cotta* with peach slices. With a spoon, drizzle the port reduction in lines or swirls across the plated *panna cotta* and peaches.

Please Don't Pick the Daffodils . . .

. . . unless they are growing in your garden!

Springtime on the islands means daffodils, thousands of them. We don't know who first started planting them along the roadsides, but the brilliant idea caught on. Friendly neighbours sometimes give new property owners a welcoming bag of bulbs to plant by their driveway. The result is a spring swath of vibrant yellow along many roadsides. The deer don't eat daffodils and none of us pick them, so they delight the eye of residents and visitors alike. We grow extra in our gardens for that longed-for burst of spring colour and fragrance in the house.

Spring daffodils at Miners Bay, Mayne Island.

Mocha Mousse

This rich mousse is the ultimate coffee dessert.

A temporary collar of aluminum foil is added to the dish to make it higher and is later removed. The result—a mousse that is about an inch taller than the dish—very impressive! For a professional finish, gently turn the dish on its side and press the exposed edge of the mousse into finely grated chocolate.

Makes 6 to 8 servings

2 envelopes unflavoured gelatin
½ cup (125 mL) strong coffee
8 ounces (225 gr) Belgian chocolate, chopped
Splash milk
3 egg yolks
¼ cup (60 mL) coffee liqueur
1 cup (250 mL) whipping cream
7 egg whites
¼ tsp (1 mL) cream of tartar
Pinch salt
⅓ cup (80 mL) sugar
Whipped cream

Mount Maxwell Roasters, the new kid(s) on the block, show their wares at a Salt Spring Saturday market.

Take a length of aluminum foil that will go all the way around the rim of the mousse dish, and fold the foil lengthwise in thirds to form a rigid strip. Tape it around the rim of the dish.

Sprinkle gelatin over the coffee in a saucepan, heat just until gelatin has melted and then allow to cool.

Place chocolate in a bowl and melt in the microwave. Then mix in a splash of milk to prevent the chocolate from turning to fudge, and cool.

When the chocolate is cool, beat in egg yolks and coffee liqueur. Mix well.

In a separate bowl, whip cream until beaters leave tracks in it. Clean beaters.

In another bowl, whip egg whites, adding cream of tartar and salt when frothy. Then slowly add sugar and continue beating whites until stiff peaks form.

Mix chocolate mixture, cream and gelatin mixture together gently.

Fold combined mixtures into egg whites.

Pour batter into mousse dish. Chill for at least 4 hours in fridge.

Just before serving, remove foil collar and decorate mousse with additional whipped cream.

Java Jitters and Raven Dark

Yes, Java Jitters and Raven Dark are Gulf Island coffees, and their names evoke the brews that help Gulf Islanders—including us—wake up and function.

Gulf Islanders may not grow coffee, but we consume it and are passionate about its quality, the politics of growing it and how it gets into our cup. The result is that island coffee companies typically have extensive websites introducing their growers and roasters, and explaining how each business considers the environment and social issues raised by its activities.

Pender is served by Moonbeans Coffee Roaster, a business that resettled here from Vancouver in 2003, and brings coffees from around the world to the local grocery store.

Galiano Coffee Roasting Company describes itself as a "family company run by a small and diverse group of socially-minded island parents." Roast master Janice Oakley operates in a little shed in the woods, and the product is distributed in brown paper bags stamped with the name of the roast and the date roasted, so you can keep track of its freshness. We bring home big bags of Raven Dark every time we visit the island.

A Pender coffee shop expresses the island ethos.

Salt Spring Coffee started on Salt Spring Island, where it still maintains a foothold, but it has since established a new roasting operation on the Lower Mainland, where the company is now expanding to serve new markets. Salt Spring Coffee takes the environment seriously—it claims the first life-cycle carbon neutral coffee in Canada—and customers are encouraged to take home a free package of spent grounds to compost.

Perhaps most imaginative is Ometepe Coffee, which supplies Salt Spring with coffee grown on the island of Ometepe in Lake Nicaragua. A group of Gulf Island residents formed the Ometepe–Gulf Islands Friendship Association in 1988. Volunteers bring in coffee, then roast, package and sell it to Salt Spring residents and others. Profits from the operation are ploughed back into Ometepe Island and elsewhere in that region of Nicaragua. Over $25,000 a year has been invested in schools, a first-aid facility, a micro-bank and a rescue operation for glue-sniffing boys. This ultimate "feel-good" formula certainly enhances the flavour of our morning cuppa.

Celebrating Spring

Galiano Inn, Galiano Island

An air of sleepy contentment surrounds the Galiano Inn, which is on the edge of Sturdies Bay and within sauntering distance of the Sturdies Bay ferry. Despite its extensive facilities and nearness to the village, the inn is serene even at the height of the summer season. This is due in part to the ambience of the Japanese-style gardens surrounding the comfortable modern villas, and the friendliness of the easygoing staff.

Then there is the food. Local foods inspire the menu at this tranquil oceanfront inn, and its wine cellar is superb. Chef Dean Hillier and sommelier Richard Massey have both been at the inn for some years and are incredibly skilful. For the first time ever we threw ourselves on the mercy of a sommelier and asked Richard to use his wine expertise to pair a wine with our dinner selections—duck for one of us and lamb for the other, choices that made choosing the wine challenging. The ensuing conversation was an eye-opener and his wine choice—Formiga, an unusual red from Catalunya (Catalonia)—paired so well with both dishes that it made the meal one to remember.

Chef Dean Hillier

Chef Dean boarded the Vancouver-to-Galiano ferry seven years ago. "Other than one year off, I've never left," he remarked, with a shy smile. "I really enjoy the local foods and easy access to some interesting items. For example, Galiano Inn smokes its own salmon."

"I studied at VCC [Vancouver Community College]. My mother was a cook and I helped in her kitchens when I was in high school. Then I went into it professionally. I am very fond of both sushi and Indian food, and sometimes they influence me. I slip in a hint of Indian at the restaurant, like the coriander in my lamb shank, and I never overcook fish."

There are many options for dining al fresco at the Galiano Inn.

Sommelier Richard Massey

For many people, the idea of consulting a sommelier is daunting, but don't hesitate at Galiano Inn. Richard Massey, originally from Nelson, BC, has been with Galiano Inn for seven years and is approachable, enthusiastic and knowledgeable, and has put together what is probably the best wine cellar on the Southern Gulf Islands. "Owner Conny Norden is totally supportive," he explained. "If I am travelling and discover an unusual or incredible wine, I have carte blanche to acquire it for the cellar."

Worldwide vintages are found here, but local wines are equally supported, and there is an impressive selection both on the wine menu and in the inn's wine store. "We have a unique *terroir* here in the Gulf Islands," Richard explained. "No other place in the world can produce wines like these; they are very food friendly. In classic areas wine and food have evolved together, and that's happening here. It's becoming natural to team Pinot Noir from a local vineyard with a Pacific salmon dish."

Celebrating Spring Menu for Six

Created by Chef Dean Hillier, Galiano Inn, Galiano Island
Wine pairings and tasting notes by Galiano Inn sommelier Richard Massey

Wine Pairings

GREEN PEA SOUP WITH CRÈME FRAÎCHE

2010 Garry Oaks Pinot Gris

(Garry Oaks Winery, Salt Spring Island)

This Salt Spring Island grown Pinot Gris received a gold medal at the Northwest Wine Summit. Stone fruits on the palate with Chablis-like minerals are tightly wound in this softly rounded island white. I like the way the minerality of this wine works with the green peas, and the roundness is a good match with the added richness the *crème fraîche* contributes.

LEMON MINT QUINOA SALAD WITH BEET-INFUSED OIL

2010 Morning Bay Estate Bianco

(Morning Bay Vineyard & Estate Winery, Pender Island)

My preferred wines from Morning Bay on Pender Island have always been the ones grown and produced on the estate. I love both the estate biancos. This crisp, cool-climate, food-friendly wine features bracing acidity that holds up to dishes containing citrus and salads dressed with vinaigrette.

SWEET CHILI BROILED SALMON, SNOW PEAS AND PEA SHOOTS

2009 Saturna Island Pinot Noir

(Saturna Island Vineyards, Saturna Island)

This lighter, European-style Pinot Noir is a great accompaniment to the "medium impact" cooking technique of broiling. The snow peas and pea shoots keep the dish light and as fresh as spring. The extremely soft and approachable tannins of this wine do not interfere with the salmon, acting as a stage to highlight and promote the wonderful West Coast salmon flavour.

ORANGE GLAZED RHUBARB TART

Salt Spring Vineyards Blackberry Port

(Salt Spring Vineyards, Salt Spring Island)

The sweetness of this wine, tasting of local island blackberries, is a great counterpoint to the slightly sour rhubarb. The accompanying vanilla bean ice cream cools the fortified alcohol.

Chef Dean Hillier with Galiano Inn's wood-fired pizza oven.

Richard Massey brings a choice wine from the cellar.

Green Pea Soup with Crème Fraîche

This fresh, light soup is made richer by the optional addition of cream. *Crème fraîche*, used here as a garnish, is commonly found in supermarkets in the United Kingdom and the rest of Europe but less easy to obtain in Canada. It takes only minutes to make at home. Just remember to do so 24 hours before you plan to use it. Thick whipped cream can be substituted for the *crème fraîche*.

Makes 6 servings

Crème Fraîche
1 cup (250 mL) whipping cream
2 Tbsp (30 mL) buttermilk

Stir together the whipping cream and buttermilk in a glass jar. Cover. Let stand at room temperature (about 70F/21C) for 8 to 24 hours, or until thickened.

Stir again, and refrigerate. Use within 10 days.

Green Pea Soup
1 cup (250 mL) diced onion
2 Tbsp (30 mL) butter
4 cups (1 L) vegetable stock
3 lb (1.4 kg) shelled fresh garden peas or frozen peas
Salt and pepper
¼ cup (60 mL) finely chopped mint leaves
Cereal cream/half-and-half (optional), water or stock
½ cup (125 mL) *crème fraîche*
Mint sprigs, for garnish

In a pot, sauté the onion in butter until tender.

Add stock and bring to a boil.

Add the peas, reduce the heat and simmer until the peas are soft. Season with salt and pepper.

While peas are cooking, combine ⅛ cup (25 mL) of the chopped mint with *crème fraîche*. Set aside to allow flavours to meld.

When peas are tender, cool for a few minutes, then place in blender with remaining mint. Blend till smooth. Do this step in batches if necessary.

Return pea mixture to pan and gently reheat. Thin, if necessary, with cream, if using, or with water or stock. Adjust seasonings.

Divide soup among 6 bowls, add a spoonful of the minted *crème fraîche* in the middle, top with a mint sprig and serve.

Safety Tip: Never blend hot liquids in a blender with a closed lid. They can explode out of the blender all over the kitchen—messy as well as dangerous! Always, cool before blending or use an immersion mixer.

Lemon Mint Quinoa Salad with Beet-Infused Oil

If you don't have a juicer, and can't find beet juice in the supermarket, the retained liquid from a jar of pickled beets is an easy substitute. Quinoa has become popular in recent years and is also available in red and black varieties.

Makes 6 servings

Beet-Infused Oil

> 1 large raw beet, trimmed
> Grapeseed oil

Juice the beet in a juicer.

Pour beet juice into a small pan, and cook until juice has been reduced by three-quarters. Cool.

Blend reduced beet juice with same amount of grapeseed oil until emulsified. Store, covered, at room temperature until needed.

Quinoa Salad

> 2 cups (475 mL) quinoa
> 2 cups (475 mL) water
> ¼ cup (60 mL) fresh lemon juice
> ¼ cup (60 mL) olive oil
> 3 cloves garlic, minced
> 1 cup (250 mL) grape tomatoes, halved
> ½ cup (125 mL) chopped parsley
> 2 green onions, chopped
> 2 Tbsp (30 mL) chopped mint
> Salt and pepper

Place quinoa and water in a pot and boil quinoa till tender, 10 to 15 minutes. Cool.

In a small bowl, whisk together lemon juice, oil and garlic.

In another bowl, mix cooled quinoa, tomatoes, parsley, onion and mint.

Add the lemon and oil mixture and toss. Season with salt and pepper and toss again. Cover and let stand for 1 hour to allow the flavours to develop.

Divide quinoa mixture among 6 plates and drizzle with the beet-infused oil.

Sweet Chili Broiled Salmon, Snow Peas and Pea Shoots

This easy recipe is delicious served hot but just as good served cold the next day, when the flavour of the caramelized topping has permeated the fillet. It's worth cooking extra to be sure there are leftovers.

The essence of a successful stir-fry is a hot pan and quick cooking. Basically, the vegetables are heated rather than cooked.

Dean advises: "Broiling gives salmon a better flavour than baking. Do it four inches from the grill."

Makes 6 servings

Sweet Chili Broiled Salmon
¼ cup (60 mL) sweet chili sauce (Thai chili sauce)
2 Tbsp (30 mL) soy sauce
1 to 2 Tbsp (15–30 mL) grated ginger
6 salmon fillets

Whisk together chili sauce, soy sauce and ginger.

Line a baking sheet with foil and spray with nonstick cooking spray.

Place salmon skin side down on baking sheet and spread with marinade. Let stand 30 minutes.

Preheat broiler. Spoon any remaining marinade on salmon.

Broil salmon for 6 to 8 minutes, depending on thickness. Meanwhile, make the pea stir-fry.

Snow Peas and Pea Shoots
2 Tbsp (30 mL) safflower oil
3 cloves garlic, minced
1 tsp (5 mL) grated ginger
3 cups (700 mL) snow peas
3 cups (700 mL) pea shoots
2 Tbsp (30 mL) rice wine
1 Tbsp (15 mL) soy sauce
1 tsp (5 mL) sesame oil

Heat oil in a large sauté pan, add garlic and ginger, and stir for a few seconds.

Add snow peas and stir-fry till tender, 2 to 3 minutes.

Add pea shoots, rice wine and soy sauce, and toss everything together until pea shoots are heated through.

Finish by tossing pea mixture briefly with the sesame oil.

Place salmon on plate with the pea stir-fry.

Orange Glazed Rhubarb Tart

Don't feel guilty—buy some frozen puff pastry and give yourself a break! Serve slices of this wonderful spring tart with a good vanilla bean ice cream.

Makes 6 servings

> **1 cup (250 mL) orange juice**
> **1 Tbsp (15 mL) fresh lime juice**
> **½ cup (125 mL) sugar**
> **1 lb (454 gr) rhubarb stalks, cut diagonally into ¼ inch (0.6 cm) thick pieces**
> **1 sheet puff pastry, defrosted**
> **1 to 2 tsp (5–10 mL) orange zest**

Preheat oven to 400F (205C). Grease a cookie sheet.

Mix orange and lime juices with sugar in a bowl. Add rhubarb, toss and let stand.

Roll out puff pastry into a 7 by 11 inch (18 by 28 cm) rectangle. Transfer to prepared cookie sheet.

Make a border around the edge of the pastry by scoring a line, 1 inch (0.6 cm) from the edge, all the way round. Use a knife, but do not cut all the way through the pastry. With the tines of a fork, prick the centre surface of the pastry, up to the border.

Strain rhubarb, reserving the juice, and spread rhubarb over the pastry shell, inside the scored edges. Bake for 30 minutes until rhubarb is soft and the pastry edges have risen and are golden.

Meanwhile, place reserved juice in a pan and cook until juice has been reduced by half or is syrupy.

Brush glaze over the baked tart while still warm, and sprinkle orange zest on top.

Galiano Inn looks out on the east end of Active Pass, with Mayne's Georgina Point lighthouse beyond. It's not always as serene as this — from here we've watched two ferries and a pod of orcas crowding the channel.

Summer

An Ode to Island Visitors

Breakfast arrives at Salt Spring Vineyards B&B.

In winter, Gulf Islanders dream of summer's lazy beach or deck days. In summer, we occasionally dream of winter's cozy, quiet, "sitting-by-the-stove" days. In reality, summer is busy.

This is the season of casual dining, salads and picnics, and finger foods for both invited and unexpected guests. The ferries are full; so is our social calendar. Visitors bob back and forth on the ferries. We bob back and forth between our burgeoning gardens, kitchens, the car and the washing machine. We juggle cooking island delights, touring the beauty spots with guests, changing beds for the next set, attending our favourite island activities or catching some sun with a quiet martini on the deck, and we thrive on all that summer offers!

We not only enjoy our visitors but also appreciate the essential role they play in our island economies. Thanks to visitors, our farmers sell out at the markets and so can expand next year's crops. Our vineyards do a roaring trade in wine sales and secure another year's operational budget. The honesty-stand produce is snapped up as soon as it's put out, encouraging our small organic gardeners to plant more. Thanks to our visitors' awareness, enjoyment and demand for locally produced organic food, our supplies are increasing year by year. Summer is showtime for the very best aspect of island living—the food produced here—and islanders delight in sharing it.

Summer is also party time. This is the season of salmon barbecues and lamb roasts, crab feasts and vineyard picnics, outdoor concerts and fishing derbies. The islands are hopping but in a relaxed way. After all, what's the hurry? We're all on island time!

So come and visit, and we will do our favourite thing—show you our special places in their summertime glory—for every islander is convinced his or her particular island is the most exquisite in this beautiful part of the world.

Right: Taste of summer on the Gulf Islands—lamb chops are seasoned with lavender and rosemary.

Opposite: On summer Saturdays, farmers, bakers, singers and artists gather at a central point to sell their wares. While kids gather round a storyteller or musician, islanders and visitors buy fresh produce, pick up a loaf or a book, taste snacks, sip coffee and gossip with neighbours.

Previous page: Eroded sandstone in Retreat Cove, Galiano Island.

Farmers' Markets

For most Canadians, the official start of summer is June 21, but on our islands, summer is a state of mind, heralded by the first farmers' market, no matter what the date. Farmers, gardeners, artisan bakers, cooks and chocolate makers gather to offer their vast array of produce: vegetables and cut flowers, herbs and garlic, plums and pears, jellies, jams and marmalades, relishes and vinegars, fruit pies, breads, cakes and a wonderful muddle of muffins.

Out come the shoppers, baskets on arms, ready to savour the free samples, socialize their way from the first stall to the last and load up on the best the islands have to offer. It's a colourful, noisy, bazaar-like scene and a favourite summer ritual.

Featured alongside the fresh produce are the wares of our local artisans: jewellery, pottery, woodwork, candles, soaps, dried flowers, clothing, paintings, books, toys and instruments. At Salt Spring's Saturday market in Ganges, the craft stalls now outnumber the produce stands, though the determined shopper can still easily ferret out the culinary treats. Salt Spring has now started a "produce only" market on Tuesday afternoons.

On the smaller islands, food remains front and centre on Saturdays. Stalls open for business at 9:00 a.m. sharp, by which time there are usually several lineups of shoppers eager to nab the freshest, biggest and ripest produce. The goat cheese invariably sells out quickly, as do the buckets of spectacular sunflowers. The vegetables never have time to wilt in the sun, and most are gone long before noon. Eventually the vendors pack up and head home to tend their crops and prepare for next week's rush. We carry home the serendipitous makings for several meals. It's such an inspiring way to shop.

Arugula and Fennel Lemon-dressed Salad

Gone are the days when "salad" meant a heap of shredded store-bought iceberg lettuce. Salad greens love temperate West Coast weather, and Gulf Island farms and gardens produce a wonderful variety of tasty greens. Fennel and arugula are great examples. They grow easily on the Gulf Islands and are delicious paired with a touch of lemon.

Makes 6 servings

⅓ cup (80 mL) extra-virgin olive oil
¼ cup (60 mL) fresh lemon juice
1 tsp (5 mL) lemon zest
½ tsp (2.5 mL) salt
6 cups (1.4 L) arugula leaves
30 grape tomatoes, halved (optional)
2 small fennel bulbs, thinly shaved with a mandoline or very sharp knife
½ cup (125 mL) toasted pine nuts
½ cup (125 mL) freshly shaved Asiago cheese

Make the dressing by whisking the oil, lemon juice and zest, and salt together in a small bowl; set aside. Place arugula leaves in a large salad bowl. Sprinkle tomatoes, fennel and pine nuts over top. Toss with the lemon dressing immediately before serving. Top with the Asiago shavings.

The Art of Garden Salads

Fresh garden salads should be considered a summer art form. The ritual of walking to the vegetable plot, basket on arm, scissors in hand, is a soothing aesthetic experience as well as a productive one.

There's such pleasure in choosing each fluted lettuce leaf, some crinkled, some red tinged, anticipating the bite of arugula and the scent of chopped mint. Clip a few tiny kale leaves here, add the mustard taste of wasabi greens there. The creative combinations are endless. Top it off with a spectacular scatter of edible flowers.

Here are some suggestions:

• Lettuces: butter, red sail, romaine

• Greens: arugula leaves, mustard greens, wasabi greens, Chinese greens, endive, chicory

• Herbs: mints, oregano, dill, fennel, marjoram, chives

• Edible flowers: chive flowers, pansies, calendula, marigolds, nasturtiums, bergamot, jasmine, squash blooms, borage, violets

• Berries: strawberries, raspberries, blackberries, loganberries, blueberries

Above: Edible nasturtium and borage blossoms garnish the assorted greens on offer at the Salt Spring Farmers' Market.

Right: A garden at Wave Hill Farm overflows with salad possibilities. *Jan Mangan photo*

Raspberry/Blackberry Vinaigrette

Tender leaf salads from the garden cry out for a light dressing such as a simple but fragrant raspberry or blackberry vinaigrette made with a fruit-infused vinegar. Making the vinegar infusion is so easy, you will wonder why you didn't try it years ago. Ready in several weeks, it makes a great gift, especially if you print the raspberry vinaigrette recipe on a small card and tie it to the neck of the vinegar bottle with a decorative raffia bow.

Makes about 1 cup (250 mL) vinaigrette, plus 1½ cups (350 mL) berry vinegar leftover for another use

Vinegar

   1 cup (250 mL) freshly picked raspberries or blackberries
   2 cups (475 mL) white wine vinegar

Place berries in clean wide-mouthed glass jar.

Pour vinegar over them and screw down top.

Place on a dark shelf and leave for 2 to 3 weeks to infuse, giving the jar an occasional gentle swirl.

Strain vinegar and discard the solids.

Strain again through a paper coffee filter to remove any fine solids.

If not using immediately, pour berry vinegar into decorative bottles and cork.

Seal bottle tops by dipping cork and neck edge in melted wax.

Vinaigrette

   ½ cup (125 mL) homemade raspberry or blackberry wine vinegar
   ½ cup (125 mL) light-tasting olive oil
   1 tsp (5 mL) Dijon mustard
   1 tsp (5 mL) maple syrup
   ½ tsp (2.5 mL) finely chopped fresh oregano
   ¼ tsp (1 mL) black pepper
   Handful of fresh raspberries or blackberries if available

In a jar with a tight-fitting lid, combine all ingredients except berries. Shake well.

Toss with salad just before serving.

Garnish tossed salad with berries and serve.

A Drizzle of Hazelnut Oil

A new business on Salt Spring Island is creating a buzz. Saltspring Sunrise Premium Edibles (see "Sources" section, page 234) is marketing a delicious, certified organic, cold-pressed hazelnut oil made from local nuts. The company's walnut oil is just coming into production, and pumpkin oil will in the near future. Hazelnut oil is my second favourite oil to drizzle on salad greens (my first being truffle oil, but I haven't discovered a local producer for that). Of course, Dave's nut allergy means he keeps away from these pretty little jars, but when he's not within smelling distance, I indulge by drizzling a little hazelnut oil over a variety of salad greens, or a lunchtime platter of sliced tomato, basil leaves and goat cheese. Hazelnut oil is at its best when used to add a sprinkle of flavour to a finished dish, rather than in the cooking process. High heat breaks down the delicate structure of specialty oils.

Watch for Saltspring Sunrise oils in local food stores and in delis on both the Gulf Islands and Vancouver Island. These oils definitely fall into the luxury food category, but what a delightful treat!

Andrea's Kitchen Mantra

Written on the wall above our kitchen counter is Andrea's favourite quote:

"Approach love and cooking with reckless abandon."

(This is widely attributed to her icon, the Dalai Lama, and she was dashed to discover a site full of his authenticated quotes denied this. However, as folklorists we are both quite happy to live life according to words of wisdom from Anon.)

Garden Pea and Avocado Hummus

Andrea grew up in working-class England with tinned peas and could never abide their metallic taste. Tiny frozen peas, discovered in Canada, were much better, but never a favourite of either of us. We ate them because our kids loved them and glued them to their forks with mashed potatoes. Freshly picked garden peas are an entirely different vegetable. We love snipping the pods off the plant and smelling the faint trace of sap left on our fingers. The aroma intensifies with each satisfying pop as we shell them. Then there's that first burst of raw green in the mouth as we sneak a few. There is nothing more satisfying than the barely boiled, mint-sprigged ambrosia of sweet garden peas for supper—a dab of golden butter slipping over the green globes, a grind of pepper freckling them. If you have to share your bounty, this recipe is a wonderful way to do so.

Serve this hummus as a dip with any crackers, but it is particularly good paired with Mae's Wetcoast Crackers (page 183) or fingers of freshly toasted pumpernickel bread or even multigrain Melba toast.

Makes 6 appetizer servings

> 1½ cups (350 mL) freshly picked garden peas
> ¼ cup (60 mL) boiling water
> 1 large avocado, peeled and chopped
> 1 clove garlic, diced
> 2 Tbsp (30 mL) lime juice
> ½ tsp (2.5 mL) sea salt

In a small saucepan, briefly cook peas in the boiling water until just soft. Drain, cool peas in cold water and pat dry in a tea towel.

Place the cold peas in a blender with the avocado and remaining ingredients. Process to a smooth green purée. Serve.

Max & Moritz operate the Spicy Island Food House at Galiano ferry terminal.

Waiting for Ferries

Filling in time at the ferry dock is an inescapable part of Gulf Island life. Activities while waiting for ferries include napping in the car, reading, working on a laptop, chatting with fellow travellers (the ferry system itself being a common topic of conversation), and playing Frisbee or Hacky Sack. On Saturna, Galiano and Pender, however, there's another option—food with a view.

The lineup at Lyall Harbour, Saturna, is conveniently situated beside the Lighthouse Pub and Restaurant, which offers good food and a delightful deck overlooking Navy Channel. Often there's time for a quick beverage while ferry watching in comfort.

Pender and Galiano Islands both have interesting ferry dock food outlets. Galiano has a bright red van—Max and Moritz—famous in ferryland for serving home-cooked Indonesian food. Pender has The Stand, which serves what one newspaper critic dubbed "the best home-made hamburgers in BC." The gigantic "Hummer" burger has to be seen to be believed. But on all islands, get in line early and allow time for your order. All three places cook the food fresh for each customer.

If you're a visitor, relax and enjoy the ferries as part of the holiday. Take something with you to nibble (such as our Pea and Avocado Hummus, page 75) and allow time in your schedule for the ferry to be late. Stuff happens, and in summer the ferry fleet moves the equivalent of about two-thirds of the entire population of Canada to and fro on the West Coast—an amazing feat.

The *Queen of Nanaimo* pulls away from Village Bay, on Mayne Island.

Porter Pancake Canapés with Lox

Murray Hunter, the brewmaster at Salt Spring Island Ales, developed this recipe using his Dry Porter. Porter is as great in cooking as it is to drink. It's especially good for making beer breads and pancake batters. There is only one disadvantage to making pancakes with beer—they must be cooked as soon as the liquid is added. The chemical reaction that makes the pancakes light and fluffy is lost if the batter stands. If you need lots of pancakes and want to double this recipe, make it in two batches.

To use as canapés, make the pancakes bite-sized. For regular-sized pancakes, use 1 Tbsp (15 mL) sugar in the batter, make the pancakes larger and serve with butter and maple syrup, or yogurt and berries.

Makes 24-30 canapé pancakes

> **Oil or butter for coating skillet**
> **1 cup (250 mL) flour**
> **1 Tbsp (15 mL) baking powder**
> **½ tsp (2.5 mL) salt**
> **½ tsp (5 mL) sugar**
> **1 egg**
> **¼ cup (60 mL) milk**
> **½ cup (125 mL) Salt Spring Island Ales Dry Porter**

Toppings
> **Lox, *crème fraîche*, and capers or chopped spring onion**

Preheat a skillet or griddle over medium heat. Lightly coat with oil.

In a large bowl, stir together the flour, baking powder, salt and sugar.

In a separate bowl, whisk the egg and milk together, and then add the porter.

Immediately whisk the wet ingredients into the dry ingredients until just blended—a few lumps are fine.

Spoon 1 to 2 Tbsp (15–30 mL) batter onto the hot griddle for each small pancake. When bubbles rise to the top of the pancakes, turn them and cook until browned on the other side.

Serve immediately, topped with lox and a dab of *crème fraîche*, garnished with capers or chopped spring onion.

Salt Spring Island Ales

There is nothing like beer to cool your thirst on a hot summer's day, and now that need can be met locally. "Drink beer with nature" is the slogan for Salt Spring Island Ales, and nature and its care plays a large role in the production of these local brews. Gulf Islands Brewery (see "Sources" section, page 234), which makes these ales, is situated in Salt Spring's pastoral Fulford Valley, at 270 Furness Road. The wooden barn housing the equipment is built from trees harvested on-site, and the water used in the beer comes from a natural spring. The brewery uses locally grown hops and recycles spent grain by donating it to Salt Spring cattle farmers, mushroom growers and bakeries. This is local sourcing and recycling at its best.

The hops are harvested at the peak of freshness and immediately trucked up the road to brewmaster Murray Hunter. "They go from vine to kettle in about one hour," he says. "They're alive and kicking when we throw them in. I'm hoping you'll be able to smell and taste that freshness in the final product." This is an unusual approach in making beers, for which, unlike wine, terroir is not usually a factor.

Salt Spring Island Ales are organic. They are hand crafted and hand bottled in small batches, unpasteurized and unfiltered. The beer comes in several brews from a light ale to a full-bodied porter. The brewery also produces some specialties, such as Heatherdale Ale, made for the famous Butchart Gardens near Victoria.

Almost all Salt Spring restaurants carry the company's products, and Salt Spring Island Ales are found widely on Vancouver Island. They can also be ordered through the company's website.

A tasting room is open on Fridays and Saturdays throughout the summer, and tours are available by appointment at other times. Customers can buy all the ales on site, including party kegs. The company is also starting a new "Growler Program" so that regular clients can buy refillable two litre jugs—another great way to help the environment.

Below: Hops are grown and picked on the island for use in brewing.

Below right: Salt Spring Ale makes a batch of brews.

Salt Spring Spanakopita

This recipe features Spicy Chili Feta, a specialty of David Wood's Salt Spring Island Cheese Company. The recipe is also an opportunity to use some infamous Gulf Island nettles. It works just as well if you spurn nettles and use spinach from your garden or the grocery store. Spanakopita is delicious hot or cold.

Makes 12 appetizer servings or 6 entrées

> 2 bunches spinach or the equivalent quantity of new nettle tops
> 1 large Spanish onion, chopped
> 1 large clove garlic, finely chopped
> ½ cup (125 mL) butter
> 2 cups (475 mL) Spicy Chili Feta, drained
> Salt and pepper
> Nutmeg, for grating
> 1 Tbsp (15 mL) chopped fresh dill
> 12 sheets phyllo pastry

Preheat oven to 350F (175C).

Using gloves, strip the leaves from the nettle stems. Wash leaves and wilt them in a small amount of boiling water. Drain and cool nettles, and then squeeze out as much remaining liquid as possible. This is important, as wet greens result in soggy spanakopita. Roughly chop the greens and set aside.

In a frying pan, gently sauté the onion and garlic in a little of the butter, until onion is opaque. Set aside to cool.

Crumble feta into a bowl, and add the cooled nettles and onion mixture. Season to taste with salt and pepper, and add 6 or 7 rasps of nutmeg and the dill. Thoroughly combine ingredients.

Melt remaining butter. Brush a little over the bottom and sides of a large baking tray.

Cover the bottom of the tray with one phyllo pastry sheet, brush with butter, top with another sheet and brush again with butter; repeat until you have used 6 sheets. Brush butter on top sheet. (Don't worry if the sheets break—just fit them together with a slight overlap.) Spoon the nettle mixture on top and spread evenly across the phyllo pastry, leaving bare a narrow edge of pastry around the perimeter. Continue forming layers of phyllo pastry and melted butter, sealing the edges all around the filling. Butter the top layer.

With a sharp knife, gently score halfway through the top layers of pastry to indicate portion sizes.

Place baking tray on the middle rack of oven and bake for 35 to 40 minutes, or until the pastry on top is crisp and golden.

Remove from oven. Cut through the lines on the pastry to the bottom of the tray. Depending on the size of the pieces, use a fish slicer or spatula to lift them.

Packages of phyllo pastry of various sizes are found in the frozen food section of grocery stores. The thin sheets are rolled up together in a plastic bag. To use, thaw overnight and then unroll and peel off the number of sheets specified in the recipe. Immediately cover these with a slightly damp cloth to keep them from drying out. Quickly reroll the remaining sheets, place in the plastic bag and freeze for later use. (Phyllo is one of the few foods that can safely be refrozen.)

David Wood sells his cheese at Salt Spring Farmers' Market.

Moonstruck uses milk from its Jersey cows.

Opposite: Salt Spring Island Cheese Company's beautifully packaged chèvres are available across Canada.

Salt Spring Island Cheese Company

Nothing is nicer than a Gulf Island picnic, and nothing is better to take along than cheese. Don't miss visiting a wonderful cheese company on Salt Spring Island.

David Wood's Salt Spring Island Cheese Company was established in 1996 and sells its products across Canada. David specializes in beautifully packaged sheep and goat cheeses, often with an edible flower accent. Visitors are welcome to visit the year-round farm shop on Reynolds Road, near Fulford Harbour, and enjoy taste testing, buying the cheeses and viewing the cheese-making process through windows. Salt Spring Island Cheese Company produces a wide range of cheeses, from soft chèvres to hard cheeses, blue cheeses and two brined fetas (one plain and one with chilies). The company, which has an informative website (see "Sources" section, page 234), has a stall at the Saturday market at Ganges, where David is often seen cheerfully serving customers.

Moonstruck Cheeses

Moonstruck Organic Cheese Inc., founded in 1998 by Julia Grace and Susan Grace, uses milk from their organic herd of purebred Jersey cows. Cheese maker Julia makes a variety of cheeses—such as Camemberts, cheddars and blue cheese—including Beddis Blue.

Moonstruck cheeses can be found in BC outlets and at the farm store—on Beddis Road on Salt Spring Island—open from May to the end of September and in the winter by appointment. A selection of Moonstruck cheeses is available at Salt Spring's Saturday market or online from the company's website (see "Sources" section, page 234).

Beddis Blue and Fig Tart

This is a lovely summer luncheon entrée featuring Moonstruck Cheese's Beddis Blue cheese paired with fresh figs. Serve this tart with a garden salad.

Figs are found in late summer and early fall at farmers' markets and in the small island stores that regularly stock local produce. During August and September, check out Galiano's Daystar Market, Southridge Store on Pender Island and Deacon Vale's farm gate store on Mayne Island. Also watch for honesty stands as you drive around the islands, and screech to a halt when you spot a sign that says "Fresh Figs."

Makes 6 servings

Pastry Shells

> 1 recipe 'Never Fail' Pastry (page 161)
> Several handfuls of dried beans

Preheat oven to 400F (205C).

Cut out rounds of parchment paper the same size as the removable bottoms of six 4 inch (10 cm) tart tins. Grease tins.

On a floured surface, roll out pastry. Cut out 6 circles of pastry large enough to line a tart tin, and line each tin with pastry.

Prick the bottoms of the pastry shells and chill for 15 minutes.

Cover the bottom of each pastry shell with a round of parchment paper, place a small handful of beans in each shell and bake for 10 minutes.

Remove beans and parchment paper, and continue baking shells for another 5 minutes, or until the pastry feels dry to the touch. Let shells cool in the tart tins.

Figs ripen in late summer and early fall.

Filling

> 1 ounce (28 gr) salted butter
> 1 small onion, finely chopped
> 7 sprigs fresh thyme (6 to garnish plates, optional)
> 2 eggs
> 1/3 cup (80 mL) whipping cream
> Pinch each sea salt and pepper
> 3 fresh figs, each cut into 8 slices
> 2 ounces (57 gr) Beddis Blue cheese, crumbled
> Grated nutmeg (optional)

Preheat oven to 400F (205C).

Melt butter in a pan and sauté the onion with a sprig of thyme until onion is transparent.

Discard thyme, drain and cool onion, and then divide onion among the 6 tart shells.

Continued on next page

In a bowl, whisk together eggs, cream, and salt and pepper.

Place four fig slices in each tart, divide the cheese equally among them and fill each shell with the egg mixture.

Grate nutmeg, if using, over the surface of each tart.

Bake tarts for 20 to 25 minutes, until the centres are firm and the pastry edges are golden.

Cool for 10 minutes before carefully removing the tarts from the tins.

Garnish each tart with a thyme sprig and serve.

The Crab Boat's A-Coming, Hurrah, Hurrah!

Every Saturday between Easter and Thanksgiving, a steady stream of people can be seen heading towards Pender's Port Browning Marina, carrying a motley array of large pots, pans or buckets. Sometime around noon—give or take a bit—the crab boat, *Fortune IV*, docks and you should be in line. Later in the day, *Fortune IV* may still be there, for the fisherman visits family on Pender, but the crabs will be sold out! These are the large Dungeness crabs, big enough that one will feed two people. We've watched folks buy these live beauties up to 10 at a time, taking advantage of good prices, the large size of the crabs and the fact that fisherman, Jeff Douglass, will kill and clean them if you are too squeamish to do the dirty deed yourself.

Barbecued or boiled, fresh Dungeness crab, cooked and eaten immediately, is so sweet and meaty you will spurn frozen crab meat forever.

Jeff has family on both Pender and Saturna, so he takes a day out of his regular runs to the Vancouver wholesaler and brings his crabs to the islands. We love him for it. Though some islanders own crab traps, only the small rock crabs can be caught at the end of the dock; Dungeness crabs are found in mid-channel and so are out of reach unless you have a boat.

Most people enjoy this local sustainable delicacy simply cooked by dropping the crabs into rapidly boiling seawater and leaving them for 10 minutes. They are then cleaned under cold running water and served with crab crackers, melted garlic butter for dipping and forks.

Alternatively, try the following delicious Ginger and Green Onion Crab recipe.

Ginger and Green Onion Crab

The large, meaty Dungeness crabs found in the deep channels between our islands are big enough to serve two people, so adjust this recipe accordingly for extra guests. It's crucial to deep-fry only one crab at a time so that it can be whisked out of the pan before you overcook it.

On some islands you can buy live crab off the boat, but if you prefer you can usually have it killed and cleaned before you take it home.

Makes 2 servings

Sauce
    2 pinches white pepper
    6 Tbsp (90 mL) water
    1 Tbsp (15 mL) oyster sauce
    ¾ tsp (4 mL) cornstarch
    ½ tsp (2.5 mL) sugar
    ⅛ tsp (0.5 mL) fish sauce
    ⅛ tsp (0.5 mL) roasted sesame oil

In a small bowl, mix sauce ingredients together. Set aside.

Crab
    1½ to 2 lb (680–900 gr) Dungeness crab
    3 Tbsp (45 mL) cornstarch
    Vegetable oil for deep-frying and stir-frying
    2 inch (5 cm) fresh ginger, peeled and sliced into 10 to 12 pieces
    3 green onions, cut into 2 inch (5 cm) lengths

Clean the crab and cut in half. Pat dry with paper towels and place crab in a large bowl.

Sprinkle crab with cornstarch and toss to coat the pieces.

Pour 2 to 3 inches (5–8 cm) vegetable oil into a deep pan and heat to a shimmer. Drop in the two crab pieces and quickly deep-fry. As soon as the shells turn red, immediately remove crab from the pan and drain off excess oil. Set crab aside on paper towel.

Heat 1 Tbsp (15 mL) additional vegetable oil in a wok. Add the ginger and stir-fry for a few seconds, until aromatic. Add the crab pieces and stir a few times to reheat. Add the reserved sauce and green onion, and toss the crab a few times until it's well coated with sauce. Serve immediately.

La Berengerie's Seafood Gratinée

Huguette Benger, owner of Galiano Island's La Berengerie, delights in cooking local fish and offered us her version of a classic French gratin—seafood baked with a cheese sauce.

This recipe looks complicated because of the three steps—making the stock, making the sauce and assembling the dish—but it's not. It is the perfect dish to put together after a Saturday visit to the dock to buy fresh fish direct from the boat. The Salt Spring fish boat *Crab Dancer* regularly calls at both Galiano and Mayne Islands in the summer months. The docking times are posted on the local notice boards. Join the lineup, and you might find yourself standing next to Huguette or Orian Finnie, the current chef at La Berengerie.

Makes 4 servings

Stock

> A little olive oil
> 1 shallot, chopped
> 3 cloves garlic, chopped
> Pinch each cayenne, oregano and paprika
> 12 local prawns (in the shell)
> Glass of dry white wine
> Salt and pepper

In a sauté pan, heat olive oil on medium heat and gently cook shallot and garlic for 3 minutes. Season with cayenne, oregano and paprika.

Add prawns and cook until they just change colour.

Add white wine, salt and pepper. Cover and cook 5 more minutes.

Remove from heat and let cool. Remove prawns and transfer stock to a bowl. Shell prawns and reserve their flesh separately.

Sauce

> A little butter and olive oil
> 3 cloves garlic, chopped
> 1 celery stalk, chopped
> 1 shallot, sliced
> 1 star anise
> Pinch each cayenne, dill seed, orange zest and paprika
> 1 ounce (28 gr) Pernod
> 1 roasted red pepper, peeled, seeded and chopped
> ½ lb (227 gr) mushrooms, sliced
> ½ cup (125 mL) whipping cream

In a fry pan on low heat, melt a little butter with an equivalent amount of olive oil, and sauté garlic, celery, shallot and star anise with the cayenne, dill seed, orange zest and paprika for 5 minutes.

Add the Pernod and reserved stock, and stir in the red pepper and mushrooms. Cook for 5 more minutes.

Add the cream, bring mixture to a boil, lower the heat and simmer the sauce for 5 to 10 minutes.

Assembly

- **4 local scallops**
- **1 salmon steak, 6-8 oz (170-225 gr)**
- **1 piece of halibut , 6-8 oz (170-225 gr)**
- **1 piece of red snapper, 6-8 oz (170-225 gr)**
- **½ cup (125 mL) grated Emmental cheese**

Preheat oven to 350F (175C).

Wash scallops and fish and pat dry. Remove any skin and bones from the fish, and cut it into bite-sized pieces.

Arrange scallops, fish and reserved prawns in an ovenproof dish. Cover with the reserved sauce. Top with grated Emmental.

Bake for 15 minutes, or until browned and bubbling. Serve immediately.

La Berengerie and La Boheme

For 30 years, Galiano's La Berengerie restaurant has served both residents and visitors with local food in creative and eclectic "hints of Mediterranean" and "Fusion" recipes that have kept customers returning. Owner Huguette Benger is still hands-on, though her restaurant partner, Orian Finnie, currently does most of the cooking. Huguette, originally from Avignon, France, is so passionate about food she has written her own cookbook featuring many of La Berengerie's favourite recipes. But like us, she encourages even novice cooks to "experiment, never follow a recipe *à la lettre.*"

Galiano artist Keith Holmes captured the buzz found in and around La Berengerie in a delightful painting, and when it was unveiled islanders had fun identifying themselves dining. To perfect the ambience, Huguette encourages art shows, poetry readings and live classical music in her restaurant. She hosts festivals, and sometimes an artistic flea market takes place in the grounds. During the summer months, the bohemian atmosphere spills outside under a colourful canopy and becomes Café Boheme, a lively outdoor annex run by Huguette's son Nicolas. It presents a casual menu with ethnic and vegetarian choices served at tables gathered around a large outdoor stone fireplace.

The diners and atmosphere at La Berengerie on Galiano are captured by resident artist Keith Holmes.

Salt Spring Vineyards Stuffed Grape Leaves (Dolmades)

Joanne McIntyre has no problem with the main ingredient for this recipe—grape leaves. The rest of us have to know someone with a grapevine. Luckily, grapevines are common on the islands, for long before viticulture became the hottest Gulf Island form of agriculture, pioneers tucked grape stock from the old country in with their goods and chattels. The islands abound with these ancient vines that wind along massive trellises, shelter porches and decks, and occasionally produce grapes.

Grapevines frame the pasture at Wave Hill Farm on Salt Spring.
Jan Mangan photo

David too had a dream. "I'd like to be able to sit under a grape arbour in the sunshine," he admitted as we laboured, heaving rocks for a lavender terrace. "I want to sit back, eyes closed, and be able to stick out my hand and pick a few grapes." Since Dave is ever indulgent of my gardening habit, when I spotted some old grape stock being sold as a fundraiser at the farmers' market, I promptly bought him two short, sturdy vines. Like many old island vines, they are flourishing in less than ideal conditions. In a couple of years, Dave's garden chair will be shaded by their plentiful leaves. They've produced no grapes, though, so I was glad to have this recipe from Joanne, so Dave can nibble on his own dolmades.

The recipe is in two parts. First brine the grape leaves, and then use the brined leaves to make Joanne's dolmades. The brined leaves will keep for a year. If you are lucky enough to have a grapevine of your own, you can use the very young tender leaves without brining—rinse and blanch them to soften them and then completely remove the stem. Be careful: leaves on the vine toughen up quickly. Tough dolmades are dreadful. It's best to brine grape leaves early in the summer when they are young and tender.

Makes 50 dolmades

Brined Grape Leaves
    4 quarts (4 L) water
    50 young grape leaves, stems completely removed
    ½ cup (125 mL) coarse salt

Sterilize two 1 pint (½ L) jars with lids and keep them warm.

Bring 3 quarts (3 L) of the water to a boil.

Divide leaves into two piles, and blanch each pile for 1 minute in the boiling water.

Drain leaves well, spread on towels, blot gently and let dry.

Make the brine by combining the remaining water with the salt in a stainless steel pot. Boil till the salt is dissolved. Let brine cool.

While brine is cooling, fold leaves envelope-style and tuck tightly into the sterilized jars.

Dev McIntyre of Salt Spring Vineyards suggests this wine pairing: "Serve stuffed vine leaves with Salt Spring Vineyard's 2009 Pinot Noir. The wine is young and fruity. Its refreshing coastal acidity pairs nicely with the flavours of the stuffed grape leaves."

Pour cooled brine into jars to within ½ inch (1.3 cm) of the rim.

Process 15 minutes in a canner, following the manufacturer's instructions. Cool and store on a dark shelf.

Dolmades

These meat-stuffed dolmades can be served as a party appetizer or as an entrée dish. The recipe can easily be halved.

    50 brined grape leaves or tender young grape leaves, blanched
    1 Walla Walla onion, diced
    4 large cloves garlic, finely chopped
    1 large carrot, finely diced
    1 red pepper, finely chopped
    4 Tbsp (60 mL) chopped parsley
    ½ cup (125 mL) uncooked brown or white rice
    1 lb (454 gr) ground veal or pork
    ½ lb (227 gr) ground lean beef or Gulf Island lamb
    ¼ cup (60 mL) olive oil
    Salt
    Zest of 1 large lemon
    Juice of 1 large lemon
    Equal parts chicken broth and Salt Spring Vineyards Pinot Noir
    Lemon wedges, for garnish

Preheat oven to 350F (175C) and grease a casserole.

Soak brined leaves in cold water for 10 minutes to desalt. Drain and soak again in fresh cold water. Drain and pat dry.

In a large bowl, mix together all the stuffing ingredients, except for the lemon juice, broth and wine.

Pinch off a golf ball–sized piece of stuffing, form into a roll and place at the base of a grape leaf. Roll the leaf, tucking in the sides as you go, to form a small parcel.

Place roll seam side down in casserole. Repeat, fitting rolls tightly together.

Sprinkle lemon juice over completed layer and make a second and third layer as needed.

Pour enough stock and wine mixture over rolls to cover them.

Weigh down the rolls with an ovenproof pie plate that will fit inside the casserole. Cover with aluminum foil, seal it around the edge of the casserole and then place the casserole lid on top. (This double seal ensures that no steam escapes.)

Bake casserole in the middle of the oven for two and a half hours.

Serve dolmades warm with extra lemon wedges.

Vine-Leaf Recipes from Salt Spring Vineyards

Food and wine go together like . . . well, you know the many sayings. Salt Spring Vineyards owners Dev and Joanne McIntyre have a new take on food pairings, as they not only have a wine-tasting room with a fridge full of local cheese to tempt your taste buds and wallet, but also have built a delightful bed and breakfast suite over it. It is both the ultimate place to stay for wine lovers and a breakfast lover's delight. Joanne McIntyre is a great cook, and her vineyard breakfasts, delivered to the room in a basket, are both innovative and beautifully presented. We weren't surprised when, on hearing about our book, she immediately produced a two-in-one recipe featuring grape leaves. Joanne often uses grapes creatively in her cooking; roasted grapes, fresh pressed grape juice, and grapes in sauces and salsas. It's amazing how creative you can be with a vineyard as your front yard.

Lavender and Lemon Butterflied Lamb

The key to this simple dish is the lovely marinade. Don't be taken aback by the use of lavender; remember, it's related to rosemary so is perfect with red meats. When finally spread over the grill, the butterflied leg cooks evenly and quickly. Slice it on a board at the table for your ravenous guests who, we hope, have brought along salads, buns and a local red wine, so you too can party!

Makes 6 to 8 servings

- 4 cloves garlic, finely chopped
- 3 sprigs lemon thyme
- 2 bay leaves, each broken into 3 pieces
- 1 cup (250 mL) Salt Spring Vineyards Blackberry Port
- ½ cup (125 mL) lavender or white wine vinegar
- ½ cup (125 mL) fresh lemon juice
- 3 Tbsp (45 mL) grated lemon zest
- 1 Tbsp (15 mL) Dijon mustard
- 1 Tbsp (15 mL) dried culinary lavender buds (ground in spice grinder or cleaned coffee bean grinder)
- 1 Tbsp (15 mL) grated fresh ginger
- 1 butterflied leg Gulf Island lamb (about 4 lb/2 kg deboned meat)
- 2 lemon wedges per person, plus 2 extra

Whisk together all ingredients except lamb and lemon wedges, and pour into an 8 by 10 inch (20 by 25 cm) glass pan. Spread butterflied leg of lamb cut side down in the marinade.

Cover and marinate in the fridge overnight. Turn over the following morning and leave in the marinade until ready to barbecue.

Oil grill rack and preheat grill to medium.

Drain lamb and lightly pat dry. Save the marinade for basting the meat on the grill.

Grill lamb, basting as needed, on medium heat for about 10 minutes on each side, or until an instant-read thermometer inserted horizontally into thickest part of meat registers 125°F (52C) for medium-rare.

Transfer lamb to a carving plate. Squeeze 2 lemon wedges over lamb and let stand, loosely covered with foil, for 10 minutes.

Cut lamb into slices and drizzle with any juices that have accumulated on the carving plate. Serve with remaining lemon wedges.

If you enjoy celebrating Canada Day with a barbecue party on your deck, this is the perfect recipe. It just needs a bit of forethought, for first you need to buy a butterflied leg of lamb, and prepare it the day before cooking.

A butterflied leg is one that has been split open down the length so the leg bone can be removed. The boneless meat is then usually rolled up and tied. The roll can be seasoned and roasted on the rotisserie as is, but rotisserie cooking takes both time and attention.

We like to keep things simple. We cut the string, unroll the meat and marinate it in a shallow dish, turning halfway through.

The Saturna Lamb Barbeque

Canada Day (July 1) is celebrated with pizzazz on the Southern Gulf Islands with an event of epic proportions. Since 1949, Saturna—the quietest and most reclusive of the Gulf Islands—has thrown the biggest annual public party, known as the Saturna Island Lamb Barbeque.

It began when a ram belonging to Saturna pioneer Jim Cruickshank fell down the well. He'd been trying to raise sheep through the hard winter of 1949/50, and that finished him. He gave up and sold his flock, all but the last two lambs. These he offered to barbecue for a school picnic and to raise funds for the community hall.

Jim used a style of cooking he'd learned in Argentina, in which the carcass was supported on an iron framework in front of a slow wood fire. The lamb was so delicious that the community decided to repeat the event the following year.

Sixty years later, the Saturna Island Lamb Barbeque has become a major event. Each year Saturna Islanders work for weeks to pull it off. Twenty-five or more lambs are raised to feed more than a thousand guests. Cords of wood are chopped and hauled for the fire, and gallons of Spanish rice and coleslaw prepared. The barbecue has moved with the times, though, and vegetarian guests can now order an alternative meal. So Jim's farewell gesture lives on, and the funds raised still support community facilities on the island.

The barbecue attracts celebrants from up and down the West Coast. They arrive by sail and motorboat and jostle for mooring space in Winter Cove. Rain or shine, everyone comes early to stake out a spot in the nearby park. Newbies watch with bemusement as old hands hike in at 8:00 a.m. with folding chairs, backpacks full of snacks and drinks, blankets and even collapsible awnings strapped to their backs.

The lambs are still roasted, Argentinian style, on vertical spits erected around a gigantic bonfire. As the lamb cooks, it's turned and basted with a secret marinade sloshed on with large switches of fresh rosemary and mint. Live music, games and races entertain the crowd. There is a craft market, hamburger stand and beer tent. At midday, everyone stands to sing a lusty version of "O Canada" despite the distracting savoury aroma that by this time hangs over the island. Midafternoon, and it's finally time. We line up to tuck into the traditional fare: plates loaded with slices of succulent lamb accompanied by buns and generous servings of Spanish rice and coleslaw. There is even a cookie for dessert. Suddenly, all is quiet except for the smacking of lips.

Local lamb roasts beside an open fire.

Asian Chicken to Go

Since summer is the time for casual meals on the deck or picnics on the beach, we love easy, tasty, adaptable dishes. This elegant main course chicken dish can be made well ahead and served hot or cold. It is also easily portable picnic fare, so perfect for summer. Use locally raised free range "happy hens" and your chicken will be hormone and antibiotic free, and so will you!

Makes 4 servings

2 lb (900 gr) organic chicken drumsticks or thighs
8 large cloves garlic, finely chopped
1 cup (250 mL) Gulf Island white wine
¼ cup (60 mL) soy sauce
3 Tbsp (45 mL) grated fresh ginger
Juice and zest of 2 lemons

Wash and dry chicken. Place in a bowl.

Add all the other ingredients and toss to coat chicken.

Cover and marinate in the refrigerator for at least 2 hours, or overnight, stirring occasionally.

Preheat oven to 350F (175C).

Place chicken in a shallow roasting pan, spoon some solids from the marinade on each piece and baste with the marinade.

Roast chicken for 30 to 40 minutes, basting at least once, until well browned. (Discard any leftover uncooked marinade.)

Serve hot or cold.

Sacred Mountain Lavender

Two acres of organic lavender—over 60 varieties, both culinary and non-culinary—blooming from June to September and a farm shop full of home-made lavender products make Salt Spring Island's Sacred Mountain Lavender farm a site worth seeing. As well as having the delight of wandering the fields, you can pick up some unusual and beautifully packaged edible lavender products in the farm shop. Culinary lavender is creeping into mainstream use. Long an ingredient in *herbes de Provence*, lavender is also present in several Sacred Mountain food products. Lavender pepper and salt, lavender sugar, chocolate and lavender brownie mix and lavender jellies are just a sample. Then there are the more usual soaps, bath bombs, lavender water and sachets. Lavender lovers can also find a full range of Sacred Mountain products for sale at the Sacred Mountain booth at the Ganges Saturday market.

Top: Sacred Mountain lavender jelly and lavender chocolate cake mix.

Above: Jacqueline Sutton shows growing Spanish lavender and some of her products.

A field of lavender gladdens the eye at Salt Spring's Between The Covers B&B.

Lavender and Rosemary Red Wine Jelly

A stunning jelly, simple to make, lovely in colour and delightful in taste. I gave this for Christmas gifts last year. Everyone loved it and one recipient phoned to say she kept going to the fridge with a teaspoon, and when could she have another jar!

This versatile, soft-set jelly pairs well with meats, such as lamb, pork or poultry. Spread over a round of Brie cheese, the jelly is a pretty appetizer. It's also lovely with scones, served spooned over ice cream or mixed into whipped cream.

Makes eight ½ cup (125 ml) jars

½ cup (125 mL) culinary lavender buds
½ cup (125 mL) fresh rosemary leaves, chopped
Zest of 1 lemon
½ cup (125 mL) lemon Juice
2 cups (475 mL) robust red wine
4 cups (1 L) sugar
3 ounce (85 gr) pouch liquid pectin

Sterilize eight ½ cup (125 ml) jelly jars with lids and keep warm until needed.

Place the lavender and rosemary in a Dutch oven.

Add the lemon zest, lemon juice and wine to the pot, and bring to a boil. As soon as the mixture boils, remove from the heat. Cover the pot and let mixture steep for 30 minutes.

Strain the mixture through a sieve lined with a double thickness of dampened cheesecloth. Press on the herbs to extract as much liquid as possible. Discard the herbs.

Strain the liquid a second time through a sieve lined with a coffee filter to removed any small particles and keep the jelly clear.

Combine the strained liquid and sugar in the pot. Bring to a boil over high heat, stirring often. When the mixture reaches a full boil that cannot be stirred down, stir in the pectin, following the manufacturer's instructions.

Remove from heat. Skim off any foam that has formed.

Pour jelly into the hot, sterilized jars, leaving ¼ inch (0.6 cm) head space. Wipe the rims clean. Seal with new tops. Process the jars in a canner for 10 minutes.

Remove and let cool. You will hear pops as the lids seal. Store any unsealed jars in the fridge and eat first.

Herbed and Spiced Butters

Fresh or dried herbs mixed into butter add a rich sparkle of taste to veggies and meats without the trouble of making a sauce and so are the perfect accompaniment for a casual summer meal.

Here is the basic recipe, but note it is a "reckless abandon" type recipe. Use any of your favourite herbs or spices. If you overdo the herbs, add more butter. Make the herbed butter ahead, store it in the freezer, slice off what you need when you need it and you are an instant gourmet cook! Use it to top steak, fish or chicken, or dot it on steamed vegetable or potato dishes. Feel free to experiment—spread garlic-dill butter on cheese scones or lavender-lemon butter on plain scones.

Makes about 20 servings (1 Tbsp / 15 mL per serving)

½–1 cup (125–250 mL) finely chopped fresh herbs (See below for possible combinations)
1 cup (250 mL) butter, at room temperature
Sea salt and freshly ground pepper/ground spices of choice
1 tsp –1 Tbsp (5–15 mL) liquid such a citrus juice or flavoured oil, or a touch of honey (adjust depending on the softness you prefer for the butter)

Beat herbs into the softened butter.

Add seasonings and any ground spices to taste, and beat until combined.

Beat in the liquid.

Spread a sheet of plastic wrap on the counter and form the butter mixture into a log shape (if butter is too soft, cool in the fridge for 10 minutes). Wrap tightly and roll log in plastic, label and freeze.

To use, unwrap the frozen log, cut off the number of slices needed, rewrap it and return unused portion to the freezer. Keep slices in the fridge until ready to use.

Parking regulations are strict in the Gulf Islands.

Some favourite combinations:

Chopped garlic and parsley

Curry powder, parsley and hot sauce

Cinnamon and honey

Tarragon, garlic and lemon juice

Mint, lemon zest and juice

Chives and orange juice

Dill and lemon zest

Basil and truffle oil

Cilantro, garlic and lime juice

Garlic and anchovy fillets

Rosemary, lavender and lemon zest

Go ahead—have fun and create your own special butter.

Breezy Bay Farm on Saturna Island is a hub of constant activity, particularly in the spring and summer. It is the only certified organic farm on Saturna and the only one that sells its products off the island. The farm also hosts some community plots tended by individual islanders who promise to follow its strict organic principles. Scattered across a field on the spring morning we visited, people were engaged in digging, stringing seedling supports or sowing seeds in the newly warmed ground.

Owners Bill and Flo House were way ahead of the game; their spring field was already sprouting, for they produce a variety of fresh herbs, such as chives, mint and dill, as well as their beloved summer crop, basil. They ship the herbs to Vancouver for distribution to Thrifty Foods stores.

This land has been farmed since Saturna's early settlement days, when remittance man Gerald Payne arrived from England and began clearing it. The historic Payne House still stands, overlooking the farmlands, and is now run as Breezy Bay Bed & Breakfast. Gerald Payne wouldn't recognize his farm, though. He planted an orchard, ran a few sheep and lived with his wife and kids in Victorian splendour, roughing it with a cook and maid. He would never have envisaged his farm as such hard-working land or dreamed of basil as a cash crop. Basil is a tender herb, but it flourishes in dry Saturna summers. Flo has developed a way of packaging it in a plastic casing, so the herb stays fresh while being distributed to Lower Mainland and Vancouver Island stores. Watch for the Breezy Bay label in the produce department when you are grocery shopping.

Hey Pesto! A Summer Delight

Fresh basil means summer is finally here. Basil, like Gulf Islanders, revels in long hot days, and the turning of its pungent leaves into the savoury spread called pesto creates one of summer's greatest gifts.

Making pesto is quick and easy. Once you have made the basic basil recipe, then it is easily adapted to create tasty summer herbal treats from a variety of garden-grown herbs. Parsley, arugula or garlic scapes (the long flower stalks) married with a variety of cheeses all make delightfully different pestos that can be used to heighten sauces, coat pasta, add depth to stew, season meatballs, garnish new potatoes, flavour soup—the list is endless.

The only problem is keeping it. Fresh pesto is usually stored in the fridge in a small jar with a layer of olive oil on top to keep out the air and stop the pesto from darkening. It must be used within two or three weeks.

But I love pesto and like to keep it around all year. The preserving problem is now solved, thanks to zip-sealed freezer bags. Spoon your pesto into small resealable bags, press out the air and seal. Lay the bag on a cookie sheet, evenly spread out the pesto so it's flat, and freeze in the bag. Once frozen flat, the bags are easily stored in the deep freeze. When pesto is needed for a recipe, open a bag, break off the amount of pesto required, reseal the bag and return it to the freezer. Hey, pesto—a taste of summer all year round.

Pesto Potato Salad

This is potato salad with a summer makeover. If you don't grow your own herbs, look for fresh basil and parsley at honesty stands and farmers' markets. If you have time and like a more intense flavour, dry the tomato halves in the oven (or in the sunshine) ahead of time.

Makes 6 servings

5 medium potatoes
½ lb (227 gr) green beans
1 cup (250 mL) cherry tomatoes, halved
2 cloves garlic, chopped
⅓ cup (80 mL) packed basil leaves
⅓ cup (80 mL) vegetable oil
¼ cup (60 mL) hot water
2 Tbsp (30 mL) white wine vinegar
¼ tsp (1 mL) pepper
½ cup (125 mL) packed parsley sprigs
⅓ cup (80 mL) grated Parmesan cheese
⅛ tsp (0.5 mL) salt
Several whole lettuce leaves, washed and patted dry
A few shredded basil leaves, for garnish

Peel and cook potatoes. When cool, slice into ¼ inch (0.6 cm) thick slices.

Trim green beans, cut into 2 inch (5 cm) pieces, steam, drain and cool.

Combine potatoes, beans and tomatoes in a large bowl. Set aside.

Make pesto dressing by blending garlic, basil, oil, water, vinegar and pepper until smooth.

Add parsley, Parmesan and salt, and pulse until smooth, scraping down the sides of the blender as needed. Check seasoning and adjust to taste.

Pour basil pesto over potato mix. Turn potatoes gently to coat them with dressing.

Line a serving bowl with lettuce leaves. Fill with pesto potato salad. Garnish with the shredded basil, chill and serve.

Substitute sliced mushrooms and sliced green beans or chopped red pepper and diced precooked squash for the tomato and corn.

Substitute crumbled blue cheese or goat cheese for the cheddar.

Tomato, Corn and Dill Risotto

On a hot summer day, who wants to use the oven? A simple yet sophisticated risotto dish is the answer. If you own a barbecue with a side ring as well as a grill, you can stir the rice in a leisurely manner, wine glass in hand, while chatting with guests lounging on the deck. A true risotto needs low heat and lots of stirring to let the rice develop the creamy texture of the traditional Italian dish, but the resulting taste is worth the effort. The key to great risotto is to use a good heavy-bottomed pan, take your time and stir often. Penderites have a bumper sticker that reads, "What's the hurry? I'm on Pender time." For this dish, we need one that reads, "What's the hurry? We're on risotto time." Serve this unusual risotto with warm crusty artisan bread and chilled white wine.

Makes 4 servings

> 2¼ cups (535 mL) chicken stock
> 2 cups (475 mL) milk
> 2 Tbsp (30 mL) butter
> 1 onion, chopped
> 2 cloves garlic, chopped
> 1 cup (250 mL) arborio rice
> ½ cup (125 mL) dry white Gulf Island wine
> 1 large tomato, skinned, deseeded and diced
> 1½ cups (350 mL) corn kernels freshly cut from the cob
> ¼ tsp (1 mL) each salt and pepper
> ½ cup (125 mL) grated White Grace Cheddar from Moonstruck Cheese
> Handful fresh dill, finely chopped, small sprigs dill, for garnish

Combine the chicken stock and milk in a saucepan. Heat until simmering, then keep warm.

In a large saucepan, melt the butter on medium heat and fry the onion until softened. Add the garlic and stir for a few seconds until fragrant. Stir in the rice and keep stirring for 1 minute. Add the wine and stir until absorbed.

Begin to add the warm stock/milk combination ½ cup (125 mL) at a time, stirring frequently so the rice does not stick on the bottom of the pan. Wait until the liquid is almost absorbed before adding the next portion of liquid.

Add the tomato and corn with the last ½ cup (125 mL) liquid. Keep gently stirring until the rice is fully cooked but slightly chewy and the corn tender. The stirring process takes about 20 minutes to this point.

Stir in the salt, pepper, cheese and dill, and then quickly spoon the risotto into a hot serving dish and scatter some dill sprigs on top. Serve immediately.

Farmers' Market Spanish Rice

If you are on Galiano or Saturna, you will be aware that both names have Spanish origins. It's fun to give a nod to this Spanish heritage by cooking Spanish rice as a tasty alternative to plain rice. Here is the easiest way to make Spanish rice when on one of the islands: head to the nearest farmers' market and buy an onion and some freshly made salsa!

Makes 4 to 6 servings

> 2 Tbsp (30 mL) oil
> 2 Tbsp (30 mL) chopped onion
> 1½ cups (350 mL) uncooked long grain white rice
> 2 cups (475 mL) chicken broth
> 1 cup (250 mL) chunky farmers' market salsa

Heat oil in a large, heavy skillet over medium heat. Stir in onion, and cook until tender, about 5 minutes.

Mix in rice and stir often until it begins to brown.

Stir in chicken broth and salsa. Reduce heat, cover and simmer for 20 minutes, until liquid has been absorbed.

Fluff and serve.

Peek into History: A Touch of Spain

Three hundred years ago, Spanish explorers sailed Gulf Island waters in small gutsy galleons. It is fitting that their explorations are still remembered in the smattering of Spanish place names across the islands. In 1792, Commander Dionisio Alcala Galiano of the Spanish navy left his name behind on Galiano Island. Bragging rights for the first charting of Saturna Island go to the crew of the schooner *Santa Saturnina*. A plaque at East Point honours the ship's captain, José María Narváez y Gervete, and his name graces Narvaez Bay. Reminders of these early contacts are also at Dionisio Park, Mount Sutil and Bodega Ridge.

The Spanish connection is celebrated annually on Saturna and Galiano. Both islands built replicas of the launches that landed the Spanish seamen on shore. Saturna Islanders celebrated the bicentennial of the island's discovery by Europeans by building the *Saturnita*, and Galiano residents built the *Nina*, a copy of the Sutil's longboat. Both islands take turns hosting races in which these boats compete with each other, and we all cheer on the fiercely competitive rowers.

A customized marrow waits for the right child to discover it. Her name was scratched with a pin when the vegetable was small—a great way to get kids interested in gardening.

Mark Lauckner—Saving a Seedy Heritage

While spending an afternoon on Mayne Island enjoying the galleries and studios, we wandered into the Mayne Island Glass Foundry and within minutes found ourselves deep in a discussion about heritage seeds with owner/artist Mark Lauckner. It's wonderful how a passion for growing things shows up in unexpected places. In no time flat, the gallery was left behind to look after itself as we tramped through the drizzle to inspect Mark's garden at the back. Here were no superb vegetables waiting to be picked, but a different take on a gardener's pride and joy—a variety of overripe vegetables that Mark was monitoring while the seeds developed.

An ardent saver of heritage seeds, Mark soon had us viewing the garden as he did, not as just a food source, but as a seed bank for varieties of tomatoes, carrots, squash, garlic and so on that have nearly died out.

Mark has been involved with the heritage seed movement since 1980 and has written numerous articles advocating seed saving and the use of rare varieties of vegetables. He is quietly part of a growing effort to repopularize endangered heritage varieties and to stop major seed producers from creating a monopoly of genetically modified seeds. He's doing his bit to ensure global food security. So if you are on Mayne Island in the summer, drop into the glassworks to see his artwork but also ask about buying heritage seeds so you too can enjoy the luscious flavours of long-forgotten vegetable treasures that will, in turn, produce seeds you can plant.

Ten Terrific Sandwich Fillings

The scenic hikes on the Southern Gulf Islands often demand a packed lunch; the ever-changing scenery is far too compelling to turn back for a meal. There is nothing better than leaning against a log enjoying the view before you and munching on a sandwich made from island artisan bread and local farmers' market or honesty-stand products. Here are some sandwich filling suggestions to help you savour your surroundings.

• Moonstruck's White Grace Cheddar, sliced tomato and arugula

• Roast pork and honesty-stand plum sauce

• Egg salad and farmers' market salsa

• David's Cream Cheese (see page 20), avocado and local wine jelly

• Salmon paté from Salt Spring Fishery and Christina's Pea Sprouts (see p. 188)

• David Wood's goat's cheese and farmers' market tapenade

• Garden Pea and Avocado Hummus (see page 75) topped with sliced apple and chopped dates

• Freshly ground organic peanut butter and Deacon Vale Farm Jalapeño Jelly

• Sliced barbecued lamb with Lavender and Rosemary Red Wine Jelly (see page 95) and thinly sliced onion

• Gravlax (see page 23) with fresh watercress

Pick up a rosemary loaf baked by Heather Campbell, Salt Spring's "Bread Lady," (see page 214) and delectable sandwich fixings at the farmers' market.

Chocolate Lavender Cake

Chocolate and lavender are a lovely combination. This recipe makes a beautiful summer birthday or special occasion cake. Cake batter can also be baked in mini bundt pans for pretty individual presentations.

Makes 8 to 10 servings

Cake

 ¾ cup (180 mL) milk
 2 Tbsp (30 mL) dried culinary lavender
 6 egg whites
 1¾ cups (430 mL) all-purpose flour
 ½ cup (125 mL) cocoa
 2 tsp (10 mL) baking powder
 ¼ tsp (1 mL) salt
 ¾ cup (180 mL) softened butter
 1½ cups (350 mL) sugar
 3 tsp (15 mL) vanilla extract

Preheat oven to 350F (175C). Cut disks of parchment paper and line the bottoms of two 9 inch (23 cm) round cake pans. Grease the paper and pans liberally with butter, and dust lightly with cocoa powder.

In a small saucepan, heat milk and lavender to just before the boiling point. Immediately remove from heat and let steep for 20 minutes. Strain milk through a fine sieve lined with muslin or through a basket-type coffee filter. Discard lavender and set milk aside to cool.

Whip the egg whites till they form soft peaks, and set aside.

Sift together flour, cocoa, baking powder and salt, and set aside.

Cream butter and sugar. Gradually add the cooled lavender milk and vanilla while beating.

Alternately fold the beaten egg whites and flour mixture into the butter mixture till combined and not streaky.

Pour batter into the cake pans and bake for 30 to 35 minutes, until tops spring back when touched. If using mini-bundt pans, check cakes after 20 minutes.

Cool cakes on a baking rack for 10 minutes, then remove from cake pans and peel off parchment paper.

Continued on next page

Note: To prevent the cakes from sticking in the mini bundt pans, liberally butter the pans and dust lightly with cocoa powder. After removal from the pans, prick the baked surfaces with a fork to allow absorption of the lavender syrup.

Syrup

1½ cups (350 mL) sugar
⅓ cup (80 mL) dried culinary lavender
1½ cups (350 mL) water

Combine sugar, lavender and water in a small saucepan.

Bring mixture to a boil, and boil until the syrup thickens.

Strain syrup and set aside. Discard lavender.

Filling and Topping

1 cup (250 gr) whipping cream
Grated dark chocolate, for garnish
3 sprigs fresh or dried lavender

While cakes are still warm, level the top of each layer by carving off the curved portion. Prick the cake layers with a fork and, using a spoon or ladle, drizzle ½ cup (125 mL) of the reserved lavender syrup over the top of each layer. Allow the cake to soak up the syrup. Cool completely.

Whip the cream until thick. Top one layer of the cooled cake with half the whipped cream.

Place the second layer, cut side down, on top of the cream.

Decorate cake with the remaining whipped cream. Cover cream with grated chocolate and lay lavender sprigs across the middle.

Cooking with Lavender

We planted lavender in two raised terraces around a small but walkable spiral labyrinth. It is a relaxing, pleasantly scented garden of contemplation that I walk regularly. We planted several varieties and shades. Some, like Royal Purple and Grosso, are strongly coloured and extremely pungent. They were developed for their essential oils, and I use them in potpourri or dried flower arrangements. These lavenders should not be used as a culinary herb. Though they won't hurt you, they are too strong and bitter to use successfully in cooking.

The culinary varieties of lavender, such as Hidcote and Provence, are soft in both colour and fragrance. They bloom along the front of the beds within easy reach of plucking, and I use them in a variety of ways.

Related to rosemary, lavender is best used with discretion. While the whole bud tossed into hot water makes wonderful lavender tea, the bud is too harsh to use whole in most recipes, so try the following techniques.

Check your recipe, and instead of leaving the lavender buds whole, infuse them ahead of time in the liquid to be used. Cool the liquid and pour through a sieve or coffee filter, pressing on the lavender buds to extract all their flavour. Discard the solids. Add the liquid to the recipe where specified.

If the recipe contains little or no liquid, grind the lavender buds in a clean coffee grinder. You can also mix the lavender buds together with sugar in the recipe, and then blend in a blender or food processor until there are only fine pieces. Use the sugar in the recipe as noted.

Foxglove Farm Strawberries with Balsamic Sabayon

Forget ice cream—this recipe takes the delight of fresh local strawberries to new heights by adding a sublime sauce—sabayon. Use it the day it is made, as sabayon will separate if kept overnight.

Makes 8 servings

> 4 Tbsp (60 mL) sugar
> 3 egg yolks
> 1½ Tbsp (22.5 mL) balsamic vinegar*
> 1 cup (250 mL) whipping cream
> 3 baskets (6 cups/700 mL) local strawberries, hulled

Place some water and ice in a large bowl. Refrigerate until needed.

Bring some water to a simmer in the bottom pan of a double saucepan. The water in the lower pan should not touch the bottom of the upper pan.

In the upper pan, whisk together the sugar and egg yolks. Beat well until light in colour. This is best done with an electric whisk.

Place the upper pan over the simmering water in the lower pan, and continue to beat the sabayon until it becomes very pale, thickens and falls in ribbons from the beaters (do not overcook).

Remove from the heat. Whisk in the balsamic vinegar.

Place the pan containing the sabayon in the prepared bowl of iced water, and continue whisking until the sabayon is completely cooled (approximately 10 minutes).

In a separate bowl, whip the cream until it forms thick peaks.

Gently combine the whipped cream with the sabayon, and refrigerate until ready to serve.

Divide the strawberries among the dishes, and spoon the sabayon over the berries. Serve immediately.

*Aged balsamic vinegar is the best, but ordinary balsamic vinegar will also work well, though its flavour is not as complex as that of aged balsamic vinegar.

Foxglove—More Than a Farm

The 120 acre (49 hectare) Foxglove Farm on Salt Spring Island, headed up by the indefatigable Michael Ableman, his co-founder and partner Jeanne-Marie Herman, and their farm partners Sean and Dorie Hutchinson, is a wonderful example of a heritage farmstead given an imaginative new lease on life.

The farming here is serious—extensive fields of organic fruits and vegetables, large productive greenhouses, orchards, goats and chickens, grains and legumes. But this is also a place of learning; Foxglove Farm is also the Centre for Arts, Ecology & Agriculture.

The centre offers diverse programs, retreats and workshops that run from one day to a week. There is a choice of accommodations, from deluxe cabins to camping sites, and you can learn how to start a mushroom-growing operation, take a cooking class with a well-known chef, make cheese, build an outdoor wood-fired oven, hone storytelling skills or learn how to retrofit solar technology. The centre offers a seemingly endless variety of public programs, classes and events.

While first and foremost a farmer, Michael Ableman is also an author and photographer, and is well known for his books on sustainable and guerrilla farming, and the issues relating to food in our modern world. He's also behind SOLEfood, an urban farming project run in a parking lot in Vancouver's Downtown Eastside, and is a source of moral support and information for many Gulf Island farmers.

Despite the diversity in the Foxglove operation, food production is front and centre, and volunteers come from around the world to work here. The farm produce is sold at Salt Spring's Saturday and Tuesday markets, and Salt Spring Islanders can sign up to be part of the Community Shares Program. They commit to paying up front at the beginning of the growing season and get a weekly discounted share of the produce throughout the season. This innovative partnership between the farm and consumer benefits both.

Foxglove produces not only standard vegetables and fruit, but some high-end luxury items as well, such as artichokes and quince, persimmons and figs. In spring, this is the place to come for its signature crop, asparagus.

To find out more about Foxglove Farm and the Centre for Arts, Ecology & Agriculture, check the farm's extensive website (see "Sources" section, page 234).

A young assistant helps out at the Foxglove farmers' market stall. *Jan Mangan photo*

Fennel edges this field of artichokes on Foxglove Farm.

Multicoloured carrots are a Foxglove specialty.

Rose Petal Meringues

June is a favourite month for weddings and roses. There is no better way to add a WOW factor at the end of a celebratory meal than with these meringues flavoured with rose petals.

All roses petals are edible, but many Gulf Islanders cultivate old-fashioned rose varieties that have wonderful fragrances. These are the ones to use for this recipe. Or pick a few of the wild roses from the roadside (never from parks). They too have a wonderful fragrance that transfers to food.

This looks like a long and complicated recipe, but all three sections are easy. Just plan ahead. Make both the crystallized rose petals and the meringue shells well before the event to allow them to dry.

Makes 8 to 10 filled meringues

Crystallized Rose Petals

To make these delights, you will need to gather a large handful of fragrant rose petals. Make sure they are organic, clean and dry. You will also need a pair of small scissors, a small clean paintbrush, a teaspoon and fork, and a baking sheet covered with parchment paper.

Wild roses.

> 20 fragrant rose petals
> 1 egg white
> A few drops of water
> 1 cup (250 mL) sugar

Use scissors to carefully clip off the bitter white portion at the base of each rose petal.

Combine the egg white with a little water and beat lightly with a fork.

Place the sugar in a blender and pulse a few times to make it finer. Pour sugar into a saucer.

Holding one petal at a time, carefully paint each side with the egg white mixture. Drop the petal onto the sugar and use the teaspoon to sprinkle sugar over all surfaces.

Using a fork, carefully transfer sugared petal to the baking sheet. Repeat the process until all the petals are coated.

Place the baking sheet in a cool dry place to allow the petals to dry and crystallize completely.

Once dried, store the crystallized petals in an airtight container. They will keep for months. They can be used not only in the meringue recipe below, but also to decorate cakes and cookies. Other edible flowers can be preserved using this method (see sidebar, page 111).

Meringues

- 3 egg whites
- ¾ cup (180 mL) sugar
- 1½ tsp (8 mL) rose water
- Tiny drop red food colouring (optional)

Preheat oven to 120F (49C). Line two baking sheets with parchment paper.

In a metal bowl, beat egg whites until foamy. Gradually add sugar and beat until mixture holds soft peaks.

Continue beating while dripping in the rose water. Beat until mixture is stiff and glossy.

Beat in food colouring, if using. If desired, first divide meringue mixture in half and colour one portion only.

Pipe or spoon 16 to 20 small mounds of meringue mixture onto the prepared baking sheets.

Place baking sheets in the oven and leave them there for 1 hour, checking that the meringues are not getting brown.

Turn off the oven but leave the meringues inside until they are fully dry and the oven has cooled. Leave them in overnight if necessary.

Carefully lift the cold meringues from the parchment paper using a spatula. Store them in an airtight container. They will keep for several weeks.

Rose Filling and Assembly

This must be done immediately before serving or the filling makes the meringues go soft.

- 1 cup (250 mL) heavy whipping cream
- 8 finely crushed crystallized rose petals
- 1 tsp (5 mL) rose water
- 8–10 whole crystallized rose petals
- Icing sugar
- One fresh rose for decoration

Whip together the cream, crushed rose petals and rose water until the mixture is very thick and holds stiff peaks.

Sandwich a spoonful of the cream mixture between two meringues.

Perch a crystallized rose petal on top.

Arrange on a silver platter, dust with a little icing sugar and garnish platter with the fresh rose. Serve immediately.

Crystallized Flowers

These edible flowers and leaves can be successfully crystallized using the same method as for rose petals:

Freesia blossoms (remove from the green stems)

Mint leaves

Pansy petals

Lemon balm leaves

Violets

Fresh (not dried) lavender sprigs

Nasturtium flowers and buds

Rose buds

Borage flowers

Beautiful Blueberries

Blueberries are the perfect summer fruit—so perfect they need no adornment! There are several blueberry farms on the islands, so fresh blueberries can be purchased in season at the farmers' markets. In a good year, watch for the "U Pick" signs on the roads and take the family along to help gather the fruit.

Blueberries are wonderful served alone, sprinkled over granola or ice cream, or accompanying a slice of cake. They are also the easiest of island fruits to preserve. Simply spread on cookie sheets and freeze. Once frozen, they can be stored in resealable bags and kept for the winter. What could be easier?

Summer Pudding

Summer pudding is a lovely, traditional, no-bake, make-ahead dessert for a hot summer day. It can be made with any soft summer fruit, but it's best with those with a rich tart flavour, such as raspberries, red and black currants, and blackberries. A mix of blackberries and red currants is our favourite.

This recipe is an approximation. Use whatever size bowl you wish, cook the amount of fruit needed to fill it and use as many slices of bread as necessary to completely line the bowl. If using a large bowl, add an extra layer of bread slices across the middle of the filling to keep the structure solid.

Makes 6 servings in a 4 cup (1 L) bowl

> **4 cup (1 L) non-reactive bowl**
> **½ cup (125 mL) sugar (or more to taste)**
> **1 Tbsp (15 mL) lemon juice**
> **1 Tbsp (15 mL) water**
> **1 to 1½ lb (454–680 gr) washed, mixed soft summer fruits**
> **Approximately 8 slices white bread, crusts removed***
> **Whipped cream**

In a saucepan, stir together the sugar, lemon juice and water, and bring mixture to a gentle boil. Add the fruits and stew very gently until they have softened but still retain their shape.

Using a round cookie cutter or glass, cut a circle from the first slice of bread. Place the circle in the base of the bowl.

Line the rest of the bowl with the bread slices by placing them against the sides, slightly overlapping both the bottom circle and each other. Cut and taper them as needed. The trimmings will be used to fill any gaps on top.

Fill the lined basin with the stewed fruits, and cover the top of the fruit with more bread slices and the trimmings. Again, overlap the bread pieces, making sure to leave no gaps.

Place a weighted saucer on top of the pudding. (A large can of tomatoes works well). Place the bowl on a plate in case the juices overflow. Leave overnight in the fridge to allow the bread to absorb the juices.

Just before serving, run a knife around the edge of the pudding, and turn it out onto a plate with a rim to catch any juices.

Cut the pudding into wedges and serve with whipped cream.

*Any white bread works, but brioche is particularly tasty.

Andrea's Fall Fair Blue Ribbon Blackberry Pie

There is no great secret to making a Blue Ribbon winning pie other than "fast and fresh and make the pastry top attractive." Pastry is always best tossed together quickly, as doing so incorporates more air and keeps fat cold. Freshly picked berries are at the peak of their flavour. I usually make the pastry first and then let it rest in the fridge while I go out to pick the berries. I get up early to make the pie the morning of the competition, so it's really fresh and full of flavour.

Makes 6 to 8 servings

1 recipe 'Never Fail' Pastry (page 161)
6 cups (1.4 L) freshly picked blackberries
1 cup (250 mL) sugar
3 Tbsp (45 mL) cornstarch
1 tsp (5 mL) lemon juice
1 tsp (5 mL) grated lemon zest
2 Tbsp (30 mL) unsalted butter, diced
1 small egg, beaten
1 tsp (5 mL) sugar, for garnish

Prepare the pastry and use half to line a 9 inch (23 cm) pie plate.

In a bowl, lightly toss together berries, 1 cup (250 mL) sugar, cornstarch, and lemon juice and zest.

Mound filling into pie shell and dot with butter.

Roll out the rest of the pastry to make the pie top. Cover the filled shell with pastry, sealing edges and trimming to fit. Cut a slit in the top of the pie to let out steam.

Use trimmings to decorate the top by forming them into decorative leaves and berries.

Brush decorated pie with beaten egg and sprinkle evenly with 1 tsp (5 mL) sugar.

Bake at 375F (190C) for 45 to 60 minutes, until pastry is golden and filling is bubbling. Cool before serving.

Frozen Wild Blackberry Parfait

If you don't want to bake pie on a hot day, a frozen fruit parfait is an elegant and refreshing, make-ahead summer dessert. Mounded into stemmed glasses or champagne flutes, and garnished with fragrant mint and lavender, a fruit parfait is a wonderful way to celebrate summer.

To make the blackberry purée for this recipe, simply blend fresh blackberries and strain to remove the seeds.

Makes 4 servings

> **2 cups (475 mL) blackberry purée**
> **1 cup (250 mL) sugar**
> **2 ounces (57 gr) Cassis***
> **Juice of 1 lemon**
> **3 egg whites**
> **1½ cups (350 mL) whipping cream**
> **A few whole blackberries and 4 mint leaves and lavender sprigs, for garnish**

In a bowl, mix blackberry purée with ½ cup (125 mL) of the sugar, and the Cassis and lemon juice.

In a separate bowl, whip the egg whites till foamy, and gradually add the remaining sugar and whip until stiff peaks form.

In a third bowl, whip the cream until thick.

Fold the whipped cream into the purée, and then gently incorporate the egg white mixture until evenly coloured.

Spoon mixture into individual ramekins, parfait bowls or stemmed glasses, and freeze immediately.

Just before serving, remove from freezer, garnish with a few whole blackberries, and top with a mint leaf and lavender sprig. Serve immediately while still frozen.

*Cassis (blackcurrant liqueur) is available in liquor stores.

Wild and Free: Blackberries

Blackberries are the most savoured and abundant of free foods. You cannot miss them on the islands, for in August the thorny stems of the plants, glinting with plump purple berries, line sunny stretches of island roads. It's a common sight during blackberry season to see cyclists stopping for an impromptu snack, hikers with purple-stained lips and fingers, and serious pickers with laden baskets destined for jam-making sessions.

Delicious eaten fresh, blackberries also freeze well for use throughout the year. Islanders serve them in muffins, pies, puddings and sorbets, make blackberry vodka, liquor or wine, and even dye homespun wool with them.

Picking is normally a peaceful and leisurely pleasure, but last year we were taught a new method.

"Hey, Andrea!" came the shout from a passing truck that slowed to see how my foraging was going. "Wanna know how to do that a whole lot faster?"

"Sure," I said.

"Ya need a Shop-Vac."

"A Shop-Vac?" I repeated blankly.

"Yeah, you hold the blackberry bunch out, put the tube underneath. It sucks them off like a hot damn. Not a leaf among them."

I looked up and down my isolated stretch of road. "Don't you need an electric outlet for that?"

"Hell, no. Shoved a generator on the back of the truck. Loaded up with four hundred-foot cords, four guys and four Shop-Vacs. We hit both sides of the road and vacuumed up 28 pounds in 15 minutes."

I chuckled. "That's a whole lot of jam."

He grinned. "It's a whole lotta hooch. Good stuff too." He pipped the horn and drove off.

I looked down at my meagre pickings in the ice cream pail and laughed out loud. We own neither a truck, a generator nor a Shop-Vac, but it was a lovely day and I'd not only time to forage, I'd garnered another great island story.

Pender Lavender and Lemon Scones

Imagine sunshine, sparkling ocean, a flower-filled deck and off-island friends visiting for the afternoon. There are two options, depending on the company:

The relaxed option—lazily sip a crisp white island wine accompanied by local cheese and crackers (see Mae's Wetcoast Crackers, page 183).

The "impress everyone" option—afternoon tea with fresh scones.

Here is my favourite scone recipe. It's never failed me no matter how I tweak it. If you like plain scones, leave out the lemon and lavender; the scones will still be delicious. Some alternative flavours are suggested below, but of course you could throw out all my suggestions and just add half a cup of regular plumped raisins!

These scones are best fresh from the oven but can be made ahead and frozen for up to a week. Serve warm scones just with butter, or spoil everyone with blackberry jam, whipped cream and pot of Earl Grey tea. Or up the ante by raiding your garden for a handful of mint and lemon balm, and make a pot of fresh herb tea.

Makes 12 scones

> 2 cups (475 mL) all-purpose flour
> 2 Tbsp (30 mL) sugar
> 3 tsp (15 mL) baking powder
> Pinch salt
> Finely grated zest of 1 large lemon
> 1 tsp (5 mL) finely ground dried culinary lavender
> ⅓ cup (80 mL) butter
> 2 eggs
> ½ cup (125 mL) buttermilk (plus a little extra if needed)
> Sacred Mountain lavender sugar

Preheat the oven to 400F (205C). Line a baking sheet with parchment paper or a silicone mat. Grease and set aside.

Sift flour, sugar, baking powder and salt into a medium bowl. Stir in lemon zest and ground lavender with a fork, until evenly mixed

Rub the butter into the flour mixture until it is like fine bread crumbs.

In a small bowl, whisk together 1 egg and the yolk of the other with the buttermilk. Set remaining egg white aside.

Pour the liquid into the flour mixture, and whisk together with a fork to bring the dough together. If the mixture seems too dry, add a little buttermilk as needed.

Tip the dough onto a floured surface. Knead quickly and lightly (don't overwork). Pat the dough down to a thickness of approximately 1 inch (2.5 cm).

Using a 2 inch (5 cm) floured cookie cutter, cut the dough into circles (or cut into wedges) and transfer them to the prepared baking sheets.

Using a pastry brush, lightly brush the tops of the dough circles with the remaining egg white and sprinkle each with lavender sugar.

Bake the scones for between 15 and 20 minutes, until risen and golden.

Become Queen of Scones—Be Adaptable

Have fun adapting this scone recipe with the following local seasonal ingredients.

Lemon and Cranberry Scones:

Omit lavender, and add ½ cup (125 mL) plumped, dried cranberries.

Apricot Scones:

Omit lemon zest and lavender, and add ½ cup (125 mL) chopped fresh apricots and ½ tsp (2.5 mL) cinnamon.

Citrus Blueberry Scones:

Omit lavender, and add ½ cup (125 mL) fresh or frozen blueberries plus zest of 1 large orange.

Lavender and White Chocolate Scones:

Omit lemon zest, and add 3 ounces (85 gr) chopped white chocolate.

Chocolate Cherry Scones:

Omit lavender and lemon zest, and add 2 ounces (57 gr) chopped dark chocolate and ½ cup (125 mL) chopped dried or fresh cherries. (We like using "Crow Bar" from the Salish Sea Chocolate Company on Salt Spring Island; see story page 219.)

Wonderful—Now you are ready for your own stall at the farmers' market!

A Close Call

The Anglican Church Women of Pender Island hosted a summer garden tea party for many years, in the grounds of an elegant historic home. Ladies in the community donned gauzy dresses and unearthed incredible hats to celebrate in full tea party regalia.

One year, the organizers' white gloves got into a bit of a twist. Horrors! In place of the clotted cream ordered especially for the occasion, sour cream arrived.

Fortunately, the Vancouver Island dairy responsible for the mix-up stepped in quickly to resolve the problem. Half an hour before the first party-goers began lining up for scones, the clotted cream arrived—delivered by chartered seaplane. Those were the days!

Citrus Blueberry Scones

The Wine and Beer Islands

Five vineyards and a brewery are on the Southern Gulf Islands. Take a tour to add a delightful focus to a vacation and tasty beverages to your al fresco picnics or oceanside dinners.

Three of the vineyards and the brewery (page 78) are found on Salt Spring Island. Pender and Saturna Islands each have one vineyard. All five vineyards welcome visitors to their tasting rooms during the summer. To visit the wineries or brewery in the winter, phone to make an appointment.

You can actually stay at Salt Spring Vineyard, in the lovely bed and breakfast retreat above the tasting room. Local musicians play on the deck on summer weekends, and picnic tables around the pond encourage visitors to linger. This vineyard hosts occasional summer dinners among the vines and celebrates the harvest with the Grape Stomp Festival. Yes, this is your opportunity to take off your shoes and tread on the grapes in traditional fashion!

As this book went to press, Pender's Morning Bay Vineyard changed hands. It will now be known as Sea Star Estate Farm and Vineyards. New local owner, David Goudge, says the vineyard will continue, and a complementary organic farm will be developed on the property. He looks forward to continuing to host a variety of community events and we are all invited to visit next season.

The Southern Gulf Islands are emerging as a new Canadian wine region, and one to be taken seriously. The wines developed here pair particularly well with the food of the region and are gaining recognition across Canada.

Sommelier Richard Massey lives on Galiano and oversees the wine cellar at the Galiano Inn. A strong supporter of local wine, he has contributed the following comments to help us understand this vibrant new island industry.

Richard's Wine Notes

The Southern Gulf Islands are home to a dedicated community of grape growers producing crisp, cool-climate, food-friendly wines.

Around the world wine and food have evolved together, and this evolution is no different on the Gulf Islands. As I watch each new vintage, it becomes clear that these local wines are expressing the aspects of their origin more and more distinctly. The combination of the chosen varietals and unique environmental factors is producing grapes with a natural balance of fruit and acidity. Acidity is the vital element to food and wine pairing. It provides the crispness, purity and vibrancy that intensify the flavour of a food—similar to squeezing fresh lemon on salmon.

Gulf Island wines are generally delicate and fresh. They contain lower alcohol levels and more mineral character than the typical Californian or Australian examples. Wine lovers are discovering they enjoy the more restrained character and complex fruit flavours these wines offer. Consequently, island wineries have all but completely eliminated the common practice of supplementing their production with Okanagan fruit.

Drinking local is not only delicious but also ethically, economically and environmentally smart. These wineries are owned by passionate families who often farm "beyond organically." By purchasing local wines, we contribute to the local economy while reducing the greenhouse gas emissions associated with transporting products long distances.

When choosing a Gulf Island wine, be sure the grapes are estate grown and seek out varietals such as Ortega, Bacchus and Auxerrois for whites, and Marechal Foch, Pinot Noir and Leon Millot for reds. This will ensure a true Gulf Island taste experience with the purity of an early morning Pacific breeze.

Richard's Favourite Picks from Southern Gulf Island Vineyards

(presented in alphabetical order)

Garry Oaks Winery, Salt Spring Island
I love the Pinot Gris, particularly the 2010. Stone fruits with a seam of mineral and citrus tension. This wine has a tendency to become more supple and round as it comes to temperature. Pair with local mussels, a few friends and a seaside patio!

Morning Bay Vineyard and Estate Winery, Pender Island
My preferred wines from Morning Bay are from grapes grown on the estate, lovely aromatic blends that are a great match with foods from the ocean. Try the Estate Bianco or rosé-styled Chiaretto (KEY-ah-RET-toe) with shellfish and fruit salad.

Tapping a distinctive *terroir*, island vintners and brewers share their products, often paired with locally sourced foods.

Our picturesque island vineyards are the perfect place to pick up wine to enhance our meals, whether by sipping it or cooking with it. Here are some hints to help you get the most flavour per splash:

In your cooking, use only wines that you enjoy drinking. If you do not like the taste of a wine in a glass, you will not like the flavour in the dish you added it to!

Don't overpower. A small quantity of wine will enhance the flavour of the dish. Most of the alcohol in the wine evaporates while the food is cooking, so only the flavour remains. Boiling down wine concentrates the flavour, including acidity and sweetness, so it's important not to use too much.

Give the wine time. Wait 10 minutes or more to taste, before deciding to add more wine.

Do not add wine to a dish just before serving. The wine should simmer with the food, or sauce, to enhance the flavour. If added late in the preparation, wine can impart a harsh quality.

Salt Spring Vineyards, Salt Spring Island

A favourite from Salt Spring Vineyards is the Karma, a traditionally produced *méthode champenoise* sparkler. Keep an eye on this delicious wine, as the owners have expressed a commitment to further its complexity and concentration in upcoming vintages. Also, their organic Blackberry Port shouldn't be missed. Enjoy it with high-quality bitter chocolate.

Saturna Island Family Estate Winery, Saturna Island

The Saturna Winery's Pinot Noir is light in colour and delicate on the palate. Expect rhubarb and sour cherry flavours wrapped in mouth-watering acidity. We pair it with salmon in the restaurant, and it's equally delicious alongside thin-crust pizza and soft cheeses.

Pinot Noir and Blackberry Chili Sauce

An easy red wine sauce with a hint of sweet heat. A special treat; serve with roast pork or grilled chicken.

Makes 1 cup (250 mL)

> 1 cup (250 mL) Gulf Island Pinot Noir
> 1 jalapeño, seeded and finely minced
> ½ cup (125 mL) seedless blackberry jam
> 2 to 3 tbsp (30-45 mL) butter

In a saucepan, bring wine to a boil. Turn heat to medium and stir frequently until wine is reduced to the consistency of heavy cream.

Add the jalapeño and stir for 2 minutes. Remove sauce from heat.

Immediately whisk in the blackberry jam and butter until blended and glossy. Serve hot.

Celebrating Summer

Chef Bruce Wood of Bruce's Kitchen, Salt Spring Island

Chef Bruce Wood, famous in Ontario for cooking fresh organic food before it became mainstream, wanted to be closer to his food sources, so he upped and moved to Salt Spring Island in 2007.

He opened Bruce's Kitchen, then the smallest restaurant in the Gulf Islands—a tiny lunchtime takeout and eat-in space with a few tables. Simply decorated with shelves of his homemade preserves and sauces, and pans and pots hanging from the ceiling, it had the air of a home kitchen and Bruce cooked right there in front of you. His "eat in for lunch, take us home for dinner" concept caught on as word spread. "Fresh organic food," islanders said, "bought straight from the local producers," and "no menu but a daily chalk board." People began to line up.

Pressure mounted, so once a week Bruce began offering Friday night dinners, a three-course prix fixe menu of seasonal food for 20 people, all the tiny restaurant could squeeze in. Again word went around, and you had to book ahead to get a seat. The smallest restaurant became a big success.

Passionate about fresh seasonal food, Bruce began to share his expertise. He'd developed a talent for teaching so decided to mentor Gulf Island Secondary School students in the cooking program; they work as apprentices in his kitchen. The success of this project, and his success as a chef, lies in his down-to-earth approach.

"I don't do 'chef recipes,'" he told us. "They drive you crazy and put you off cooking."

Success brought changes, and Bruce's Kitchen had to expand. He moved into a larger space in Grace Point Square, Ganges, and acquired a liquor licence.

"I'm focusing on BC wines and a strong local list," he said enthusiastically. "There are some great wines from the Gulf Islands and the Cowichan Valley."

The new restaurant isn't quite how he envisions it yet. "Gotta make changes to the space—open it up so you can see me cooking in the kitchen again. Can't do it all at once though."

But never fear, larger premises haven't changed the essentials. "Fresh, local, seasonable, sustainable and organic" remains Bruce's mantra, and you still have to book ahead for the Friday night dinners. Contact him through his website where he does a weekly posting of current seasonal menus.

Top: Chef Bruce Wood multi-tasks in the kitchen, preparing food, guiding his assistants, and planning the next task in an unbroken flow of activity.

Bottom: Grace Point Square, Ganges—Bruce enjoys his kitchen so much he has named his restaurant after it.

Celebrating Summer Menu for Six

Created by Chef Bruce Wood, Bruce's Kitchen, Salt Spring Island

Bruce Wood's style of cooking is both joyous and practical. Since this is a summer menu, he has made full use of the barbecue. "Everyone has one and it's quintessentially summer, so why not use it?" he said, in his down-to-earth manner.

Eggplant, Tomato and Chèvre "Oreo" with Aged Balsamic Glaze

This is Bruce's playful take on the ubiquitous cookie. The dark layers of eggplant and the white chèvre filling resemble one of the great milk-dunking treats.

Makes 6 servings

> ½ cup (125 mL) good quality balsamic vinegar
> ½ cup (125 mL) red wine
> 3 Tbsp (45 mL) cane sugar
> 2 large eggplants
> 2 very large, ripe beefsteak tomatoes
> 2 cloves garlic, slivered
> 1 tsp (5 mL) chopped fresh basil
> 1 tsp (5 mL) fennel seeds
> Pinch chili flakes
> Sea salt and freshly milled black pepper
> ¼ cup (60 mL) extra-virgin olive oil
> 1 lb (454 gr) soft Salt Spring Cheese Company chèvre, formed into 6 evenly sized discs
> 2 fistfuls local salad greens

Preheat barbecue to medium high.

In a small pan, bring vinegar, wine and cane sugar to a boil, and boil until reduced by one-third. Pour into a bowl and cool.

Slice the eggplants into twelve 1 inch (2.5 cm) thick slices. Slice the tomatoes into twelve thick slices.

Combine the garlic, basil, fennel, chili flakes, and salt and pepper with the oil in a large bowl. Gently toss the tomatoes and eggplant in this mixture until it is distributed over them.

Place the eggplant slices on the barbecue and grill, turning them until evenly and lightly blackened (about 4 to 5 minutes per side). Remove from grill.

On a greased baking sheet, build 6 stacks of eggplant, tomato, chèvre, tomato and eggplant.

Place the baking sheet on the barbecue and close the lid. Heat just until the chèvre begins to soften (check every minute).

Divide the salad greens between 6 salad plates, place an eggplant stack on the greens, drizzle with the reserved balsamic glaze and serve warm.

Cedar-Planked Salmon with Gravlax-style Sweet Mustard Sauce

Cooking salmon on a cedar plank imbues the fish with a sweet smokiness that is not overpowering. This recipe combines the traditional First Nations technique of cooking the salmon on a cedar plank with a Scandinavian approach to the seasoning. This dish is excellent whether eaten hot or cold.

Be sure to buy untreated cedar for the plank; most grocery and fish stores now sell the planks in packages. They are about ½ inch thick, 6 inches wide and 12 inches long (1.2 by 15 by 30 cm). Soak the plank in water for an hour or more before using.

Makes 6 servings

Sweet Mustard Sauce

½ cup (125 mL) mayonnaise
½ cup (125 mL) sour cream
2 Tbsp (30 mL) brown sugar
2 Tbsp (30 mL) strong, grainy mustard
Sea salt and freshly milled black pepper

In a bowl, whisk all ingredients together. Cover and refrigerate until needed.

Salmon

¼ cup (60 mL) brown sugar
4 Tbsp (60 mL) chopped fresh dill
2 tsp (10 mL) coarse sea salt
1 tsp (5 mL) mustard seeds, roughly cracked
½ tsp (2.5 mL) coarsely ground black pepper
Six 6 ounce (170 gr) boneless wild salmon fillets
1 lemon, halved
¼ cup (60 mL) brandy or dark rum

In a bowl, mix together brown sugar, dill, salt, mustard seeds and black pepper.

Place the salmon fillets in a 9 by 11 inch (23 by 28 cm) glass pan and rub fillets with the lemon. Gently pat seasoned sugar mixture onto the fillets, and drizzle with brandy. Cover and refrigerate for a minimum of 1 hour or as long as 48 hours.

Preheat the barbecue to medium high.

Place the salmon fillets on the wet plank and put it on the barbecue. Close the lid and cook until the salmon is opaque and flakes easily, approximately 12 to 14 minutes. (The plank will smoke and char—it's supposed to.) Remove the salmon from the plank, and serve hot with the mustard sauce.

Salt Spring Chèvre and Cherry Clafouti with Rye Caramel Sauce

Local cherries, glorious harbingers of summer! When plucking and eating that first juicy bunch from the orchard, you know that a world of culinary treats is unfolding. Here cherries are combined with a rich chèvre custard. The chèvre, from Salt Spring Island Cheese Company, gives the clafouti a lovely tang and is better than any packaged cream cheese you can find in the grocery store.

Makes 6 servings.

Cherries

   6 cups (1.4 L) freshly picked local cherries, washed, pitted and patted dry
   2 Tbsp (30 mL) minute tapioca
   1 cup (250 mL) cane sugar

In a bowl, mix the cherries with the tapioca and sugar till coated. Set aside.

Custard

   12 ounces (340 gr) absolutely fresh soft Salt Spring chèvre
   3 Tbsp (45 mL) sugar
   1 tsp (5 mL) vanilla extract
   4 large eggs, separated
   2 tsp (10 mL) flour
   4 ounces (113 gr) whipping cream

In a bowl, cream the chèvre with sugar and vanilla.

Add the egg yolks and beat to combine. Whisk in the flour and whipping cream.

In a separate bowl, whisk egg whites until stiff. Fold egg whites into chèvre mixture. Set aside.

Clafouti

   1 Tbsp (15 mL) soft butter
   4 almond biscotti, finely crushed
   ¼ tsp (1 mL) freshly grated nutmeg
   Prepared cherries
   Prepared custard

Preheat oven to 375F (190C).

Rub the inside of six ramekins with butter. Place some biscotti crumbs in each ramekin and tilt and swirl until the inside of the ramekins is well coated.

Combine the reserved cherries with the custard mixture, and divide among the ramekins. Sprinkle with grated nutmeg.

Stand ramekins on a baking sheet lined with parchment paper, and place in the oven.

Bake clafoutis for 25 minutes, or until the custard is brown, puffy and set. Meanwhile, prepare the Rye Caramel Sauce.

Rye Caramel Sauce

Make this while the clafouti is baking.

> ¼ cup (60 mL) raw sugar (Demerara or turbinado)
> 1 Tbsp (15 mL) unsalted butter
> Half vanilla bean, split
> ¼ cup (60 mL) rye whisky
> 1 cup (250 mL) whipping cream

In a large heavy bottomed pot, melt the sugar with the butter. Add the vanilla bean and slowly add the rye to the mixture. It will steam and hiss, but don't worry.

Add the cream and stir well. If the sauce is lumpy, continue stirring until smooth.

Bring mixture to a boil and cook for 3 to 4 minutes. Remove from heat and remove vanilla bean.

Just before serving the clafouti, gently reheat the sauce (if necessary) and drizzle decoratively over each warm clafouti.

Fiddler's Cove, Saturna Island.

Fall

Fall's Mellow Fruitfulness

Fall surprises us. Despite sunny days, we suddenly notice the maple leaves have golden edges and there's a new smell in the air—a tinge of woodsmoke. On the early morning run for the ferry, we drive through mist hanging in the hollows near the golf course, and after a rainstorm shaggy mane mushrooms burst forth in our driveway. Fall is here in all its glory.

This is the season when islanders lock their cars, not to prevent a crime wave but to prevent unwanted squash, zucchini or boxes of apples appearing on the backseat!

Fall is the season of excess. We can, jam, freeze and feast on the bounty our orchards, farms and gardens produce. Don't mention you could use a few pears or several bags will magically appear on your doorstep.

Freezers are stocked with blackberries and spring lamb. Friendships are forged or fractured over the divulging of the "secret chanterelle gathering spot." The grape harvest is anxiously monitored, then picked, woodpiles are augmented and the timing of the full moon checked so that next year's garlic crop can be planted as traditional folk wisdom decrees.

Bigleaf maple leaves glow on sunny days.

The fall colours are glorious. Vivid gold maples and orange pumpkins vibrate against a blue sky and a backdrop of dark green conifers. Gardens are full of dahlias and Michaelmas daisies, the markets are full of squash and our pantry shelves groan with the weight of jewel-like jars of jams, wine jellies, syrups and herbal vinegars, not to mention quarts of canned pears, peaches, tomatoes and a variety of chutneys and relishes.

One restless night, I crept into my pantry, switched on the light and took comfort from the packed shelves. One more day's canning would give us enough fruit for the winter months, plus Christmas. We have a pact with our friends—only homemade or locally made consumables for gifts! I decided to make some garlic jelly and another batch of pear and ginger marmalade, then crept back to bed, soothed by the island's bounty.

Fall Beautiful Beginnings

Red Rock Crabs

The summer visitors have left, the crab boat has stopped calling and you still fancy crab. What to do?

Buy a licence and a crab trap, and hang the trap off the end of the dock. Both Dungeness and red rock crabs are in season all year round, but when catching your own you are most likely to catch red rock crabs unless you have a boat and can lower your trap in the deeper waters.

Red rock crabs are much smaller than the crab boat's Dungeness crabs, so you will need two to three for a recipe. Take a measure when you go crabbing, and check the sizes for "keepers" posted on your fishing licence. Also follow the law and sustainable fishing practices, and throw back any females.

Rock crabs are small, tasty, and easy to catch.

Red Rock Crab and Cheese Dip

Hot crab dip is such a tasty treat for fall's cooler evenings. If your crab trap is empty and the crab boat isn't around, this recipe also works with tinned or frozen crab. Serve this hot crab dip with crackers.

Makes 8 servings

1½ cups (350 mL) flaked fresh uncooked crabmeat (3–4 rock crabs)
1½ cups (350 mL) grated Gulf Island hard cheese
1½ cups (350 mL) local cream cheese or goat cheese
¾ cup (180 mL) organic mayonnaise
½ cup (125 mL) sour cream
¼ cup (60 mL) dry Gulf Island white wine, plus extra if needed
2 Tbsp (30 mL) thinly sliced and chopped elephant garlic
1 Tbsp (15 mL) chopped fresh dill
2 tsp (10 mL) lemon zest
Pinch cayenne pepper
Salt and pepper
1 green onion, chopped, for garnish
Crackers

Check the crabmeat and remove any shards of shell.

In the base of a double boiler, bring water to a boil, making sure it will not touch the base of the top saucepan.

In the top of the double boiler, stir together the crabmeat, hard cheese, cream cheese, mayonnaise, sour cream and white wine.

Cook mixture, stirring often, until cheese is melted, the crabmeat is opaque and the sauce is bubbling.

Meanwhile, chop together by hand (or pulse in a blender) the elephant garlic, dill and lemon zest till the mixture forms a fine paste.

Stir garlic mixture and cayenne into the crab mixture. Cook for another 5 minutes to allow flavours to meld and sauce to return to a slow boil. Add extra white wine if dip seems too thick.

Taste dip, and season as desired with salt and pepper.

Scrape into a pretty casserole and place under a hot broiler until browned and bubbly.

Garnish with green onion and serve with crackers.

Nasturtium Leaf Mini-wraps

On a mellow September evening, serve this lovely and creative hors d'oeuvre at dinner. It uses the cheerful nasturtiums that continue to riot and brighten the garden long into the cooler months—I even picked some for the table on Christmas Day one very mild winter! Also featuring garden herbs and homemade cream cheese, this recipe was created by master gardener Brian Crumblehulme of Mayne Island, who is a creative chef specializing in local foods. Nasturtiums are one of the easiest edible plants to grow. Their leaves, flowers and seeds can be eaten and have a delightful peppery taste. The young green developing seeds can be picked and pickled and are sometimes referred to as English capers. Just don't forget to leave some to ripen, so you can save them for planting the following year.

Makes 4 servings

> 1 cup (250 mL) David Rotsztain's homemade cream cheese (page 19)
> Handful fresh chives
> Mint sprig
> Several leaves fresh basil or oregano, depending on the season
> 1 tsp (5 mL) caraway seeds
> 1 Tbsp (15 mL) finely grated orange zest
> 8 large nasturtium leaves, stems removed
> 4 nasturtium flowers, for garnish

In a bowl, soften or whip cream cheese until easily spreadable.

Chop the herbs and combine them with caraway seeds and orange zest.

Stir herb mixture into cheese. Cover and refrigerate overnight to allow the flavours to meld.

Rinse freshly picked nasturtium leaves and pat dry.

Divide the cheese mixture into 8 pieces and roll into cylinders

Wrap a nasturtium leaf around each roll of cheese, securing each with a toothpick.

Place 2 rolls on each plate and garnish with a nasturtium flower.

Serve immediately.

A vibrant window box of nasturtiums decorates an island business.

Brian Crumblehulme Still Cooks!

It seems that there is almost nothing Renaissance man Brian Crumblehulme hasn't tried. Currently known for his newspaper articles on gardening and growing food, he is also one of Mayne Island's two elected Island Trust representatives. Brian has been a chef, teacher, chemist, researcher, architect and ballet dancer! He and his wife, Mary, have built schools in Nepal and spent time consulting and teaching in the Republic of Georgia, Ukraine and Kazakhstan. Despite his multitude of interests, two passions have been constant since he was six years old—growing food and cooking it.

After washing up on the shores of Mayne Island, Brian and Mary built Fernhill Lodge where for some years they ran a notable bed and breakfast operation. It featured many of Brian's own recipes using delights from their garden (see Nasturtium Wraps, page 131). Once retired from the B&B business, Brian turned his attention to raising awareness about the need for sustainability and expanding knowledge of local food. "It makes no sense constantly trucking food in on the ferries when you can grow your own," said Brian. "Think of the carbon footprint!"

He and two other Mayne Islanders, Peter Judd and Richard Iredale, put their heads together and decided to raise local awareness by holding a 100-mile dinner with a speaker. This was so successful they made plans some months later to up the ante by holding a 100-kilometre dinner. This too was successful, so the idea evolved into planning for the weekend-long Good Life Festival—a sharing of ideas for living green on the islands, featuring the 30-Mile Potluck Dinner, where almost all the food was made and produced on Mayne Island.

"The biggest obstacle for producing an authentic all Mayne Island potluck was finding flour and oil or fat," said Brian. "We eventually had to cheat on the flour, as despite Mayne pioneers successfully growing wheat here, no one was growing it today. We went to Red Rooster Bakery on the nearby Saanich Peninsula. He organically grows and grinds his own. The fat problem was easier; we used what the pioneers used—bacon fat and beef lard!"

The chemist in Brian popped to the fore. "Much-maligned lard is why homemade pastry and old-fashioned chips [french fries] taste so good, know why?"

I didn't.

"Because lard can cook at a much higher temperature than the light oils. This means potatoes crisp, puff and don't absorb the fat, and pastry is super light and flaky."

I know he's right. My pastry has won me several baking prizes, because lard is the not-so-secret ingredient (see 'Never Fail' Pastry, page 161). I just didn't understand the chemistry behind it. Thanks, Brian.

Rainforest Mushroom Soup

We know it's fall mushroom season when the shaggy manes suddenly appear in the middle of our driveway. (We have tried to encourage them to grow elsewhere, to no avail.) Then we don slickers and head to the forest edges with baskets so we can make our favourite mushroom recipes, among them this soup. A variety of edible mushrooms grows on the Southern Gulf Islands, but unless you are sure you can correctly identify them, check out the farm stores where knowledgeable pickers take their baskets. The Farm Gate Store on Mayne Island, Daystar Market on Galiano, Southridge Farms Country Store on Pender and the Saturna Grocery Store all carry fresh or freshly dried mushrooms, and Salt Spring has a wonderful commercial grower—Salt Spring Exotic Mushrooms (see sidebar, page 140)—that supplies fresh mushrooms year-round. Any variety of edible mushrooms, such as oyster, shiitake or chanterelle, will work in this seasonal soup.

Makes 8 appetizers or 4 main course servings

¼ cup (60 mL) plus 1 tsp (5 mL) butter
4 cloves garlic, minced
2 cups (475 mL) sliced shallots
9 cups (2.2 L) sliced fresh mushrooms
½ cup (125 mL) dry sherry
½ cup (125 mL) dry white wine
¼ cup (60 mL) all-purpose flour
Salt and pepper
8 cups (2 L) chicken or vegetable stock
½ cup (125 mL) whipping cream
Fresh parsley leaves, for garnish

In a large frying pan, melt ¼ cup (60 mL) butter and sauté the garlic and shallots until translucent. Stir in the mushrooms, and sauté until they are beginning to soften and release juices.

Add the sherry and wine. Turn up the heat, and when the liquid is boiling, reduce heat to medium-low; keep stirring until liquid is reduced to a glaze. Set pan aside.

In a large saucepan, melt remaining butter, add the flour, salt and pepper and stir until mixture thickens. Keep stirring, and gradually add the stock. It will begin to thicken. Keep stirring until the mixture is smooth.

Stir in the reserved mushroom mixture, and simmer until mushrooms are tender. Do not boil. Check and adjust seasoning.

Stir in the cream, ladle soup into bowls and place a fresh parsley leaf in the centre of each. Serve immediately.

Note: This is a chunky soup. If you prefer a smooth one, before adding the cream, purée the soup in small batches in a food processor. Return soup to pan, reheat gently and then stir in the cream.

A Word of Caution

Collectors of wild mushrooms must be cautious, and being something of a mycologist—a student of mushrooms—is important. Some of the best edible mushrooms are not easy to identify and can be mistaken for others that are unpleasant to eat or (at worst) poisonous. However, you may be able to hook up with a local naturalists' club for a fungus foray, on which a specialist will teach how to separate the good from the dangerous. But also bear possible allergies in mind. Sadly, people who regularly eat store-bought white mushrooms may be allergic to some wild species, so use caution when trying unfamiliar varieties for the first time. Also be careful what you consume with them; some, like shaggy manes, undergo a chemical reaction if consumed with alcohol that makes them poisonous to some sensitive people.

Wild and Free: Chanterelles and Other Tasty Mushrooms

It's yellow and a little slimy, and it grows in the woods. Would you eat it?

While you might be suspicious, lots of Gulf Islanders steal out to their favourite secret spot, collect tasty chanterelle mushrooms and take them home to eat or preserve.

Chanterelles, shaggy manes, giant puffballs, shaggy parasols and other wild mushrooms are a lovely addition to fall meals. These fungi usually sprout after a rain and may decay within a few hours or a day, so mycophagists (eaters of mushrooms) regularly check their favourite harvesting spots. Each mushroom species grows in a specific type of habitat, some in grassy areas, others in woodlands; therefore, in fall you see islanders peeking behind the bushes along the road or slowly hiking a woodland trail carrying a basket.

Fungi are mainly composed of water and so don't add much nutrition to your diet. But they contain a broad range of chemicals, which can provide exquisite flavour. The canny cook will make mushrooms the main ingredient of an omelette or use a small quantity to add flavour to soups, stews and sauces.

Right: Tasty chanterelles thrive in the Gulf Islands.

Pear, Goat Cheese and Walnut Flan

The delight of wandering the Gulf Islands in fall is seeing our beautiful orchards in full fruit. The islands grow an amazing array of apples and pears. Many are delicious heritage varieties, unknown in stores, as they have no shelf life. Use them or lose them is the real situation with some of the tastiest fruit. Here is an easy way to use the luscious pears you spotted at a farm stand, and who can resist topping them with local walnuts?

Makes 12 appetizers or 4 to 6 main course servings

8 inch (20 cm) unbaked pastry shell
2 large ripe local pears
2 Tbsp (30 mL) lemon juice
10 ounces (283 gr) soft goat cheese
3 eggs
¼ cup (60 mL) whipping cream
1 Tbsp (15 mL) chopped fresh dill
1 Tbsp (15 mL) chopped fresh parsley
1 tsp (5 mL) curry powder
Dash hot sauce (optional)
½ cup (125 mL) chopped, toasted local walnuts
1 green onion, finely chopped, for garnish

Preheat oven to 400F (205C). Prick pastry shell all over. Bake shell blind in the middle of the oven for 15 minutes, or until shell is golden. Remove from oven and cool.

Peel, halve and core pears. Slice thinly lengthwise and sprinkle with lemon juice.

In a bowl, beat half the goat cheese until creamy. Whisk in eggs, cream, dill, parsley, curry powder and hot sauce (if using) until mixture is smooth.

Attractively arrange the pear slices in the pastry shell.

Pour the egg mixture over the pears. Crumble the remaining goat cheese on top. Sprinkle with the toasted walnuts.

Bake in the middle of the oven for 45 minutes or until flan is golden and firm.

Serve warm or at room temperature, sprinkled with the green onion.

Most farms in the Gulf Islands operate on a small scale. *Jan Mangan photo (right)*

Discovering Farms on Salt Spring

It is no surprise that the biggest Gulf Island—Salt Spring—has the most agriculture, and visitors to it can explore over 30 farms selling a variety of organic produce. The farms range from tiny operations like Small Earth Farm, which produces vegetables for the Saturday market by using no-tillage permaculture and only hand tools, to the large market garden operation behind Harbour House Hotel that provides fruit, vegetables and grains year-round for the hotel restaurant. Hotel visitors can request a garden tour. Seeing the lush array of produce first-hand makes you want to rush into the restaurant and start ordering.

Some farms grow only fruit and vegetables; one is the Salt Spring Centre of Yoga, whose extensive garden is farmed as an extension of its yoga practices and spirituality. Orchards scattered across the island are tended with passion and intensity by growers such as Harry Burton. He cherishes heritage fruit and is a prime mover and shaker behind the Salt Spring Apple Festival. Several Salt Spring farmers raise organic beef, pork, chickens, turkeys and lamb, and some of them post signs offering farm-gate sales. Two historic farms sell meat—heritage-breed pork at Bullock Lake Farm and lamb at Ruckle Farm, where you can also buy beautiful fleece and wool. There are scatterings of greenhouses growing the more exotic fruit, such as melons and tender eggplants, and berry farms, apple pressing operations, and chicken and egg sales. The most original operation is Elizabeth Buchanan's bicycle-power-ground flour—she pedals away on her stationary bike, keeping fit, while it grinds the flour she then sells at the market, along with a wide variety of home-baked vegan treats.

The variety of farms and products is astounding, and we wish we had room to showcase them all. A brochure listing all the organic farms may be found at both the Saturday and Tuesday markets or at the Salt Spring Island Visitor Centre in Ganges.

Dan Jason's Thanksgiving Beans

The title of this Dan Jason recipe summarizes how he feels about the earth and growing food. It is the perfect potluck dish to share at an island Thanksgiving celebration. Dan says "celebrate your actions, for this recipe is especially festive when the main ingredients are from your garden." We agree.

Serve these beans with warm fresh bread.

Makes 6 to 8 servings

> 1 cup (250 mL) dried home-grown organic beans
> 4 medium onions, coarsely chopped
> 2 large cloves garlic, chopped
> 4 Tbsp (60 mL) cooking oil
> 1 medium-sized winter squash, peeled, cubed and cooked
> 2 Tbsp (30 mL) chopped orange zest
> 1 Tbsp (15 mL) chopped jalapeño pepper
> ½ cup (125 mL) raisins
> ½ tsp (2.5 mL) cinnamon
> ½ tsp (2.5 mL) allspice
> ½ tsp (2.5 mL) nutmeg
> ¼ tsp (1 mL) ground cloves
> 2 large tart apples, peeled, cored and cubed
> 6 cups (1.4 L) chopped Italian plum tomatoes.
> Salt and freshly ground pepper
> Sour cream (optional) and freshly chopped cilantro, for garnish

Soak the beans for a minimum of 4 hours or overnight. Drain.

Place beans in a large pot, cover with fresh water, bring to a boil, reduce heat and simmer for 1 hour, or until beans are tender. Drain. (Do not add salt while cooking beans, as it toughens the skins.)

In a large skillet or Dutch oven, sauté onion and garlic in oil until golden.

Stir in squash, orange zest, peppers, raisins, cinnamon, allspice, nutmeg and cloves, and simmer uncovered for 20 to 30 minutes.

Stir in drained beans, apples and tomatoes. Simmer for 10 to 20 minutes, or until apples are soft.

Season with salt and pepper.

Ladle beans into bowls and serve hot with sour cream (if using) and chopped cilantro.

Mushroom and Blackberry Port Vol-au-Vents

The fruity richness of Salt Spring Vineyards Blackberry Port adds a lovely depth to mushrooms. This is a showy dish that's great for dinner parties.

Makes 6 servings

- 2 Tbsp (30 mL) olive oil
- 2 large field mushrooms, sliced
- 3 celery stalks, finely chopped
- 2 cloves garlic, crushed
- 1 onion, cut into thin wedges
- 2 cups (475 mL) rich vegetable stock
- 1 cup (250 mL) red wine
- 2 sprigs fresh thyme
- ½ cup (125 mL) Blackberry Port
- 1 Tbsp (15 mL) redcurrant jelly
- Salt and pepper
- 6 large (4 inch/10 cm) prebaked vol-au-vent cases
- Flat leaf parsley, for garnish

Heat 1 Tbsp (15 mL) of the oil in a large pan. Add mushrooms and sauté for 4 to 5 minutes, stirring until lightly browned. Remove with a slotted spoon and set aside. Add remaining oil to the pan.

Sauté the celery, garlic and onion over low heat, stirring occasionally, for 5 to 6 minutes. Add stock, wine and thyme, and bring mixture to a boil. Reduce heat and simmer until liquid is reduced by one-third.

Add the blackberry port and redcurrant jelly. Bring back to a boil and continue cooking for 10 minutes, until liquid is reduced by half and is thick and syrupy.

Season to taste, discard the thyme and stir in the mushrooms. Simmer for 5 minutes, or until tender.

Preheat oven to 375F (190C).

While the sauce is simmering, pry out the centre of the precooked vol-au-vents and reheat centres and cases in the oven for 3 minutes.

Place hot vol-au-vent cases on individual plates. Using a slotted spoon, spoon the mushroom mixture into the cases, dividing it equally among them. Garnish with the parsley, and top with the little pastry centres. Serve immediately, offering remaining sauce in a gravy boat.

David and I are experimenting with growing mushrooms, shiitake and oyster, on inoculated logs. So far no luck! This is a long process, and if we are lucky we might see results in 18 months to two years. Thank goodness for Salt Spring Exotic Mushrooms (see sidebar, page 140), a company that produces fresh mushrooms year-round and regularly has a booth at the Ganges Saturday market (photo opposite). Wild island mushrooms are also found in season at Daystar Market on Galiano and the Farm Gate Store on Mayne, so buy plenty for this fall recipe.

Salt Spring Exotic Mushrooms

Beautiful overflowing baskets of plump fresh organic shiitake and oyster mushrooms are found weekly at the Salt Spring Saturday market. They are the local product of Adam and Rebecca Gold's Salt Spring Exotic Mushrooms, the Gulf Islands' only commercial mushroom farm. This family-run operation grows beautiful fresh Japanese mushrooms for the culinary market. The mushrooms are harvested every couple of days, so they are always at the peak of perfection. The company also distills mushrooms for therapeutic purposes.

Salt Spring Exotic Mushrooms sells oyster and shiitake mushrooms at the Ganges Market.

Salt Spring Exotic Mushrooms is more than a business; it's a sustainable lifestyle. The 30 acre (12 hectare) family farm also has an orchard, a berry plantation, field crops, flower crops, medicinal and culinary herbs, a woodlot and a pond for aquaculture.

"We live a beautiful rural lifestyle and strive to nourish ourselves while nourishing our environment," says Adam. "We recycle and reuse."

This is a family that tries to live by recycling and reusing. The farm vehicles are run on recycled vegetable oil (biodiesel), and the wood medium for growing the mushrooms is waste wood from a Vancouver Island pulp mill. After its use as a growing medium, the wood goes into compost used to better the farm's soil, and the excess water from the mushroom operation is diverted to irrigate the orchard.

Adam and Rebecca sustainably harvest timber for heat, have their own well, and grow their own meat, mushrooms, fruit, vegetables and herbs year-round.

"We do our best to close our loop so we create a light footprint on the earth." They share their sustainable-lifestyle skills with the local community by offering apprenticeships, employment, tours and permaculture courses.

Adam is currently expanding the orchard and berry plot, so watch for sales of their products in the future.

The Gourmet Delight of Gulf Island Lamb

"I am vegan, unless I can buy eggs from happy hens. Then I discovered there was meat from happy chickens and happy lambs available here. Guess I'm a happytarian."

—A Gulf Islander

"It's the salt-laden wind that makes the Gulf Islands' lamb so delicious," declared an old-timer. "The salt settles on the land and is present in the grass, so the grazing lambs come already seasoned."

Whatever the reason, the spring lamb raised here tastes special.

Spring lamb refers to an animal born in the spring and butchered in the late summer or fall when it's meaty but still tender. Sadly, our famous Gulf Island sheep farms are declining. New government regulations came into force requiring local sheep farms to send their lambs to be butchered on the mainland in large government-inspected facilities. Since this meant trucking animals both on the ferry, then over 100 kilometres (62 miles) away, many sheep farmers gave up. Part of following organic farming practices is respecting animals and not stressing them out.

Luckily, Jacques Campbell of Campbell Farm on Saturna Island persevered with the government red tape and was eventually allowed to build a small slaughter facility, surrounded by pasture, on her farm. Once again, island sheep farmers had access to a small, caring, island facility where their lambs could remain stress-free to the last second. Relaxed lambs mean no adrenalin is present in the meat, another reason why Gulf Island lamb is so tasty and tender.

As we write this book, Salt Spring Island is working its way through the government bureaucracy in order to obtain permission to open a mobile butchering facility. It will travel to the individual farms so the animals will not have to be moved, thereby assuring that their stress will be kept to a minimum. We hope this will mean that sheep farming on Salt Spring will once again be front and centre.

Gulf Island farmers keep several varieties of hardy sheep—including these Cotswolds.

Sheep farms often advertise whole or half lambs for sale, and many are pre-ordered for local grocery stores or restaurants, or for islanders who stock their freezers. However, some farmers keep a selection of individual cuts of lamb that they are happy to sell. Watch for signs offering farm-gate lamb, or ask around at the farmers' markets and phone the farms direct (see "Sources" section, page 234). In order not to disturb the livestock, please do not go to the farms without an invitation.

Rolled Shoulder of Lamb Stuffed with Herbs, Capers and Anchovies

Rolled shoulder of lamb is a less familiar cut than the popular leg roast, but many lamb lovers consider the shoulder to be more flavourful than the leg. Once a lot of trouble to prepare, the shoulder is now sold ready boned and rolled. It does, however, require a slightly different cooking technique.

The roll looks attractive when sliced. Don't be scared by the anchovies in the recipe— they add a depth to the meaty flavour and no fishy taste.

    6 anchovy fillets in oil (drain and reserve oil)
    2 large cloves garlic
    2 tender rosemary sprigs about 2 inches (5 cm) long
    Large handful fresh parsley leaves, stalks removed
    Grated zest from 1 large lemon
    1 Tbsp (15 mL) drained capers
    1 Tbsp (15 mL) lemon juice
    1 Tbsp (15 mL) oil from the anchovies
    1 tsp (5 mL) grainy mustard
    1 boned shoulder of lamb, about 1.5 to 2 kg (3 to 4 lbs)
    Freshly ground black pepper
    4 ounces (125 mL) red wine
    4 ounces (125 mL) water

Preheat oven to 500F (260C).

Finely chop or pulse the anchovies, garlic, rosemary, parsley, lemon zest and capers till well mixed and almost a paste. Scrape into a small bowl. Add the lemon juice, anchovy oil and mustard, and combine well.

Cut and discard the string on the rolled shoulder of lamb. Spread the meat out, fat side down. Spread the stuffing over the meat. Grind a generous amount of black pepper over the stuffing. Re-roll the meat and tie it securely with new string.

Place roll, seam side down, in a roasting pan, and transfer pan to the centre of the hot oven. Roast for half an hour, until lamb is nicely browned.

Pour the wine and water around the lamb (not over it). Turn the oven down to 350F (175C), and cook meat for a further 15 minutes per 18 ounces (500 gr). If roast weighs over 4.5 lbs (2 kg), then cook for 12 minutes per 18 ounces (500 g). If the roast is not crispy and brown on top, put it under a hot broiler for a few minutes.

Remove roast from the oven and let rest for 15 minutes before carving. The meat should be pink in the centre (medium rare). Do not overcook or the meat will toughen. It will continue to cook as it rests.

Make a gravy with the pan juices, thickening them if desired.

Slice across the lamb roll, and serve slices immediately with the gravy.

A Touch of Island Reality

An island couple wishing to provide organic food for their family decided to buy a young lamb from a nearby farmer and raise it in their field to provide meat for their freezer in the fall. The couple had four children, and the kids loved visiting the field every day to lean over the fence to give the animal fattening treats. Soon the lamb recognized them and would charge across the field, baaing to greet them. The youngest child named it "Thunder."

Thunder prospered all summer and grew so tame the kids could take it for walks. Then September and school started, and Dad wanted to fill the freezer.

One day the dreadful deed was done, and after a reasonable amount of time Mother anxiously cooked a lamb roast, wondering how she was going to explain it to the kids. The meat smelled wonderful and everyone tucked in. She need not have worried.

"Doesn't Thunder taste good?" said the youngest child. "Can I have seconds?"

Sex in the Garden for a Backyard Bounty

If your zucchini did not develop, your tomatoes were a disaster and your fruit yield dismal, you have pollination problems. The islander's solution? Call Linda!

Linda Gilkeson is the Gulf Island gardener's best friend, whether you know her personally or not. She is a master gardener with a PhD in entomology, and her book *Backyard Bounty*, a year-round guide to growing organic food in our area, is on almost every island gardener's bedside table. If it's not, it should be!

Linda is tireless—writing, teaching courses and workshops up and down the BC coast on organic gardening, pollination and pest management techniques. She also produces her own food in her extensive Salt Spring garden. Her dry humour and practical approach mean her workshop on pollination, called "Sex in the Garden," is always packed.

Her message is loud and clear—grow food year-round! "Ignore most gardening books," she says happily. "In this climate it's easy to grow food every month; you just can't grow warm weather crops in winter. Cold weather crops are great. If I had to go to the moon with only one veg, I'd take Swiss chard. I grow it 12 months of the year. Love it. In fact, I have it with scrambled eggs nearly every morning. I sauté it with mushrooms and olives, then add the eggs, seasoning and whatever herbs are around. Lovage and chives in spring, tarragon early summer—anything goes."

Another favourite food is purple sprouting broccoli. "I adore it. So tender, tasty and quick to cook. Dunk it for 30 seconds in boiling water. Pity it's only around for 12 weeks in early spring. Then there's honey figs, so sweet you nearly faint when tasting them for the first time. Easy to grow if you get the right type of tree. Did you know you can freeze them? I just found a pack I'd forgotten when rummaging in the freezer. Mmmm, that's like finding gold."

I started to laugh. If I hadn't stopped her, Linda would have listed every growable fruit and vegetable as her favourite.

Always generous both with her time and knowledge, Linda shares gardening information through Linda's List, a monthly email newsletter of seasonal things to do for trouble-free food production in your garden. Sign up on her West Coast Gardening website (see "Sources" section, page 234).

Caramelized Onion and Zucchini Galette

The lovely, rustic presentation of a galette is both attractive and adaptable. You can mix and match the filling ingredients to suit whatever fall vegetables you have on hand, and the annual proliferation of zucchinis is the perfect excuse. Add some sausage slices if you like, or mushrooms. The permutations are infinite and the result a feast for the eyes as well as the taste buds.

Makes 4 to 6 servings

> 2 medium zucchini, sliced
> 1½ tsp (7.5 mL) salt
> 1 Tbsp (15 mL) butter
> 1 tsp (5 mL) olive oil
> 1 large onion, thinly sliced
> 3 cloves garlic, minced
> ½ recipe 'Never Fail' Pastry (page 161)
> 1 cup (250 mL) grated Asiago or any hard island cheese
> ¼ cup (60 mL) Salt Spring Island Cheese Company feta cheese, crumbled
> Pepper
> 1 egg yolk, beaten with 1 tsp (5 mL) water

Spread the zucchini slices over the surface of a large sieve, sprinkle with salt and let drain over the sink for about 30 minutes. Pat pieces dry before using.

Meanwhile, melt butter and oil together in a large skillet. Add garlic, onion and cook over medium heat until soft and beginning to caramelize to a golden brown. Cool.

Preheat the oven to 400F (205C).

Line a cookie sheet with parchment paper or a silicone liner and grease.

Roll out pastry into a 12 inch (30 cm) circle and place on the cookie sheet.

Mix cheeses together. Layer one-third of the cheese in the centre of the pastry, leaving at least 2 inches (5 cm) of pastry bare on all sides.

Top cheese with half the onion, then all the garlic, followed by all the zucchini and a grind of pepper, and the another one-third of the cheese. Finish off by adding remaining onion and top with remaining cheese.

To form the galette, gently lift and fold the edge of the pastry up and over the filling, pleating and gathering the edge attractively so that the pastry is like a drawstring bag that's not fully closed. The pastry will not completely cover the filling, which will be visible in the centre of the galette.

Brush the pastry with egg wash.

Bake until the pastry is a golden brown, about 30 to 40 minutes.

Serve immediately.

What Is a Galette?

Galette is a wonderfully sophisticated term for a rustic, free-form pie. Galettes are quick and unfussy to make using vegetables or fruit. As the name suggests, galettes originated in France, reputedly in Brittany. Apparently, they were first made in the form of large buckwheat pancakes folded around a savoury stuffing. These are still sold in French Canada and known as *galettes bretonnes*.

Adapted by pastry cooks, this easy method of making a pie not only has eye appeal, but is very practical. You can use pastry scraps to make small individual galettes, or quickly make one large enough to serve a family as an entrée or dessert.

Oyster Cove Sauté

For a change from eating oysters raw, try this simple recipe, but do not overcook. There is little worse than a rubbery oyster.

Makes 4 servings

> 2 tsp (10 mL) butter or olive oil
> ¼ cup (60 mL) chopped green onion
> ¼ cup (60 mL) dry white wine
> 1 tsp (5 mL) grated lemon zest
> 1 tsp (5 mL) lemon juice
> Salt and pepper
> 24 oysters, freshly shucked, plus their juice
> 8 slices hot buttered rye bread toast
> 1 lemon cut into quarters
> ¼ cup (60 mL) chopped fresh parsley
> Tabasco sauce (optional)

Melt butter in skillet over medium-low heat; add chopped onion and sauté until just softened. Add wine, lemon zest and juice, and salt and pepper, and stir briefly.

Add oysters and their juice, cover and cook just long enough for them to change colour and firm up a little. Shake pan from side to side to keep them bathed with the buttery sauce.

Place 6 oysters on each of 4 slices of toast. Divide pan juices among servings.

Cut remaining slices of toast into triangles. Garnish oyster-topped toast with a lemon quarter and chopped parsley, and serve with the toast triangles. Offer Tabasco sauce at the table.

Shellfish Safety

Because of red tide (see sidebar page 16), we recommend that visitors (or unsure locals) purchase oysters from a reputable fishboat or island store. Often the fishboat will lend you a special shucking tool if you want to eat oysters then and there on the dock. But it's easiest to buy them ready shucked and packed in their own juice.

Fresh-shucked oysters should be eaten immediately, or can be stored in the fridge for up to 24 hours.

Oysters thrive on secluded beaches.

Sustainable Oysters

In an isolated cottage perched a few feet above a small rocky beach, we had an unexpected and memorable fall feast. It was simple. "I've shucked a few oysters," said Ted. "Would you like to join me?"

We dined on many oysters, plain and unadulterated except for a squeeze of lemon or a drop of Tabasco. Some we slurped raw, others we tucked briefly under a very hot broiler. All were juicy and delicious. We chatted, sipped glasses of crisp white wine and watched the entertainment—the rising of a giant harvest moon over the ocean.

Unpolluted and undisturbed beaches where wild oysters can thrive are few and far between, so both Ted and his cove remain anonymous. He's encouraged his oysters over many years, for there were only a few when he first lived there. Through patiently harvesting only one or two at a time, and facilitating the spread of oyster larvae by returning the shells to the beach, Ted has multiplied his oysters and, there are now enough to occasionally share with friends. The result is a private sustainable fishery. Thanks, Ted (whose name has been changed to protect his beach, but he knows who he is!). We wish more people would follow your example.

Soya Nova—Soy Good!

Where else but on Salt Spring Island would the high school cafeteria carry not only local tofu as an option, but smoked tofu sandwiches, which the kids love!

Soya Nova tofu has been made on Salt Spring Island for 28 years. It's produced without fanfare. You can't see the sign for the small factory at 1200 Beddis Road, but tofu lovers know where to find it. Soya Nova products, especially the smoked tofu, are in high

Smoked tofu drying in the factory.

demand. You can visit the Soya Nova Tofu Shop and buy tofu on site, and products are also available in stores on Salt Spring Island, as well as at several restaurants on Vancouver Island, in the Thrifty Foods grocery store chain and by mail order (see "Sources" section, page 234).

Debbie Lauzon started by making tofu for herself in a blender. She learned how to do it in California in the 1960s. What started as a small kitchen-counter operation has become big business. Her three children are shareholders in her company that is run from a commercial kitchen built on her property.

Tofu making is labour intensive. Debbie and her son make it Japanese farmhouse style in an open cauldron. The process involves soaking the beans, grinding them into a slurry, cooking them and extracting the milk. Debbie mixes in a natural coagulant from the Sea of Japan, then presses the mixture and ... voila, tofu! Some is sold as regular tofu; the rest is smoked in her own smokehouse, where she uses BC wood that's certified for organic-food-grade use. Soya Nova smoked tofu is incredibly tasty, and Debbie is very proud of the fact that the product she developed is in big demand among fans across the country.

For some years Debbie had to purchase the soybeans off island, but now a farm on Salt Spring grows them for her, so her small idea grew to involve and benefit her community, something she never envisaged.

"And now I can't stop making it," Debbie said with a chuckle. "All my grandchildren are vegetarian. What would they eat if I quit?"

Mushroom, Runner Bean and Spaghetti Squash with Crispy Smoked Tofu

A tasty vegetarian dish featuring Soya Nova smoked tofu.

Makes 4 servings

> 1 spaghetti squash, halved, deseeded, roasted and cooled
> 1½ lb (680 gr) block Soya Nova smoked tofu
> 3 Tbsp (45 mL) olive oil
> 4 portobello mushrooms, sliced
> 2 cloves garlic, finely chopped
> 1 large white onion, chopped
> ¼ cup (60 mL) vegetable broth
> Handful of runner beans, trimmed and cut into 1 inch (2.5 cm) lengths
> 1 bunch washed spinach
> 1 lb (454 gr) carton soya cream
> 2 Tbsp (30 mL) chopped fresh basil
> Ground black pepper and sea salt
> Grated cheese (or cheese substitute) of your choice
> Hot pepper sauce (optional)

Scrape out the spaghetti squash fibres from the cooked halves, fluff the fibres and set aside.

Cut the smoked tofu into 8 slices. In a frying pan, heat 2 Tbsp (30 mL) of the oil, and then fry the tofu slices on both sides until crisp. Remove from pan, place on a crumpled paper towel to drain and keep warm in the oven.

Add the remaining oil to the pan, lower heat, and gently sauté the mushrooms, garlic and onion until soft.

Add the broth to the pan, and then the runner beans. Cook till beans are tender.

Add spinach and stir till it has wilted and any excess liquid has evaporated, adjusting heat as needed.

Add half a carton of soya cream. Reduce heat to a low simmer. Stir mixture, to ensure that is doesn't boil.

Stir in the reserved spaghetti squash and reheat mixture gently. Add the basil, and salt and pepper to taste. If necessary, add a little more soya cream until mixture reaches your desired creaminess.

Divide mixture among 4 warm pasta dishes or bowls, top each with 2 slices of the fried tofu and sprinkle with grated cheese.

Serve immediately with optional hot pepper sauce as an accompaniment.

Green Croquettes

This is a "sustainable cooking recipe" from the Kikuchi Family Cookbook. Sanea and Arthur Kikuchi, of Pender Island, put together this small recipe ebook and gave it to their neighbours. Each recipe featured ingredients grown in the Kikuchis' small market garden. The Kikuchis feed their family year-round from homegrown produce and sell summer excess at the island's farmers' market. Arthur also bakes and sells a sourdough bread from sprouted grains, and Sanea makes vegetarian sushi and brown rice balls. They contributed this recipe from their ebook as an example of a creative way to use garden-grown cool-weather greens. The Kikuchis enjoy these croquettes with a little sweet chili sauce.

Makes 8 croquettes

- ¼ cup (60 mL) sunflower seeds
- 1 tsp (5 mL) coriander seeds
- 1 tsp (5 mL) cumin seeds
- 8 cups (2 L) chopped green vegetables, such as kale, spinach, beet tops, chard, broccoli, green beans
- 1 small onion, chopped
- 1 tsp (5 mL) plus 1 Tbsp (15 mL) vegetable oil
- 1 tsp (5 mL) curry powder
- 1 tsp (5 mL) sea salt
- Saucer each of flour and bread crumbs
- 1 egg

In a small dry pan or skillet on medium heat, heat sunflower, coriander and cumin seeds, occasionally shaking pan, for 3 to 5 minutes, or until sunflower seeds are slightly brown. (You do not need to use oil.) Cool.

Steam green vegetables for about 5 minutes, until tender. Drain and cool.

Place sunflower seed mixture in food processor. Pulse a few times. Transfer to a bowl.

In the same pan, sauté onion in 1 tsp (5 mL) oil until translucent.

Transfer onion and cooked greens to the food processor. Cover, and pulse on and off until the mixture starts to swirl evenly.

Transfer the mixture into the bowl containing the seeds. Add curry powder and sea salt, and mix everything well.

Shape mixture into 8 flat oval patties. Coat each with flour. In a shallow bowl, beat the egg, and dip the floured patties in it. Coat patties with bread crumbs.

Oil a griddle on medium heat until a sprinkle of water sizzles gently across the surface. Add 2 or 3 croquettes. Cook each croquette until the bottom is golden brown. Flip and cook until the other side is golden brown. Keep warm until all croquettes are cooked.

Serve immediately.

Kikuchi kids show off their vegetables.

The Resourceful Kikuchi Family

Pender Islanders Arthur and Sanea Kikuchi and their four children, Kenta, Yoko, Shinta and Kota, try to grow all their own food. "Not totally possible," says Sanea with a smile. "We are rice eaters." Living modestly and constantly trying to reduce their carbon footprint, they grow vegetables in a series of raised beds surrounding their house, augmenting the soil with natural mulch from the forest, and collecting rainwater from the roof to irrigate both garden and greenhouse. They bake bread, drink homemade soya milk, and raise Japanese quail for eggs. "Quail are tiny and do not use as many resources as chickens," Arthur explains. "They are Kenta's job."

The children are home schooled and much of their learning is centred on the family garden. "Nature teaches everything," says Sanea. The children each have a family chore and their own garden bed to tend. They research organic heritage seeds and learn about finance by selling their produce at the farmers' market. Arthur and Sanea are passionate about the environment and have placed a covenant on a portion of their land, named Frog Song Forest, so it will never be developed. Concern about our current society's lack of a sustainable organic food system has led them to share their skills by teaching Pender children how to grow food in the school garden and by sharing their many recipes with their neighbours.

Versatile Tomatillos

"What do you do with those?" is the question many visitors ask when visiting my garden in the fall. They point dubiously at the tomatillos rioting over both bed and path, branches weighed down with paper lantern husks protecting the glossy green globes inside.

The tomatillo (also known as tomato verde) is my success story. Tomatoes do not grow well in my forest garden as there is not enough direct sun, but their less picky cousin, the tomatillo, thrives. Tomatillos are so productive it's hard to keep up with them, so I pick and freeze them to be dealt with later. They freeze well, spread on a cookie sheet then popped in resealable bags.

Last year I planted two tomatillo plants and they took over one entire bed, and I was picking tomatillos well into November. I mainly use the picturesque paper-lantern-wrapped fruits to make salsa verde, but they can be paired with any sautéed vegetable and are wonderful in moussaka. If I sauté them with garlic, red pepper and lemon zest, cooking until the juices have evaporated, I have a piquant sauce that is delightful with either chicken or pork. I slice and drain them, and add them to vegetable galettes, and I use them in place of tomatoes in stews. They taste like tomatoes with a citrus flavour, and can be used fresh in gazpacho, puréed in sauces or added to any recipe calling for tomatoes. They make wonderful chutney too. So, if you are having no success growing tomatoes, experiment with tomatillos—but expect them to sprawl everywhere, and make sure there is plenty of storage room in your freezer!

Island Tomatillo and Green Tomato Chutney

Tomatillos, which have an unusual appearance, are an easy crop to raise as long as you have a minimum of two plants so they can fertilize each other. Tomatillos also give a lively citrusy tang to chutney. This is a great recipe that combines tomatillos with those dreaded green tomatoes languishing on the vine in fall.

Makes five 1 pint (0.5 L) jars

6 cups (1.4 L) fresh tomatillos, husked, rinsed and chopped
4 cups (1 L) green tomatoes, rinsed and chopped
2¼ cups (535 mL) packed brown sugar
1½ cups (350 mL) chopped onion
1½ cups (350 mL) dried cranberries
1½ cups (350 mL) apple cider vinegar
½ cup (125 mL) lime juice
2 Tbsp (30 mL) chopped crystallized ginger
2 Tbsp (30 mL) pickling spice
1 Tbsp (15 mL) brown mustard seeds, toasted
1½ tsp (7.5 mL) chili powder
½ tsp (2.5 mL) salt
Zest of 2 limes

Place all chutney ingredients in a large, heavy-bottomed pot. Bring to a boil over medium-high heat, stirring until the brown sugar has dissolved.

Reduce heat to low, and simmer the chutney until thickened (1 to 2 hours), stirring occasionally to keep chutney from burning on the bottom.

Meanwhile, sterilize five 1 pint (0.5 L) canning jars, tops and rings, and keep hot until needed.

Pour chutney into the hot jars, filling them to within ½ inch (1.3 cm) of the top.

Run a thin spatula around the inside of the jars to remove any air bubbles.

Wipe the rims of the jars with a clean damp cloth to remove any food residue.

Top jars with lids, and screw on the rings.

Hot water process the jars for 15 minutes or according to the instructions that came with your canning equipment.

Remove the jars from the canner, and place them on a cloth-covered surface at least 1 inch (2.5 cm) apart. Do not touch the jars until they have cooled. The lids will make a popping sound when they seal.

Once cool, ensure that the seal on each jar is tight. Wipe, label and date jars.

Store chutney in a cool, dark area. Use within a year and refrigerate once jars are opened. Any leftover uncanned chutney can be refrigerated and used within a month.

Community Gardens

All the Southern Gulf Islands have beautiful and productive community gardens that by harvest time are burgeoning with a cornucopia of tomatoes and other goodies. But only Mayne's prize-winning garden is guarded by a Garden Goddess and the gardeners' spirits are enriched by a labyrinth.

When we visited, this organic community garden had flourishing produce in 33 plots, and the need for expansion was under serious discussion. We toured the community greenhouse, a small orchard and some community tended beds, as well as the individual beds and a children's garden—and of course we walked the labyrinth!

As with all gardens in the Gulf Islands, watering is a problem. At the Mayne Island garden, this was solved by installing several tanks attached to a large water-catchment system collecting runoff from the roof of the nearby community hall. The water supply is monitored, and no hoses are allowed. Instead, each week a chalkboard by the gate informs the gardeners how many watering cans they can fill for their plot that week. Taps are throughout the garden, and the honour system works, for everyone understands the need to conserve water.

The Mayne gardeners got a good start on their community garden project when they entered a North America—wide competition, sponsored by a tool company. The challenge was to explain gardening to an alien without using language. The islanders made a short film and were one of five winners. The reward? They were delighted to receive not only a thousand-dollar cheque, but also fifteen hundred dollars' worth of tools, which have been put to good use ever since.

Mayne's community garden is carved out of the forest and overlooked by a terra cotta "Garden Goddess."

Ron Pither, Nikky Spooner and Varalaya Farm

I first made Montana Potato Cake after buying all the ingredients, apart from the cheese and nutmeg, from the Varalaya Farm stand at Mayne Island's farmers' market.

The beautiful and unusual name Varalaya is the meld of four ancient Sanskrit words that Mayne Island farmer and organic farm activist Ron Pither believes may be the first elemental words humans spoke—water, fire, earth and air. The farm's name captures what Ron and Nikki are all about—living life responsibly and caring for their land through the basic elements first. They nurture the section of earth they steward, to keep its water clear and air pure, while providing heat and food in a sustainable way. After the name, the other two most important words on this farm are reuse and recycle.

Varalaya Farm has a busy stall in the Mayne Farmers' Market.

Working to keep the farm's carbon footprint as small as possible, Ron recycled several buildings. He skidded the farm buildings into the Varalaya sanctuary, saving them from demolition. They include the original Mayne Island lighthouse and an architect-designed, venerable farmhouse. Then came an outhouse, honeyhouse, bunkhouse, sauna, gazebo and workshops. Now they are all an integral part of Varalaya Farm, where they continue to serve a purpose.

Varalaya comprises four acres (1.6 hectares) of cultivated land in the midst of 24 acres (9.7 hectares) of forest, stream and ponds. Not only does the farmland produce market garden crops, but the forest is sustainably harvested for timber, flowers and herbs, and is a sanctuary for wildlife. In the cultivated area, Nikki and Ron raise livestock as well as a prodigious amount of organic vegetables. They also produce honey and sell jams and jellies that can be purchased in stores on Saturna and Galiano Islands, as well as Mayne. Watch for the Varalaya Farm stand every Saturday at the Mayne Island farmers' market.

Montana Potato Cake

This recipe is not named after the US state, but rather after the delicious Salt Spring Island Cheese Company's product that is one of the main ingredients. David Wood's Montana is a hard cheese with a distinctive flavour that comes from combining goat's and sheep's milk.

This recipe makes one large potato cake layered with cheese, reminiscent of the Spanish *tortilla de patatas*. It is an extremely rich dish, as it also contains butter, so a hearty slice with a simple salad makes a great vegetarian meal. When serving as a side dish for an evening meal, keep the slices small and the accompaniments simple. The dish contains no added salt, as we found there is enough in the butter and cheese. The finished potato cake makes a spectacular centre piece if wreathed by sprigs of bay or other garden herbs. It is delicious hot or cold.

Makes 4 to 6 main dish servings, 8 side dish servings

> ¼ cup (60 mL) butter
> 2 lbs (1 kg) potatoes (a waxy variety works best)
> 3 cloves garlic, chopped, divided into 3 portions
> ¼ cup (60 mL) chopped parsley, divided into 3 portions
> ¾ cup (180 mL) shaved Salt Spring Montana cheese, divided into 3 portions
> Freshly grated nutmeg
> ¼ cup (60 mL) chopped green onion

Preheat oven to 400F (205C).

Grease the bottom and sides of a 7 inch (18 cm) nonstick springform pan. Grease it well so the cheese won't stick.

Peel and thinly slice the potatoes.

Sprinkle one-third of the garlic and parsley on the bottom on the pan, cover with one-third of the potato slices and then one-third of the cheese. Repeat process, dotting second layer with dabs of butter, to form three layers of herbs, potato and cheese.

Dot top with remaining butter and sprinkle with a few grinds of nutmeg. Cover (I use the greased flat base of a slightly bigger springform pan).

Place potato cake in oven and roast for 50 to 60 minutes, until the potato is soft and the surface is a rich golden brown.

Run a knife around the side of the pan to loosen baked-on cheese, remove side and slip a wide spatula underneath the potato cake. Slide it onto a serving plate.

Garnish with the chopped green onion. Cut into slices with a serrated knife and serve.

The Oglovs' Sesame Kale Salad

The Oglovs' Pender Island garden is almost an estate. The undulating ground is tamed by terraced beds—which Stan built and Linda tends—and punctuated with Stan's sculptures. The orchard bears heritage apples, bees buzz amid a riot of flowers and vegetables tumble over the confines of staid stone walls. The garden is productive. It not only feeds the Oglovs, but they give friends and neighbours bags of apples, armfuls of zucchinis or handfuls of herbs. Dinner at the Oglovs' is a symphony of simplicity. Both are busy people, so they delight in easy recipes full of flavour. These showcase their homegrown food while allowing the cook to mingle with guests instead of slaving over the stove. The wine, music and conversation always flow. This recipe was served at one fall dinner we attended, and even Dave, who avoids kale whenever possible, enjoyed it. "It's perfect for a dinner party," said Linda as she shared the recipe. "It's made ahead and the ingredients are always available, for kale grows year-round in this climate."

Makes 4 to 6 servings

> 1 lb (454 gm) fresh kale (or chard, spinach or other cool-weather greens)
> 1 clove garlic, minced
> 2 Tbsp (30 mL) sesame oil
> 2 Tbsp (30 mL) soy sauce
> 1 Tbsp (15 mL) toasted sesame seeds
> 1 Tbsp (15 mL) apple cider vinegar
> 2 tsp (10 mL) maple syrup
> Pinch black or red pepper, or more to taste

Separate kale leaves from stems. Chop stems and greens separately.

In a saucepan, steam stems for a couple of minutes, and then add the leaves and steam until just tender.

Drain. Let kale cool enough to handle it. Squeeze out as much water as possible. Place kale in a serving bowl and fluff with a fork.

Mix the remaining ingredients in another bowl. Add to greens and toss everything together.

Chill for at least 30 minutes before serving.

Ruckle Park, on Salt Spring Island, was once part of the island's biggest agricultural endeavour—Ruckle Farm.

The historic Ruckle Farm is still a full-time going concern, though it has shrunk to 200 acres (81 hectares) from the extensive farm that Irishman Henry Ruckle developed after immigrating to Salt Spring in 1872.

Initially Henry farmed 340 acres (138 hectares) of land near Fulford Harbour. In five years, with the help of Japanese labourers, he cleared a good portion of the land and decided to set up house. He married a widow, Ella Christiansen, and adopted her infant son, and then he and Ella had three more children. Henry continued to improve his land and gradually acquired more. By the time he died in 1913, his family farm spread over 1,198 acres (485 hectares) and was the largest farm on Salt Spring.

The Ruckle Farm stand serves lemonade and cookies to park visitors.

Part of Ruckle Farm eventually became Ruckle Provincial Park, famous for its walk-in campsites on the bluffs with one of the most stunning ocean views in the Gulf Islands. The park was established by a donation from Henry Ruckle's descendants. To reach it you pass through the original core of Henry's farm, which is still producing crops. Fruits and nuts are picked from century-old trees. Lambs, raised both for meat and wool, are still herded in the traditional way with sheepdogs. Watch for Highland cattle with their shaggy hides and long horns, turkeys, chickens and a productive market garden.

Each spring on Farm Day, visitors are treated to displays of traditional farming practices. Produce is available from the Ruckle Farm stand, which may include flowers and postcards, and sometimes lemonade and cookies for hikers in need of refreshment on their way up the hill to the park. This delightful tradition was started years ago by Gwen Ruckle.

Since the road to the park winds though the farm, drive carefully and watch out for wild turkeys! The free-range flock wanders the farm at will. Turkey eggs are sold to be hatched, and you can order a turkey for your Thanksgiving or Christmas feast from farm managers Marjorie and Mike Lane.

Ruckle Farm is the oldest working farm in British Columbia still owned by the original family.

Wild Chanterelle Sauce

Sometimes you find only a few fall mushrooms when you forage for them. This sauce is a good way to share their flavour. Use it to enhance the humble hamburger, or serve it over pasta or as a gravy with red meat or game, particularly venison.

Makes 4 servings

> 2 Tbsp (30 mL) butter
> 1 cup (250 mL) finely sliced chanterelles or other wild mushrooms
> ½ cup (125 mL) minced shallots
> 1 cup (250 mL) dry Gulf Islands white wine
> 1 Tbsp (15 mL) cornstarch
> 2 to 3 Tbsp (30 to 45 mL) tomato paste
> 1 cup (250 mL) rich meat stock (or leftover gravy)
> Salt and pepper
> 1 Tbsp (15 mL) chopped fresh parsley

In a heavy-bottomed saucepan, heat the butter over medium-low heat until frothy. Add the mushrooms and shallots, and sauté until the mushrooms are soft and the shallots are translucent, about 5 minutes.

Add the wine, heat until the liquid boils and then reduce heat to low. Simmer until the liquid is reduced by a half.

Stir the cornstarch and 2 Tbsp (30 mL) of the tomato paste together. Gradually add to the stock mixture, stirring until the sauce thickens.

Season with salt and pepper to taste.

Stir in the extra tomato paste, if needed, to balance the flavours.

Stir in the parsley and cook for 3 more minutes. Present sauce in a warmed sauceboat.

To Use Dried Chanterelles

Cover the dried mushrooms with boiling water and let stand for a minimum of 30 minutes. This will rehydrate them. Drain them and pat dry, reserving the liquid.

The rehydrated mushrooms can then be used just like fresh mushrooms. The flavoursome liquid can replace water in a recipe or be saved for use in a gravy or stock.

Fall Fabulous Finishes

The Salt Spring Pie Ladies

Fall equals apples; apples equal pies.

Nowhere on the Southern Gulf Islands are apple pies celebrated with more pizzazz than at the Salt Spring Island Fall Fair and the Salt Spring Apple Festival, where pies, hundreds of them, are made and sold by the Pie Ladies.

The Pie Ladies are renowned. They range in age from keen teenagers to 90-year-olds who have been making pies for a lifetime. Of course, Salt Spring is a Gulf Island, and that means there is always a wrinkle. Salt Spring's Pie Ladies are a non-sexist group that currently includes a man.

For the fall fair, their pies are imaginative (apple-cranberry, apple-salal, apple-ginger), but for the apple festival they're apples only—but not ordinary apples. These pies are made with luscious heritage apples grown locally. At least 12 different varieties of heritage cooking apples can be tasted. So choose your slice of pie made with an apple you will never find in the stores and possibly have never heard of, such as Wolf River apples or Red Gravensteins. Their flavours are so distinctive and so unusual you will wish you had room to try a slice of every variety. But get there early. Last year 486 pies were sold out by 4:00 p.m.!

Two of Salt Spring's famed Pie Ladies prepare for the festival.
Jan Mangan photo

'Never Fail' Pastry

Pastry is such a useful basic. It can turn a fridge full of leftovers into tasty pies or pasties, or tarts fit for the most elegant dinner party. I was given this pastry recipe over 40 years ago. We had just immigrated to Canada's prairies, and I'd tried to ward off a bout of homesickness by making an apple pie. It was a disaster. The pastry was sodden lead. In fact, none of my recipes worked. I had gone overnight from being a good cook in England to having culinary disaster after disaster.

A neighbour took me under her wing and explained that Edmonton, Alberta, was over 2,000 feet (610 metres) above sea level and the high elevation affected rising agents, cooking times and how long it took for water to boil—yes, at that point I couldn't even successfully boil eggs! She gave me a recipe cut from a bag of Robin Hood flour, and I've never used another pastry recipe since. It works like a charm no matter what the elevation or country! I am in good company: I gather 80 percent of Canadian cooks over 50 years old grew up using this recipe, including some of Salt Spring Island's Pie Ladies.

I usually double this recipe and store half the pastry, wrapped in plastic and sealed in a plastic bag, in the freezer. Then I always have some ready for the next pie.

Makes one 8 inch (20 cm) covered pie

1 egg, beaten
1 tsp (5 mL) brown sugar
1 tsp (5 mL) vinegar
Ice water
2½ cups (600 mL) flour
½ tsp (2.5 mL) baking powder
½ tsp (2.5 mL) salt
½ lb (227 gr) lard or shortening

In a small measuring cup, mix egg, sugar and vinegar with a fork. Add enough ice water to make ½ cup (125 mL) liquid.

In a bowl, stir together flour, baking powder and salt.

Cut or rub in the fat until the mixture is the consistency of bread crumbs.

Mix in the reserved liquid quickly and lightly with a fork. (Add drips of extra ice water if the mixture is too dry, or a sprinkle of flour if it is too sticky.)

Gather dough together in a ball, place it in a plastic bag and chill until ready to use.

Heritage Apple Pie

Pie-lady approved and simplicity itself, this recipe showcases heritage apples. (Red-fleshed ones are a delightful surprise for guests.)

Makes 6 servings

1 batch 'Never Fail' Pastry, previous page
6–8 large heritage apples, peeled, cored, and cut into ¼ inch (0.6 cm) slices and tossed with:
> **½ cup (125 mL) sugar**
> **1 tbsp (15 mL) lemon juice**
> **1 tbsp (15 mL) orange zest**
> **1 tsp (5 mL) ground cinnamon**
> **a grating of nutmeg to taste**
> **pinch of salt**
> **2 Tbsp (30 mL) cornstarch**

2 Tbsp (30 mL) butter

Preheat oven to 425F (220 C).

Cut your ball of 'Never Fail' Pastry in half, and roll each half out to make two 12 inch (30 cm) disks (big enough to amply line a 9 inch (23 cm) pie plate). Rest disks in refrigerator until needed.

Heap spiced apple slices in the pie shell and dot with butter. Cover and seal with pastry; trim and flute the edges. Use excess pastry to decorate and cut slits to allow steam to escape.

Bake in the bottom half of oven for 45 minutes or until juices begin to bubble through the slits. If needed, cover pie rim with strips of foil after 30 minutes to prevent excessive browning.

Allow to stand for 1 to 2 hours before serving to allow filling to thicken. Serve warm or cold with either ice cream or whipped cream.

At its annual festival, Salt Spring celebrates heritage apples, showcasing their rich variety of colour, taste, cuisine and history. *Jan Mangan photo*

Salt Spring Island Apple Festival

For any serious foodie, Salt Spring Island's amazing organic apple festival is a not-to-be-missed annual event.

Imagine Fulford Hall filled with a large rectangle of tables in the centre. On display are over 350 different varieties of heritage apples—yellow apples with red flesh, tiny lime green beauties with a distinctive perfume, striped apples, shiny apples, red apples so bright they glow, and giant apples weighing in at nearly 2 pounds (almost a kilogram) each. The variety is incredible, the colours and aroma are stunning, and the names are found poetry. (Roll these off your tongue—Scarlet Surprise, Sargententi, Jonamac, Pink Princess, Northern Spry, Wolf River, Alexander, Belle de Boskoop, Tolman Sweet.)

Each set of three apples is displayed on a paper plate with a doily beneath and a card describing the variety's provenance: where and when it was first grown; its size; its flavour; its growing characteristics; its sweetness level; the time it should be picked; whether it is primarily a good eating, cooking or juicing apple; how it stores and much more.

Then you pick up a map directing you to the 16 farms with heritage orchards where you are invited to taste all the varieties. Add apple pies for sale, apple experts who will identify an unknown tree for you, apple pressers who urge you to try their juice, apple art, apple face painting, apple songs and poetry, and lunches and snacks containing apples in some form or other (apple and pumpkin soup, apple cake, etc.) everywhere you visit.

There is a reason Salt Spring is known as Apple Heaven. Passionate orchardist Harry Burton, of Apple Luscious Organic Orchards specializes in red-fleshed apples, and Harry heads up the dedicated team of growers and over 30 volunteers who put on the festival. Bob Weedon, of Whims Farm, is expert at identifying heritage apples, and Wave Hill Farm has the oldest orchard on the island (1860). Bright Farm, situated on the historic Mouat homestead, has one of the largest collections of apples on the island—over 280 varieties. You will have to pick and choose from the list, because you are not going to be able to see them all and it's so utterly fascinating you will wish the day was longer.

Jan Mangan photos

Baked Spiced Quinces

This recipe features an unusual combination of spices. Quinces (see sidebar on opposite page) were particularly beloved by the English during the reign of Elizabeth I so we've reflected their history by sharing a modern, mellower version of a highly spiced dessert recipe popular in Elizabethan times.

The spices add a little pizzazz, but the quinces are equally tasty if the spices are omitted and they are cooked with only the more conventional orange and lemon highlights (use more citrus zest if cooking without the spices). I adapted this recipe for friends who once owned Old Orchard Farm on Pender and who weren't sure how to use their quinces.

Baked quinces are wonderful served with Hastings House Vanilla Bean Ice Cream (page 233).

Makes 4 servings

> 4 quinces
> Juice of 1 lemon and 2 long strips of the zest
> Juice of 1 orange and 2 long strips of the zest
> 2 bay leaves
> ½ tsp (2.5 mL) black peppercorns
> 2 star anise
> ½ long red dried chili pepper
> 1 vanilla bean, split
> 6 cups (1.4 L) water
> 3 cups (700 mL) sugar
> Extra orange juice or water if needed

Preheat oven to 300F (150C). Grease a 7 by 11 inch (18x28 cm) baking dish.

Peel, quarter and core quinces, reserving peel and cores.

Slice quinces thickly and place in baking dish.

Sprinkle quince slices with the citrus juices and toss.

Tie reserved quince peel and cores, lemon and orange zest, bay leaves, peppercorns, star anise, chili pepper and vanilla pod inside a square of muslin or clean cheesecloth.

Place cheesecloth bag in a saucepan with the water and sugar. Simmer, stirring gently, until the sugar dissolves. Bring to a slow boil. Boil for 5 minutes.

Pour boiled spice mixture over quince slices and tuck bag containing spice mixture among them. Cover dish with foil.

Bake in the middle of the oven for 3 hours, or until quinces are tender and a deep pink colour. Check every hour to ensure there is still enough poaching liquid. If necessary, add extra orange juice or water.

Remove bag of spices, and serve fruit hot or cold.

Caramelized Almond Pears

This easy, showy finish for a fall dinner party works with any variety of pear.

Makes 6 servings

> **6 firm pears**
> **1½ cups (350 mL) prepared almond paste or marzipan**
> **4 Tbsp (60 mL) butter**
> **1 cup (250 mL) packed dark brown sugar**
> **1 Tbsp (15 mL) fresh orange juice**
> **Grated orange zest and a few sliced almonds, for garnish**

Place rack in the centre of the oven and preheat to 375F (190C).

Wash and peel pears, keeping the stem intact. Using a small sharp knife, core pears from the bottom so they stand upright.

Divide the almond paste into 6 pieces, roll each piece into a ball and stuff into the hollow pears.

In the oven or microwave, melt butter in a 7 by 7 inch (18 by 18 cm) glass cake pan.

Sprinkle the brown sugar over the melted butter, stand the pears on top, sprinkle them with the orange juice and cover the pan with foil so it forms a "tent" over the pears.

Bake pears in the oven until tender, approximately 30 minutes.

Remove foil. Baste pears with the caramelizing juices. Return to the oven and bake for another 5 minutes. Baste pears with juices again, and continue baking and basting at 5 minute intervals until the pears are golden and shiny (about 10 to 15 minutes).

Remove dish from oven and let pears cool for a few minutes before transferring them to individual plates.

Drizzle pears with the caramelized sauce from the pan and garnish each serving with orange zest and sliced almonds.

Watch for honesty stands featuring quinces, or phone the orchard farms where you've spotted a tree. Many owners will happily pick some quinces for you.

Golden Apples of the Sun

Large yellow quinces (a fruit seldom found in grocery stores) can be seen glowing in fall sunshine in many of the older island orchards.

Quinces are an ancient fruit, reputed to be the "golden apples of the sun" of Greek myth. Favourites in the Middle Ages, they declined in popularity in more modern times, though quinces are now enjoying a mild resurgence of interest, particularly in odd corners such as the Gulf Islands.

Hard and woody but with a distinctive perfumed aroma, they can be placed whole in a decorative bowl as an instant potpourri. Quinces are inedible when raw so must be cooked before being consumed. Preparing them is hard work, and you need a very sharp knife and a certain amount of strength to remove the hard core. However, the effort is worth making. When quinces are baked in the oven, their flesh turns soft and pink, and they release more perfume as they are cooking.

Fall Fairs

A quiet Friday afternoon in fall suddenly turns to bedlam. On each of the Southern Gulf Islands, people appear from all over bearing boxes, baskets and trays of fruits and vegetables, platters of scones, buns, cakes and candies, armfuls of flowers, furniture, sweaters and sheepskins, and painting and pottery, and suddenly a traffic jam of epic proportions forms around the island's community hall.

"What's going on?" ask bewildered visitors.

"Entering tomorrow's fall fair," reply the islanders, uncharacteristically rushing past instead of stopping to chat. "Gotta get our entries registered before the deadline."

The annual fall fairs are held on a Saturday at the end of August or sometime in September, depending on the island, and are the climax of a yearly round of activities. At heart each fair is a celebration of food and community, and the showcasing of skills and traditions inherited from our pioneers.

Islanders take their fall fairs seriously. Even if you didn't enter, your friends or other family members did. Blue ribbons are coveted, entries admired and judging commented on, and the serious competition is accompanied by music and song, demonstrations, food concessions and general merriment and mayhem.

There are magicians for the kids, and local dancers strutting their stuff interspersed with parades, jazz bands, rock bands, pipe bands, games and the requisite beer garden.

At the livestock pens a crowd views the island's best goats, sheep, horses and fowl. The exhibit halls are filled with tables, displaying arts and crafts, and hundreds of food-related entries: colourful garden produce, aromatic pickles and jams, and all manner of baked goods, breads and luscious berry pies.

Pender Island Fall Fair, August 2012: Over 1,400 entries competed for ribbons in categories such as Food Preparation, Fruit, Vegetables and Flowers, various Artistic Endeavours, and Livestock.

At one fall fair we know of, so many people entered the wine-making category that the judge, after the rigours of sampling, had to be driven home.

The quilting is admired, the art marvelled at and the children's entries praised—even the cake half eaten by an escaped dog received a ribbon.

At the end of the day, entries are proudly reclaimed, cups are awarded and people unwind at the community barbecue. If you listen carefully, you hear plans already being made for next year's event.

Hatake Apple and Hazelnut Rolls

Mayne Island's Helen and John O'Brian are known for great hospitality, creative ideas and a fondness for apples—apple stories, apple recipes and baskets, and boxes of apples that they sell at their gate. Helen coordinated Mayne's apple recipe book, and she and John helped rejuvenate the farmers' market. Together they instigated Mayne's May Day celebrations, helped acquire a community apple press, host house concerts at their farm and even offer beds to itinerant writers and storytellers passing through.

Old orchards are scattered throughout the islands.

Their farm is named Hatake in memory of the Japanese who farmed the land before World War II and the remnants of whose orchard the couple now tends. *Hatake* is the Japanese word for farm.

Helen not only spends time with her animals and garden, she also hand dyes the mohair wool their goats produce. This is a time-consuming process because she makes her own vegetable dyes, using an assortment of natural produce such as blackberries, onions and asparagus. She therefore keeps food fresh and simple and rarely makes dessert. But after we stayed on their delightful farm, I was inspired to create this one for her. This roll references sushi, in memory of the Japanese. The filling features the fruits of their land.

Makes 6 servings (or more as a party snack)

    4 cups (1 L) finely chopped apple
    ½ cup (125 mL) chopped hazelnuts
    3 Tbsp (45 mL) all-purpose flour
    2 Tbsp (30 mL) chopped crystallized ginger
    2 Tbsp (30 mL) liquid honey
    Zest of 1 lemon
    9 sheets phyllo pastry,* covered with a slightly damp towel to prevent them from
        drying out
    ¼ cup (60 mL) melted butter
    3 tsp (15 mL) sugar
    Icing sugar, for dusting

Preheat oven to 375F (190C). Cover a cookie sheet with foil. Have ready a sheet of parchment paper that is a little bigger than a sheet of phyllo.

In a bowl, toss together the apple, hazelnuts, flour, ginger, honey and lemon zest, and divide mixture into 3 portions.

Place a sheet of phyllo pastry on the sheet of parchment paper, and brush phyllo with melted butter. Cover with a second sheet of phyllo and brush with melted butter. Repeat process with a third sheet of phyllo.

Continued on next page

*Since this recipe requires only some of the sheets of phyllo in the package, immediately roll the rest back up and wrap well in plastic wrap. It will keep in the refrigerator for a week, or refreeze the phyllo till the next time you need it.

Using one-third of the filling, spread it in a narrow line across the bottom of the phyllo sheets, but leave 1 inch (2.5 cm) clear at the bottom edge and each side.

Fold the sides in to cover the edges of the filling, and fold the 1 inch phyllo border up over the filling. Using the parchment to assist, firmly roll up the pastry and filling like a sushi roll. Lifting with the parchment, place the roll seam-side down on the foil-covered cookie sheet.

Repeat this process with the remaining phyllo sheets and filling to make 2 more rolls.

Paint the tops of the rolls with melted butter and sprinkle each with 1 tsp (5 mL) sugar.

Place the cookie sheet in the middle of the oven, and bake the rolls until they are brown and flaky, about 30 to 40 minutes.

Remove rolls from oven and allow them to cool for 10 minutes on the cookie sheet before moving them. Slice them diagonally into bite-sized pieces and dust with icing sugar before serving.

The Japanese garden on Mayne commemorates the Japanese families who settled and worked on the Island until 1942.

Peek into History: The Japanese Contribution—Mayne Island Remembers

Japanese settlers first arrived on the Gulf Islands in the late 1890s and immediately became a vibrant part of the economy. Many took up work fishing or cutting wood to supply the Fraser River canneries. Others operated farms, herring salteries and fish-processing plants, the largest of which were on Mayne, Galiano and Pender Islands.

By the 1920s, the Japanese community (of which many members had been born in Canada) was an important and well-respected part of several island communities. It was perhaps most notable on Mayne where, by 1940, Japanese made up almost a third of the island's population.

Japanese farmers first established a large poultry cooperative on Mayne (with an estimated 50,000 hens) but by the early 1930s had turned instead to creating an extensive tomato-growing operation. From more than eight acres (three hectares) of greenhouses, the co-op produced about 50 tons of tomatoes a year, shipping huge quantities throughout the summer to Victoria and Vancouver.

All of this success was brought to a sudden end by events unfolding far away. In the months that followed the bombing of Pearl Harbor in December 1941, all island residents of Japanese origin were forced to move to internment camps in the interior of BC. Sadly, few of these people returned to the islands.

Mayne Islanders haven't forgotten their Japanese friends and neighbours. A beautiful Japanese garden at Dinner Bay now commemorates the contribution Japanese people made to the fabric of the Gulf Islands. In 2006 a plaque was unveiled at a dedication ceremony that several members of the original Japanese families attended. They had been found and contacted after some historical detective work Mayne Islanders undertook. The reunion was celebrated with great rejoicing and a reforging of friendships.

Celebrating Fall

Poets Cove Resort, South Pender Island

Climbing up a south-facing hillside that provides wonderful views of Pender's beautiful Bedwell Harbour is Poets Cove Resort & Spa—the Southern Gulf Islands' biggest resort. Guests stay in condos, time-share cottages or lodge rooms overlooking the marina, the pools and the harbour. Not surprisingly, this resort, with its spa and extensive banquet facilities, is a wedding destination in the islands.

Food with a view is *de rigueur*. Chef Steve Boudreau presides over the second-floor Aurora Restaurant, the casual Syrens Bistro (known to everyone as "the pub") on the ground floor and the private banquet area, which has its own kitchen. All three face Bedwell Harbour.

The Aurora opens to a large deck for al fresco dining on warm summer evenings. Patrons of the pub spill outside onto its patio all day long. It is so popular that there is often a queue for tables in July and August, when the marina is hopping with visiting boaters. Chef Steve has been with the resort for four years and ably takes the reins for the two kitchens by using down-to-earth Maritime common sense. He showcases his culinary skills with deceptively simple, locally based menus.

Patrons enjoy the patio at Poets Cove Resort.

Despite its opulence, Poets Cove has an ongoing mandate to be environmentally responsible, and manager Walter Kohli works on making its footprint smaller every year. "We have a Green Key Eco Rating," he said proudly, referring to a program designed for hotels and resorts to measure environmental impact. With level three out of a possible five, it demonstrates that Poets Cove "has taken significant steps to protect the environment."

The pub and marina at Poets Cove are popular with boaters.

Steve Boudreau, executive chef at Poets Cove.

Chef Steve Boudreau

"It's all about flavour—tasty, fresh and simple. That's my mantra," said Poets Cove's executive chef Steve Boudreau. His eyes twinkled. "Want to see my tattoo? Forget those fancy dragons; it's a vegetable peeler and some fennel. I'm just a simple man from Cape Breton who's crazy about food."

Poets Cove, an upscale resort destination on South Pender Island, reflects his philosophy both in the Aurora Restaurant and Syrens Bistro. The choices on the seasonal menu are limited in range but big in flavour, and often feature local delights in the daily specials. "I'd rather my kitchens produce 10 items perfectly than 20 items not so well. I involve my staff both in choosing the menu and developing items for it. It's more fun and gives them a stake in the food we send out."

Pi, the sous-chef, agreed. "For instance, we might have a little competition to see who can create the best sauce to accompany Chef's turkey terrine, or come up with a new appetizer.

Obviously Pi won one of these competitions, for Pi's Pork and Shrimp Steamed Dumplings graced the pub menu when we visited.

"I love the vegetables produced on Pender," Steve continued. "Such flavour. Those heritage tomatoes . . ." He closed his eyes to savour the memory. They snapped open again almost immediately. "Did you know we now have a contract with organic farms right here on Pender. Hope Bay Farm and Raven Rock [Farm] provide us with heritage tomatoes, micro sprouts and a variety of organic veg. I spend as much on vegetables as I do on protein," he grinned. "But it's worth it . . . the taste!"

Resort guests kayak in Bedwell Harbour.

Created by Chef Steve Boudreau, Poets Cove Resort, South Pender Island

Pan-Seared Scallops on Apple, Cauliflower and Vanilla Bean Purée

This appetizer features fresh Qualicum Beach Scallops, a sustainably cultured scallop from nearby Vancouver Island, and local apples embellished with a hint of vanilla. It's such an easy appetizer to make yet a deliciously unusual combination to present to guests.

Makes 6 servings

3 apples, diced
½ head cauliflower, chopped
4 cloves garlic, crushed
2 bay leaves
1 tsp (5 mL) salt
½ vanilla bean
Milk

2 Tbsp (30 mL) plus 1 tsp (5 mL) butter
Pinch sea salt
Fresh lemon juice
12 Qualicum scallops
1 tsp (5 mL) olive oil

Set aside ¼ cup (60 mL) of the diced apple. Place remaining apple, cauliflower, garlic, bay leaves and salt in a saucepan. Split the vanilla bean and scrape the seeds into the pan, drop in the pod and add milk to cover.

Simmer until vegetables are soft. Discard bay leaves and the vanilla bean pod, and set mixture aside to cool a little.

Purée vegetable mixture.

Return vegetable mixture to the pan and reheat on low. Stir in the 2 Tbsp (30 mL) butter and adjust the salt to taste. Stir in lemon juice to taste. Keep mixture warm. Do not boil!

To prepare the scallops, remove the tough muscle from the side of each one if this has not already been done. Pat scallops dry, and season with a little sea salt.

Heat remaining butter and olive oil in a sauté pan. Quickly sauté the reserved diced apple, remove from pan and keep warm.

Add scallops to pan. Cook for 1 minute, making sure not to touch them. You want a nice golden crust to form on the bottom.

Flip the scallops, baste with the butter mixture and cook for another minute. They should be golden outside and rare within.

Ladle a round of purée onto each plate and place 2 scallops in the middle.

Garnish with a sprinkle of reserved diced apple.

Rosemary-Crusted Rack of Lamb

Chef Steve orders whole lambs each season from Barb Grimmer's Fir Hill Farms on Pender. He recommends buying racks with chine bones removed, rib bones frenched and meat trimmed of all but a thin layer of fat.

Makes 6 servings

> **3 racks of lamb**
> **Kosher salt and freshly ground black pepper**
> **2 cups (475 mL) soft fresh bread crumbs**
> **¼ cup (60 mL) chopped fresh rosemary**
> **Approximately ½ cup (125 mL) olive oil**
> **4 Tbsp (60 mL) Dijon mustard**

Preheat oven to 475F (245C).

Season lamb with salt and pepper.

Combine bread crumbs and rosemary in a shallow bowl. Moisten with enough olive oil to make the mixture hold together. Set aside.

Heat a large dry skillet over high heat. Put the lamb, meat side down, in the skillet. Sear it on all sides for a total of 4 minutes.

Remove the meat from the skillet and paint the meaty side of the rack with the mustard. Roll meat in the reserved herb mixture to coat.

Roast meat until medium rare, 20 to 25 minutes (120F/49C internal temperature). Let the racks rest for 5 minutes before slicing.

A rack of lamb on the home barbecue.

Baby Potatoes with Olive Oil

Makes 6 servings

> **24 baby nugget potatoes, washed but unpeeled**
> **½ cup (125 mL) good olive oil**
> **Zest of 2 lemons**

Boil potatoes in salted water until fork tender.

Drain potatoes and slice them ¼ inch (0.6 cm) thick.

Toss with olive oil and lemon zest. Keep potatoes warm to allow the oil and lemon to be absorbed.

Glazed Carrots

Makes 6 servings

> **3 lbs (1.4 kg) fresh garden carrots**
> **½ cup (125 mL) vegetable stock**
> **2 Tbsp (30 mL) butter**
> **Sea salt and freshly cracked pepper**

Rinse carrots, but do not peel them. Do not remove green tops, but trim them to 1½ inches (4 cm).

Boil 3 quarts (3 L) water with enough salt that it tastes like sea water. Prepare an ice water bath in a large bowl.

Parboil carrots by submerging them in the boiling water for 3 minutes. Remove carrots from boiling water and shock them in ice water to stop the cooking process and preserve their bright colour.

Heat vegetable stock and butter in a sauté pan. Add carrots and sauté until they are hot and the sauce has reduced to a nice glaze.

Season with salt and pepper.

Apple Custard Flan

Makes 6 servings

Sweet Dough

1½ cups (350 mL) all-purpose flour
¼ cup (60 mL) sugar
Pinch salt
½ cup (125 mL) butter, at room temperature
1 large egg

Pulse flour, sugar and salt in a food processor.

Cut butter into nuggets and pulse with ingredients in food processor.

In a small bowl, whisk egg with a fork. Add egg to mixture in food processor and keep pulsing until dough just comes together. Tip dough into a bowl and form into a ball.

Chill for 1 hour in fridge.

Preheat oven to 350F (175C). Grease a 10 inch (25 cm) pie plate.

Roll out dough and line pie plate with it. (Alternatively, place dough in pie plate and press out evenly to cover it.) Prick pastry with a fork and decoratively crimp the edges.

Blind bake for 20 minutes. Set aside to cool.

Apple Filling

8 apples, each peeled, cored and sliced into 12 wedges
1/3 cup (80 mL) sugar
2 tsp (10 mL) lemon juice
2 tsp (10 mL) lemon zest
1 tsp (5 mL) cinnamon

Place sliced apples in a saucepan with the sugar, lemon juice and zest, and cinnamon. Cook on medium heat for 5 minutes. Set aside to cool.

Custard Filling

½ cup (125 mL) all-purpose flour
⅔ cup (160 mL) sugar
4 large eggs
1½ cups (350 mL) half-and-half cream
1 tsp (5 mL) vanilla extract
2 Tbsp (30 mL) apple brandy

Preheat oven to 350F (175C).

Combine flour and sugar in a bowl.

In a separate bowl, whisk the eggs and then whisk them into the flour mixture.

Heat the cream until it just foams up. Remove from heat and gradually whisk in the egg mixture, vanilla and brandy.

Arrange apple slices in concentric circles in pie shell. Fill with the egg mixture and bake for 25 minutes, or until the pastry is golden and the custard is firm.

Colourful VW on Pender Island. In the fall, islanders lock their vehicles to prevent excess zucchinis from multiplying in their parked vehicles.

Winter

The Warmth of Winter

Opposite: View from Mount
Warburton Pike, Saturna Island.

The wind howls, the rain pounds. Slicker-clad, rubber-booted and heads down, we hustle between car and house. The door opens and a warm savoury aroma spills out. Winter is the season of rib-sticking soups and stews, when a slow cooker or stockpot is the islander's best friend.

Velvet nights are all encompassing during these winter months, for we rise in the dark and the hours of daylight are short. But this has its compensations; the absence of street lights on the islands means we can marvel at the stars that sweep overhead, rivalling any city display of Christmas lights.

The woodstove glows—wise islanders own one no matter how modern their house. Power outages are a fact of life in bad weather, and woodstoves are our alternative heating and cooking source. But most of all, this is the time we hunker down. Off-island visitors are few, except over the holiday season, so islanders visit islanders. Winter means dinners with friends, potluck feasts and community gatherings.

In January, snowdrops carpet the orchard at Old Orchard Farm, Pender Island.

Almost everyone we know is a good cook, and in winter they strut their stuff, for it seems all island social occasions centre on food. Large or small, winter celebrations create the perfect excuse to share favourite dishes, be it at Thanksgiving or Winter Solstice, Hanukkah or Christmas, Ukrainian Christmas or New Year, Robbie Burns night or a plain old "beat the February blues" potluck supper. Yes, islanders have a reputation for celebrating anything that comes their way.

So forget the weather and rejoice at the tremendous gift Old Man Winter brings. For no matter how hard he blows or freezes our toes, nothing is more heartwarming than getting together, and there is no better gift than sharing wonderful homegrown, home-cooked food with family and friends. On those dark, wet, winter nights, no matter what we call the occasion, we are all celebrating something special—the enriching warmth of our island community.

Spicy Parsnip and Carrot Soup Topped with Pear

Opposite: Spicy Parsnip and Carrot Soup Topped with Pear accompanied by Dana's Caramelized Onion, Potato and Rosemary Focaccia (page 212).

Parsnips and carrots contain natural sugars that are released when heated. In this recipe the smooth, sweet flavours of these vegetables naturally balance the spiciness of ginger and garam masala. Garnished with a touch of winter pear sauce, this is a soup to remember. Both the vegetables and a variety of winter pears are easily sourced locally all winter long. They keep well and are adaptable ingredients for many recipes. If you have a garden, leave the carrots and parsnips in the soil until needed. They get sweeter with age and frost and keep better in the earth than in the fridge.

Serve this warming soup with chunks of homemade bread.

Makes 6 servings

Pear Sauce

2 cups (475 mL) winter pears, peeled, cored and chopped
2 Tbsp (30 mL) orange juice
1 Tbsp (15 mL) sugar

To make sauce, gently cook the pear with the orange juice and sugar, stirring occasionally, until pear is soft.

Mash pear mixture with a potato masher or quickly process with an immersion blender, leaving a few lumps for texture. Keep sauce warm until needed.

Soup

1 tsp (5 mL) butter
1 tsp (5 mL) olive oil
3 cloves garlic, roughly chopped
1 large onion, chopped
Thumb-sized piece fresh ginger, peeled and roughly chopped
2 Tbsp (30 mL) garam masala
4 large carrots, peeled and sliced
4 large parsnips, peeled and sliced
2 cups (475 mL) coconut milk
4 cups (1 L) rich vegetable or chicken stock
Sea salt and freshly ground black pepper
Handful fresh coriander or parsley leaves

Heat butter and olive oil in a large saucepan. Add the garlic, onion, ginger and garam masala. Gently sauté for several minutes, until the onion is soft and translucent.

Add the carrots and parsnips, and stir to coat in the butter mixture. Pour in the coconut milk and stock, season well with salt and pepper, and bring mixture to a boil.

Continued on next page

Immediately turn down the heat. Cover and simmer for 30 minutes.

Check that the vegetables are soft. Remove pan from the heat and cool mixture, uncovered, for a few minutes. Process until smooth using an immersion mixer, or blend small batches.

Taste soup, and adjust salt and pepper as needed.

Return soup to the pan and reheat to just below the boiling point.

Ladle soup into bowls, spoon warm pear sauce into the centre of each and garnish with coriander leaves.

Galiano's Soup for Seniors

Galiano Island offers the most active year-round co-operative food programs on the Southern Gulf Islands. Members of the Galiano Community Food Program cook together in the community kitchen, run Nettlefest and coordinate the community greenhouse and community gardens. The group works with both Galiano Sunshine Farm and Cable Bay Farm to grow community crops such as potatoes and garlic.

Soup for Seniors involves volunteers regularly getting together in the community kitchen to make bread and cook soup from the vegetables grown in the community plots. The resulting meals are delivered over the fall and winter months to Galiano seniors. This is a vibrant and delightful program of nourishing community care.

Galiano resident Allison Colwell, who is involved with the Soup for Seniors program, encourages everyone to make soup. She has put together a small soup recipe book to this end and sells it at her condiment stall at the farmers' market. "Served with good homemade bread and salad, soup is the perfect meal," says Allison. "Plus big batches mean you're always prepared when unexpected guests drop by at mealtime." A great island philosophy.

Mae Moore's greenhouse is both attractive and practical.

Mae and Lester's Garden for All Seasons

Singer/songwriter and artist Mae Moore lives on Pender with her husband, blues musician Lester Quitzau. They revel in a simple lifestyle in a retrofitted old island home that now has solar heat and solar electricity and is "almost off the grid." Mae is a wonderful gardener, and their organic vegetables are large and luscious. The graceful greenhouse, with its striking curved roof, extends the growing season and was designed and built by Pender's Jude Farmer. It is a work of art, but entirely practical. It even has an underground system of composting built in.

Lester and Mae's cottage is edged by a heritage orchard that Lester tends. The trees are pollinated by a large colony of mason bees, whose elaborate condo Lester built into the cottage wall.

Both Mae and Lester eat a vegetarian diet augmented by the occasional "happy hen" and buy only those items they cannot produce, such as grains and brown sugar. They sell excess produce and colourful bunches of flowers at their roadside honesty stand, but Mae also cans and freezes, so their very productive garden and orchard feeds them year-round.

Mae's Wetcoast Crackers

Mae, who is well-known on the island for her skills in the kitchen, was happy to pass on her version of those yummy but expensive Raincoast Crisps found in the stores.

Mae's crackers, not as thin or as crispy as the famous crisps, are rich in flavour and very easy to make. The grains are available within a short walk of her house (at Pender's organic Southridge Store), and she gathers the rosemary from her garden. We love these crackers served with homemade cream cheese (page 19) or just on their own as a nutritious snack.

Makes approximately 24 crackers

1 cup (250 mL) flour (spelt, wheat, rye, etc.)
½ cup (125 mL) raisins or dried cranberries
¼ cup (60 mL) pumpkin seeds
½ cup (125 mL) chopped pecans
¼ cup (60 mL) flax or hemp seeds
¼ cup (60 mL) brown sugar
3 Tbsp (45 mL) finely chopped fresh rosemary
1 tsp (5 mL) baking soda
1 tsp (5 mL) sea salt
¼ cup (60 mL) molasses
1 cup (250 mL) milk, milk substitute or buttermilk

Preheat oven to 350F (175C). Cut a sheet of parchment paper to fit the cookie sheet.

In a large bowl, mix together all the dry ingredients.

Stir the molasses into the milk, and then pour the liquid into the dry ingredients. Combine well.

Pat and spread the mixture out very thinly on the cookie sheet.

Bake for 10 minutes.

Remove from oven. Score into cracker-sized pieces. Return crackers to oven and bake for 7 to 10 minutes more. This makes a "cakey" cracker. To make them crisper, cut completely through the score lines, flip the crackers over, return them to the oven and bake for another 5 minutes.

Cool crackers and store them in an airtight container.

Note: Mae also passed this recipe to Theresa Carle-Sanders, who writes the Island Vittles blog. Theresa likes a thinner cracker so makes the following adaptation. She packs the batter into a small loaf pan and bakes at 350F (175C) for approximately 40 minutes. She then cools the loaf, freezes it until firm but not rock hard, slices it thinly and bakes the slices for another 15 minutes, taking care not to overbrown the nuts.

Duck Creek Farm's garlic is famous on Salt Spring.

Spanish Garlic Soup

The lovely Spanish place names on the Southern Gulf Islands have led to several dinner-table discussions about the Spanish explorers, how they provisioned their ships and what the seamen ate. The English explorers were famous for abysmal food, including hardtack. The Spanish sailing ships were small and crowded, dark and damp, and crew conditions obviously were miserable in bad weather. I cannot imagine that the Spanish didn't bring garlic, which would keep hung in braids and was known to have medicinal properties. I also cannot imagine that they didn't eat a version of their centuries-old national dish that is simple to prepare, as well as being nutritious and warming.

Makes 4 to 6 servings

> 30 large cloves Gulf Island garlic, sliced
> ¼ cup (60 mL) olive oil
> 5 cups (1.2 L) rich beef broth
> 1 cup (250 mL) dry sherry
> Salt and pepper
> 4 to 6 slices French bread
> Grated Parmesan cheese

In a small sauté pan, gently fry the garlic in the olive oil until garlic is fragrant and faintly golden.

In a large saucepan, heat the beef broth with the sherry. When the broth reaches a boil, add the garlic and olive oil. Season with salt and pepper to taste. Adjust heat to a simmer.

Simmer soup, covered, for about 30 minutes.

Strain out the garlic, and mash or blend it with a little of the broth. Stir garlic mixture into the soup and reheat.

Preheat oven to 425F (220C).

While the soup is reheating, prepare toast—1 slice per serving.

Generously sprinkle toast slices with Parmesan cheese, and heat them in the oven for about 3 or 4 minutes.

Place a slice of cheese toast in the bottom of each soup dish, ladle the soup over top and serve.

Duck Creek Farm

The most attractive garlic we had ever seen stopped us in our tracks when cruising Salt Spring's Saturday market. The Duck Creek Farm stall was packed with woven baskets bulging with long stems of garlic arranged like roses. The gigantic juicy bulbs were attractively striped with deep pink streaks, and so pretty I couldn't resist stopping and buying some. These palm-sized heads of pungent Portuguese garlic—sometimes called "the stinking rose"—were beautiful enough to display in a vase on my kitchen counter. This I did until the waft of their fragrance every time we passed became too much, and so we used them, one by one, for a garlic-laden dish. Despite their size they were not elephant garlic, which is very mild and in fact related to the leek. These wonderful bulbs of Portuguese garlic are the real thing and justifiably famous on Salt Spring.

John Wilcox and Sue Earle grow this outstanding garlic. John, a sixth-generation farmer from Ontario, has been farming at Duck Creek since 1999. The farm is also known for its apples and vegetables, and both John and Sue make their mark by being passionately vocal about community agriculture. "We need to repopulate our farms and find new ways to make local farming more affordable to the next generation. The way things are going, we need to become much more reliant on local food sources," said John. He projects that within the next 10 years, escalating oil prices and climatic conditions will lead to a massive shift towards local and organic small-farm food production.

Duck Creek Farm is also one of the biggest basil producers on Salt Spring, and if you are from off island, these growers have a trick that will help you get basil home without it wilting. Toward the end of the summer, when basil is in full production, they need to

Sue Earle displays Duck Creek produce for sale.

sow winter crops in the basil field. Instead of cutting the last of the basil they harvest the entire plant, roots included. A basil plant will stay fresh for approximately two weeks in a water-filled jar or plastic bag.

When we contacted Duck Creek Farm, Sue was working on a leaflet guide to all organic farms on Salt Spring, so watch for it at the market and the visitors' centre. John was working towards setting up a local branch of the National Farmers Union to support family farms. Our islands might be small, but the people here really do try to make a difference.

Sadly, as we were finishing this book and just before the 2012 garlic was harvested, we received a note from Sue saying, "My beloved John unexpectedly passed into the cosmos."

In true island fashion, everyone is rallying around Sue, and the garlic will be harvested. We look forward to buying some and celebrating the memory of a Gulf Island farmer who was a giant mover and shaker, in a way he would approve—by both eating some of his garlic and saving some cloves to replant. Sue is courageously carrying on with the farm.

Power's Out!

Power outages are the downside of island living. These beautifully forested islands take a beating in winter storms and, inevitably, down comes a tree, taking out a power line. We are powerless until the seemingly superhuman repair crews fight their way through the dismal weather to fix things.

We chose to live here, so most of us are prepared. Some folks have generators, but the bulk of us switch into pioneer mode—using flashlights, oil lamps or candles, cooking on the woodstove and hauling out the large container of emergency water until the well's pumping again.

School is cancelled and community meetings postponed, but the rest of life carries on, including hosting guests, despite no power. We just adapt the menu. The partly roasted chicken languishing in the unheated oven is rent limb from limb and dumped in a pot on the woodstove with a bottle of wine. Voila—coq au vin!

Power-out Chowder

Here is an easy and delectable woodstove recipe for a leisurely simmer-on-the-back-of-the-stove-and-share-with-friends supper. Like all the best power-out recipes, it's not really a recipe at all, more a throw-what's-defrosting-into-the-pot type of dish. Don't worry about details. The chowder will be hot and tasty.

Serves as many as need feeding

Onion, chopped
Olive oil or butter
Garlic, chopped
Potatoes, peeled and diced
Carrots (plus any other vegetables available), peeled and chopped
Bay leaf
Salt and pepper
Curry powder
Liquid, such as stock, milk or water—whatever is on hand
Fish fillets
Favourite fresh herb, chopped (dill, parsley, cilantro, etc.)
Cornstarch to thicken
Wine or water

In a large pot on the top of the woodstove, sauté onion with a little oil.

Add garlic, potatoes, carrots and any other veggies.

Stir in bay leaf, salt, pepper and curry powder to taste.

Stir for a few minutes to coat the veggies with the spices, and then add enough liquid to cover veggies by about 1 inch (2.5 cm). Cover, and simmer veggies on the back of the stove for an hour while enjoying a candle-lit card game, knitting, reading or sharing wine with friends.

Remove those slowly defrosting fish fillets from the freezer. Dice fish and drop into the simmering chowder. Add more liquid if needed, and toss in some chopped herbs. Simmer until fish is opaque and flakes easily.

Mix cornstarch with some wine, add mixture to chowder to thicken it and check seasonings. (Add more wine and cornstarch if needed.)

Serve it with bread or crackers at a candle-lit table. Offer a bottle of hot sauce to guests who like their chowder spicy, and open another bottle of wine. You will be having so much fun you won't notice the power's back on!

Christina's Pea Sprouts and Peach Salad with Balsamic Reduction

Serve this delicious salad as a starter with slices of warm ciabatta. For a main course, top with a spoonful of home-made cream cheese (page 19) and/or sliced grilled chicken breast.

Makes 2 lunch servings or 4 appetizer servings

> ¾ cup (180 mL) plus 1 Tbsp (15 mL) balsamic vinegar
> 2 Tbsp (30 mL) honey
> 2 cups (475 mL) sliced home-canned peaches
> Half English cucumber
> 4 cups (1 L) pea shoots (2 bags)

In a small saucepan on low heat, heat balsamic vinegar and honey until reduced to half the original volume. Leave to cool for 15 minutes.

Drain and pat dry the peaches.

Peel and thinly slice the cucumber.

Place the pea shoots in a salad bowl, and arrange the peaches and the cucumber on top.

Drizzle the balsamic reduction over the salad just before serving.

Christina harvests fresh pea sprouts, grown under glass, in the winter.

A Touch of Summer in the Middle of Winter

"Welcome to Christina's Garden" read the sign, and welcomed we were one sunny afternoon. Christina Pechloff lives on Mayne Island amid a small market garden, resplendent with summer flowers (which she sells by the bunch and as wedding arrangements) and beautiful sprawling vegetable patches surrounding a small greenhouse.

The greenhouse is the hub of her operation, for here is where she grows year-round pea sprouts, and sunflower and radish shoots that are becoming known across the islands.

Unlike many small market gardeners who work spring, summer and fall and then take a break in the winter, Christina never stops. She consistently produces a variety of microgreens for year-round sales. The fresh taste of these greens is particularly welcome in the winter months.

Packed full of vitamins and folic acid, yet containing few calories, a bowl of pea shoots topped with sunflower shoots and a light salad dressing is a lovely lunch. Sometimes Christine likes to add crumbled feta or dried cranberries. "Simple ideas are best," she says.

In the summer Christina's work doubles, as she makes up homegrown vegetable baskets for weekly delivery to island residents, has a steady stream of requests for wedding flowers and opens her garden to visitors on summer Sundays. But don't worry if you are not there when the garden is open. Her sprouts are available year-round through the Farm Gate Store at Mayne Island's Fernhill Centre.

Seared Tuna

Fresh tuna is light years away from canned tuna. In fact, you won't believe you are eating the same fish. This treat, with its buttery taste and texture, is low in fat and high in omega 3 oils, and takes seconds to prepare. Serve it with your favorite dipping sauce, a bowl of white rice and steamed gai lan (Chinese broccoli).

Makes 6 servings

> 1 clove garlic, minced
> 2 Tbsp (30 mL) sesame oil
> 2 Tbsp (30 mL) soy sauce (or 2 tsp/10 mL tamari)
> 1 Tbsp (15 mL) grated fresh ginger
> 1 tsp (5 mL) lime juice
> 1 tuna loin, approximately 1½ lbs (680 gr)
> Plateful toasted sesame seeds (regular or black)
> 1 green onion, thinly sliced

Place garlic, sesame oil, soy sauce, ginger and lime juice in a large resealable plastic bag and shake to mix thoroughly. Insert the tuna loin (if too big, cut in half), remove air from the bag and seal. Squeeze bag gently to coat the tuna with the marinade. Refrigerate for at least an hour or overnight.

Heat a nonstick skillet to medium-high. When the pan is hot, remove the tuna from the marinade and sear for 1 minute on every side. Tuna will be seared only on the outside and still raw inside.

Remove tuna from pan and immediately roll in toasted sesame seeds. Slice tuna into ¼ inch (0.6 cm) thick slices and garnish with a sprinkle of green onion.

Tristan's Tuna

Excited gossip rippled through the Gulf Island community. "Did you know Mayne Island is marketing sushi-grade tuna?"

We didn't know, but since tuna sashimi is one of our favourite restaurant meal choices, we did some research and discovered Tristan.

Tristan Chavrette lives on Mayne but sails the North Pacific, troll catching (a sustainable fishing practice) wild albacore tuna. The fish is chilled and flash frozen at sea. Then the sushi-grade tuna loins are vacuum packed and sold individually, or in 30 pound (13.5 kg) boxes, from his base on Mayne Island.

Currently Tristan's Tuna is carried in an increasing number of outlets across the Gulf Islands, including the Farm Gate Store on Mayne, and Southridge Store on Pender. His tuna is also available on the Saanich Peninsula and in Greater Victoria.

Watch for the tuna van on Mayne.

Slow-Grilled Hawaiian Pork Tenderloin

Not many people have the stamina to stay up around the clock to pit barbecue a whole pig as the early settlers did. This simple version of barbecued pork tenderloin fits our lifestyle much better. The pork slow roasts on the grill and is brushed with a pineapple marinade to keep it moist and give a nod to Salt Spring's Kanaka heritage. (If you want to use only local foods, substitute peaches and peach juice or apples and apple juice for the pineapple.) Serve the pork with grilled vegetables of your choice.

Makes 6 servings

> **1 fresh pineapple, peeled, cored and sliced into spears**
> **½ cup (125 mL) pineapple juice**
> **3 cloves garlic, minced**
> **½ cup (125 mL) lemon juice**
> **½ cup (125 mL) light soy sauce**
> **½ cup (125 mL) maple syrup**
> **2 Tbsp (30 mL) grated fresh ginger**
> **2 Tbsp (30 mL) grated lemon zest**
> **1 tsp (5 mL) red pepper sauce**
> **3 lbs (1.4 kg) organic pork tenderloin**

Set aside all but 2 of the pineapple spears. In a blender, pulse the 2 pineapple spears with the pineapple juice until pulped.

Add all other ingredients, except the pork, to the blender and mix briefly.

Pour the marinade into a resealable plastic bag and add the pork. Press out the air, seal the bag and squeeze the contents so that all surfaces of the pork are covered with the marinade. Marinate in the fridge for at least 2 hours or overnight.

Oil the grill and preheat the barbecue on the low heat setting.

Drain pork, reserving the marinade.

Place marinade in a large saucepan, bring to a rolling boil and boil for 1 minute to kill any possible pathogens. Pour marinade into a bowl.

Place tenderloin on the grill. Cook slowly on all four sides, turning often to prevent burning, for about 45 minutes to 1 hour. Brush meat frequently with the warm marinade.

During the last ten minutes of the cooking time, grill the reserved pineapple spears.

Remove meat from the grill when done (internal temperature should be 170F/77C).

Slice the tenderloin and serve with the grilled pineapple spears.

Peek into History: Winter Revels

For over a century, Hawaiian settlers (then known as Kanakas) hosted lively parties on Gulf Island beaches. Enticed to BC by the Hudson's Bay Company in the early 19th century, Kanakas served on sailing ships and in the fur trade. On retirement many settled on Salt Spring and adjacent islands.

The Kanaka pioneers' contribution to BC history is celebrated today at the heritage site of Maria Mahoi's house on Russell Island, and on Salt Spring. Like most other settlers, Kanakas cleared land, planted orchards and raised cattle, pigs and chickens. Their houses often faced the sea, from which they harvested fish and clams. When the wet winters came along, families dug a fire pit in the beach, lined it with big stones, lit a blazing wood fire and invited their neighbours. When the stones were hot, the pit was filled with seaweed-wrapped salmon, pork—often a whole pig—mussels and clams. Home brew kept the cooks going, and guitar music kept partygoers on their toes day and night. After a week or so the party wound down, only to start again on another beach, perhaps on the next island. A round of luaus filled the winter with festivity until farm chores started up again in spring.

Salt Spring descendants of the Kanakas regularly honour their ancestors buried at St. Paul's Catholic Church near Fulford Harbour. Each year the Kanaka tombstones are draped with cowry necklaces.

Oh, Deer!

Large populations of black-tailed deer inhabit the Gulf islands, and feral fallow deer are also seen on Mayne and Galiano. The human inhabitants of the islands are divided as to how to control the deer population. Some people love the deer and some view them as a scourge. Like many islanders, we vacillate. We photograph deer, especially the fawns that dance inquisitively up our driveway on an early spring morning. I shout insults and clatter pans though the kitchen window when they attack the garden. But we cannot be hypocrites; we are carnivores, after all, and if offered venison will cook it with pleasure, and we jump at the chance to choose a venison dish when we spot it on the menu of Galiano's Hummingbird Pub. However, we like to know the source of the meat we eat and be assured that the animal's demise was as humane as possible.

Whichever side of the deer fence you are on, please don't feed the deer. One of the causes of the deer problem on the Gulf Islands is regular feeding by humans, which has inflated the deer population.

We use a deer scare—a hosepipe hooked up to a motion detector—to help keep deer away from our garden and encourage them to browse in the natural area. Okay, so sometimes we forget to turn it off and it occasionally sprays us, our friends and the courier delivering the proofs of our latest book. That's a small price to pay for a relatively unnibbled yard.

Deer and gardens do not mix well.

Braised Gulf Island Venison—a Bit of A'right!

Venison is a healthy meat choice, as it contains very little fat. This dish is succulent and fills the house with a great aroma, so it's worth the trouble of planning ahead to allow time to marinate the meat. I once made it in England for a "Taste of Our Gulf Islands" feast we put on as a thank you to our UK family and friends. It gained the highest accolade from one very picky blunt northerner: "Nowt wrong wi' that, it's a bit of a'right." The recipe has been known in our family as 'That Bit of A'right' ever since.

Makes 6 servings

12 juniper berries
4 cloves garlic, minced
2 cups (475 mL) dry red wine (Saturna's Pinot Noir works well)
2.2 lbs (1 kg) boned venison (leg or shoulder), cut into large cubes
2 large carrots
2 onions
1 large turnip or rutabaga
3 stalks celery
Olive oil and butter
3 cloves garlic, minced
½ cup (125 mL) flour seasoned with salt and pepper
½ cup (125 mL) redcurrant jelly
2 cups (475 mL) beef stock
1 large bay leaf
1 sprig lemon thyme
2 tsp (10 mL) chopped fresh parsley, for garnish

Day 1

Place juniper berries, garlic and wine in a large resealable plastic bag.

Add venison, squeeze the air out of the bag, seal bag and marinate meat in fridge for at least 24 hours. Turn bag 2 or 3 times while marinating.

Day 2

Peel carrots, onions and turnip, and chop them and celery into large chunks.

Heat some olive oil and butter in a heavy-based Dutch oven. Fry the vegetables for 4 to 5 minutes until golden. Add the garlic, fry for 1 more minute and then set vegetable mixture aside.

Drain meat over a bowl, reserving marinade, and pat dry. Toss the dried venison with the seasoned flour.

Continued on next page

Place some more oil and butter in a hot, heavy frying pan, and fry venison in small batches until browned on all sides. Work quickly, adding oil and butter as needed. Take care not to overcrowd the frying pan. Add the browned meat to the vegetable mixture as you go.

Preheat oven to 350F (175C).

Add the redcurrant jelly and reserved marinade to the frying pan. Bring to the boil, and scrape up all the bits that have stuck to the bottom of the pan. Pour in the stock, and add the bay leaf and thyme. Stir and simmer the resulting broth for 5 minutes. Add more salt and pepper if needed.

Pour broth into the Dutch oven containing the meat and vegetables, and stir gently to evenly mix ingredients. Place pot on the stove and heat mixture to a boil.

Cover Dutch oven and transfer to the oven. Cook for about 1½ to 2 hours, or until meat is tender.

Remove pot from the oven and check the seasoning.

Sprinkle surface with a little chopped parsley and serve immediately.

Note: If the lid to your Dutch oven does not fit tightly, too much moisture will escape in the oven, and your venison will become dry and tough. Solve this by first covering the rim of the pot with a sheet of foil big enough to amply go over the edges. Place the lid firmly on top and crimp the foil around the edge. This will keep the seal intact.

Valentine's Fun on Pender

"Celebrate early," urged the Morning Bay Vineyard sign the weekend before a mid-week Valentine's Day. "Join us for a Chocolate and Merlot tasting." So we did.

On our way to the vineyard we passed a new sign—"Island Lamb"—at a friend's farm. Obviously they were gearing up for a flock of Valentine's visitors.

The chocolate and Merlot afternoon was delightful. Being red wine drinkers by preference, neither of us were strangers to Merlot, but we had never paired it with chocolate. We were seriously impressed. We both loved the complexity of the flavours, and it triggered an elusive memory in the back of my mind … a food … one with the same dark smoky taste. The full memory didn't materialize, and we eventually departed, carrying a case of Merlot in the back of the car.

We drove home past the lamb sign again. "Stop!" I yelled. "I've got it!" Poor Dave stomped on the brake. "Lamb with coffee sauce."

He looked at me with the patient quirk of one eyebrow that means he suspects I'm mad but is willing to go along with me for the entertainment.

"That's what the bitter chocolate and Merlot reminded me of. Let's buy some lamb and open the Merlot, and I'll show you."

Excited, we drove up to the farm's back door.

The light was on in the porch. The freezer was there, the lamb sign was there, but the farmers were not.

After looking around to see if they were feeding the sheep, we gave up. But this was Pender and there is always a solution. Besides, I knew our friends would hate to lose a sale. I opened the freezer, found two chops, and we absconded with them.

As soon as we got home, I weighed the lamb, phoned the farm and left a message confessing what I'd done and advising them of the cut and weight so they could let me know the price.

We continued working towards supper. I defrosted the lamb and made the coffee sauce. Dave prepped some vegetables and opened the Merlot to let it breathe. *Saturday Afternoon at the Opera* was working its way through Götterdämmerung, and the kitchen filled with tempting aromas and the rich orchestrations of Wagner.

No one phoned back, and as I trimmed the chops I was filled with guilt about whether I'd overstepped the bounds of friendship.

We set the table for our Valentine's celebration—the best cutlery, red cloth, red flowers, white candles, balloon wine glasses. Everything was ready except for the final cooking of the chops, so I phoned the farm again.

My friend answered, obviously surprised to hear my voice.

"You've not listened to your answering machine," I said.

"So I didn't," she answered. "Did I miss something?"

"Yes, a confession from me."

"Really?"

"I've stolen some lamb."

There was a peal of laughter. "You too? So did our neighbour. That'll teach us to slip out when the sign's up."

The weight lifted from my shoulders. "Let me know how much it is and I'll drop the money in tomorrow."

"No worries, Andrea. Besides, it doesn't matter. I was meaning to give you some. I've a new butcher and I wanted you to test his cut and trim for me. Consider it a gift."

Whoa! I rang off feeling really guilty. Cheek shouldn't be rewarded like this.

Dave laughed and poured the wine. "Only on Pender. How lovely of her."

We toasted our friends, knowing full well we will buy several roasts of their lamb over the season, but I have learned my lesson; next time I'll phone ahead!

As for our impromptu Valentine's dinner? Fabulous. Try the recipe for yourself.

Lamb Chops with Coffee and Chocolate Sauce

Suspend any preconceived ideas, and forget the usual mint. This sauce is a winner. It's fast and easy, and transforms lamb into a festive dish. Serve it over chops as below, or in a sauceboat with a rack of lamb. Use nothing but salt and pepper to season the meat and let the sauce do the rest. The coffee, dark chocolate and spices give a subtle Arabic flair that adds five-star depth to the meat. We love this dish because it serves up spectacular flavour with very little effort. Oh, and serve with a Gulf Island Merlot for an unbeatable pairing. Merlot shines with both chocolate and coffee flavours, and this sauce carries dark hints of both.

Makes 4 servings

> 4 meaty Gulf Island lamb chops
> Kosher salt and freshly ground black pepper
> About 1 tsp (5 mL) olive oil
> 3 Tbsp (45 mL) butter
> 1 ounce (28 gr) dark chocolate, finely chopped
> ⅓ cup (80 mL) honey
> ⅓ cup (80 mL) strong coffee
> 2 Tbsp (30 mL) Worcestershire sauce
> ¾ tsp (4 mL) lemon juice
> ½ tsp (2.5 mL) cinnamon
> ¼ tsp (1 mL) cardamom
> ¼ tsp (1 mL) mace
> ¼ tsp (1 mL) curry powder

Season lamb chops with salt and pepper. Heat a heavy, deep skillet over medium-high heat. Add olive oil and swirl to coat the bottom of the pan. Sear lamb chops for approximately 2 minutes on each side, turning only once. (If the chops are very large, do this in 2 batches.) Remove to a warm platter and keep warm.

Reduce heat to medium-low. To the same skillet, add butter and stir until melted. Whisk in chocolate, honey, coffee, Worcestershire sauce, lemon juice, cinnamon, cardamom, mace and curry powder, scraping up any browned bits into the sauce. Bring mixture to a boil and simmer for 3 to 5 minutes, until thickened.

Return chops to the skillet along with any juices that have drained from them. Turn chops to coat them with sauce, and cook them for 2 to 4 minutes per side, depending on desired doneness (cook for 4 minutes per side for medium rare).

Serve immediately with any extra sauce spooned on top of each chop.

Layered Holiday Vegetable and Cheese Pie

David and I grew up in England hearing about pies, but not just your regular apple or rhubarb pies. The north of England was famed for its "country pies"—meat pies, game pies, cheese pies and sometimes all three of those ingredients layered together. But, sadly, food shortages around the two world wars made making these pies impossible, and in our childhoods they were legendary foodstuffs described around the table at Christmas time.

Thankfully, country pies have made a deserved comeback, for stately homes with large estates, such as the Duke of Devonshire's Chatsworth House in Derbyshire, now have farm shops that sell produce and game from the estate. The most spectacular section of the farm shop is the pie section. You will find no delicately crusted apple pies here. These pies are the traditional English savoury, rib-sticking deep dish or "raised" pies. Often multilayered with a variety of meat and game, sometimes supplemented with a vegetable layer, these pies are encased in suet pastry and laced with herbs, and one slice is an entire meal. Think pheasant, rabbit and spinach pie; wild boar and Stilton pie; chicken, pork and veal pie; venison and hard-boiled egg pie—all made in 16 inch (41 cm) springform pans, the fillings stacked three inches (7.6 cm) high. You get the idea? These are the legendary pies of my heritage, so I decided to adapt the idea using local Gulf Island ingredients.

Last Christmas I made a delicious layered country pie of spinach, salmon, red peppers and wild rice. This year I decided to make a layered vegetable pie as a holiday centrepiece for my vegetarian friends. Here it is—nowhere near as massive as the Chatsworth pies, and minus the suet, but very pretty when sliced.

I confess I used yams (not locally grown), because of their colour. To eat locally, use a yellow-fleshed potato, or save a bright orange pumpkin from Halloween and roast the flesh before using it.

Makes 6 to 8 servings

Pastry

> 2$\frac{1}{3}$ cups (555 mL) flour
> 2 Tbsp (30 mL) finely grated Parmesan cheese
> Pinch salt
> $\frac{2}{3}$ cup (160 mL) water
> $\frac{1}{3}$ cup (80 mL) olive oil

Place flour, Parmesan cheese and salt in a food processor, and pulse while adding the water and oil, until the mixture forms clumps. Gather dough together in a ball and wrap in plastic wrap. Let rest in fridge for 20 to 30 minutes.

Continued on next page

Cheese and Vegetable Filling

4 small eggplants, sliced
3 medium zucchinis, sliced
2 to 3 Tbsp (30–45 mL) olive oil
4 medium yams, peeled, parboiled and thinly sliced
6 cloves garlic, chopped
Salt and freshly ground pepper
3 cups (700 mL) wilted spinach, squeezed in a towel to remove excess water
Grind of nutmeg
4 roasted red peppers, peeled and sliced
5 sprigs fresh thyme, finely chopped
3 cups (700 mL) grated hard Gulf Island cheese (any kind)
2 Tbsp (30 mL) pesto
1 small egg, beaten
Sea salt

Place eggplant slices in a sieve, sprinkle them with a little salt and allow to drain for 30 minutes to remove bitterness and excess water.

Do the same with the zucchini slices.

Pat drained zucchini and eggplant slices dry with a towel.

Heat olive oil in a large frying pan over medium-high heat. When oil is hot, cook eggplant slices in batches, adding more oil if pan becomes dry. Fry until eggplant is tender and golden on both sides. Drain slices on paper towel, blotting to remove excess oil. Let cool.

Have all the vegetables and remaining ingredients ready, and divide each into 2 equal piles.

Assembly

On a floured surface, cut off one-third of pastry, wrap in plastic wrap and refrigerate until needed. Roll out remaining pastry to a thickness of about ¼ inch (0.6 cm). Press pastry into an 8 inch (20 cm) springform pan, allowing the excess to hang over the sides of the pan. You can be quite firm with this pastry. If it breaks, overlap the broken edges and glue them together with a little water.

Fill pastry shell with layers of half of each of the vegetables as follows: yam, garlic, zucchini, salt and pepper, spinach, a grind of nutmeg, eggplant, red pepper and thyme.

Cover the final layer with half the grated cheese. Spread or dab with half the pesto.

Repeat layers with the remaining vegetables and seasonings, finishing with the remaining cheese, pesto and herbs. Brush the overhang of pastry with the beaten egg.

Preheat oven to 375F (190C).

Roll out the reserved pastry to ¼ inch (0.6 cm) thick a little bigger than the pan and place on top of the filled pie. Pinch and seal the two pastry surfaces together at the edge.

Using scissors, cut away excess pastry, leaving ½ inch (1.3 cm) extra around the rim of the pan. Roll the excess inward to complete the seal. Crimp it decoratively.

Brush the crust with beaten egg. Poke a few holes in the top of the pie to allow steam to escape as it bakes. Use the excess pastry to make decorative leaves. Arrange them on the top of the pie and brush them with beaten egg. Grind sea salt over the surface.

Place pie in oven and bake until pastry is golden brown and vegetables are tender, about 50 minutes. Cool in the springform for 3 minutes, and then remove side of pan and gently slide pie onto a warm platter. (You can leave it on the base if you are nervous about removing it!)

Serve pie on the platter, surrounded by a festive wreath of sprigs of bay and thyme. Cut into hearty wedges.

The Masselinks of Hope Bay Farm

For eight years Derek and Michelle Masselink have worked tirelessly on their small organic farm edging Hope Bay on Pender Island, determined to make the farm self-supporting. They sought to offer their growing list of customers more than the usual Brussels sprouts, chard and kale in the winter, and to somehow find techniques that would make these dreams practical. They've achieved all their objectives by thinking creatively.

"We've become a distributed farm," explained Derek. "We needed more agricultural space than was available at Hope Bay, so have made arrangements to utilize unused farmland in other locations on Pender. We currently also farm on a friend's land, pasture our lambs at the farm next door and have an arrangement to use the greenhouse owned by Pender's Home Hardware Store. "This creative thinking has allowed Hope Bay Farm to balance its bottom line, expand its crops and extend its season.

The large greenhouse expansion with new raised beds is exciting. Raised beds are practical, because they're easier on workers' bodies and stay almost weed free. The greenhouse provides a longer season for tender cash crops such as basil, and provides Penderites with a source of tasty tomatoes (with delightful names like "Indigo Rose") in November. "We're also providing microgreens year-round for Poets Cove [Resort & Spa]," said Derek.

Other aspects of the farm are also proving successful. "We have no trouble finding buyers for Michelle's sheep, both the breeding stock [and] those raised for meat. Her flock is Icelandic, so the fleeces are also in demand."

"Interestingly, we got into farming through the sheep," Derek continued. "We owned a border collie, Beth, and decided to train her as a sheepdog after watching sheepdog trials in the English Lake District. She was good, so obviously needed sheep to work with. Michelle is currently working with two dogs; the top one is Beth's granddaughter."

Continued on next page

Derek greets a customer at Pender Farmers' Market.

Derek's eyes sparkle as he talks about their future plans—a renewed box program in which islanders have a stake in the farm by paying up front for several months of weekly boxes of fresh vegetables; experimenting with new crops; and encouraging both their daughters to be part of their all-encompassing family farm lifestyle.

"The girls have been in the garden with us since they were babies. Now they each have their own garden and, at eight and twelve, are also big enough to do occasional piecework on the farm. Then we pay them for what they do. Currently both are really interested in farming."

Last winter Derek fought cancer, so it was wonderful to see him back on track and hear his enthusiastic plans. "There's nothing like cancer to make you appreciate what you've got, and reassess what you want to achieve," he said.

Hope Bay Farm is burgeoning with hope.

Salt Spring's Spice Girl: Andrea LeBorgne

The spices of life are front and centre for Andrea LeBorgne. An ardent foodie, she purchased the Salt Spring spice company Monsoon Coast about four years ago. Each year she's extended her range of products and now carries not only the company's original Indian spices, but mixes for African and Middle Eastern dishes, Chinese five spice mix and a barbecue rub.

Miniature wooden crates contain jars of selected spices needed for preparations such as butter chicken, tajine or chai tea. They are practical and attractive and take the stress out of trying to hunt for an unusual spice on island.

Andrea buys her spices in bulk and then roasts, grinds and blends them on Salt Spring. You can find her at the Ganges Saturday market, where you can purchase individual jars, as well as the multi-jar kits. Her Monsoon Coast Exotic World Spices are available in several island stores, at Granville Island Market in Vancouver and deli outlets on Vancouver Island, and by mail order from the Monsoon Coast Trading Company website.

Monsoon Coast's Butter Chicken

For much-needed warmth in the middle of winter, there is nothing like spicy heat in your food. We have several island friends who are also lovers of exotic flavours, and last year, after a Christmas party when we received not one but two delightful crates of Monsoon Coast spices as gifts, we resolved to meet as a group once a month and create a themed meal, each couple being responsible for a dish. The group managed to meet for a record of four consecutive months before schedules got in the way, and we explored Italian, Greek, Mexican and Indian foods. All were incredibly tasty, but it was the Indian food that won the most requests for recipes.

Here's Andrea LeBorgne's butter chicken recipe, using her Monsoon Coast spices. The chicken is barbecued first, giving it a much more traditional Indian flavour than cooking it entirely on the stovetop. Fortunately, in the Gulf Islands, barbecuing is practical for most of the year, as long as the cook doesn't mind getting a bit damp in our West Coast version of monsoon season.

Makes 4 servings

Freshly ground spices and grilled chicken create authentic flavour.

   10 to 12 chicken legs and thighs, skin removed, sprinkled with salt and pepper
   1 large onion, finely chopped
   2 to 3 Tbsp (30–45 mL) butter
   4 cloves garlic, crushed
   3 to 4 tsp (15–20 mL) Monsoon Tandoori spice mix (or to taste)
   2 tsp (10 mL) paprika
   1 tsp (5 mL) grated ginger
   1 tsp (5 mL) Monsoon Coast Tobago Habanero Curry mix (optional; use more for more heat)
   1 cup (250 mL) tomato sauce
   ½ to ¾ cup (125–180 mL) water
   1 tsp (5 mL) salt
   1 cup (250 mL) whipping cream
   3 Tbsp (45 mL) finely chopped fresh coriander

Barbecue the chicken over medium-low heat, turning once, until almost done (10 to 15 minutes). Do not overcook or the chicken will be dry.

Meanwhile, in a Dutch oven fry onion in the butter until onion is golden brown, about 15 to 20 minutes. Add garlic, tandoori powder, paprika, ginger and habanero powder. Fry for a few seconds, stirring to combine.

Stir in the tomato sauce, half the water and the salt. Add the chicken and stir to coat it with the sauce. Slowly bring mixture to a boil. Reduce heat and simmer, covered, until chicken is tender, about 15 to 20 minutes.

Remove lid and reduce sauce or add more water, depending on the consistency you prefer. Just before serving, add whipping cream. Stir and simmer until heated through. Garnish dish with fresh coriander.

Ribs and Beer

Let's face it! Fine dining is not always appropriate for a celebration. This is Canada. Sometimes the hockey game takes precedence, family and friends are glued to the TV and finger food is required. Bring out the ribs and beer, and the cheers will be for you as well as the next goal.

In this recipe, beer is used for precooking the ribs. Lovers of dark beer might prefer to use Dry Porter, and lovers of light beer could use Pale Ale, both products of Salt Spring Island Ales.

So, how many ribs per person? With meaty side ribs, half a pound (225 grams) per person is usual, but with baby back ribs allow 1 to 1.5 pounds (454 to 680 grams) per person because of the very large proportion of bone. The method of cooking is the same for all ribs, but obviously the cooking times will vary depending on how much meat is on the bones.

A platter of crudités, dip and warm bread rolls are good accompaniments for these ribs. Remember to provide some large napkins!

Makes 4 servings

> About 2 lbs (900 g) side ribs or 6 lbs (2.7 kg) baby back ribs
> 4 cloves garlic, sliced
> 3 to 5 whole cloves
> 2 to 3 star anise
> 1 to 2 bay leaves
> 1 tsp (5 mL) salt
> Salt Spring Island Ales beverage of your choice
> Theresa's Rhubarb Barbecue Sauce (page 45)

Cut up the ribs. Place the ribs and spices in a large Dutch oven and cover with beer. Simmer, with the lid on, for between 40 and 90 minutes, until the meat is tender.

Drain ribs and discard the liquid.

Preheat oven to 325F (160C).

Place ribs on a tinfoil-lined (for easy cleanup) roasting pan. Smear them with the barbecue sauce. Roast ribs in the oven for 60 to 90 minutes, daubing with extra sauce every 20 minutes.

Serve ribs heaped on a warm platter.

Peek into History: Island Pubs

There's a long and celebrated tradition of delightful pubs in the Gulf Islands. All serve hearty pub food and are known for quirks specific to the island they are on.

Galiano's Hummingbird Pub is famous for its little Pub Bus that ferries thirsty boaters between Montague Marine Park and the bar. Saturna Island's Lighthouse pub is where you lift a beer on the veranda while waiting for the ferry; Pender's pub at Browning Harbour Marina is famous for its bands and the not-to-be missed Pender Talent Show. Sadly, one of the oldest pubs on Salt Spring, Fulford Inn, recently closed. The inn was famous for its Christmas Carol Sing led every year by long-time island resident Valdy.

The prize for the Gulf Island pub with the most colourful history goes to the drinking establishment on Mayne Island at Miners Bay. In 1895, what we currently know as the peaceful community of Miners Bay was referred to as Little Hell. Gold prospectors bought their supplies in Victoria and then rowed across to the mainland through Active Pass, hoping to join either the Fraser Valley or Cariboo gold rush. Miners Bay was the halfway point so became the stopping-off place for the now tired and thirsty miners.

In 1892, a large private home was situated at the head of the Miners Bay wharf. It didn't take long for the owners to see their opportunity and, in 1895, they opened first as a lodging house and then as a drinking establishment to meet the miners' needs. Currently operating as the Springwater Lodge, the picturesque building is the oldest continuously operated hotel in British Columbia.

Springwater Lodge, Miners Bay.

Andrea's Roasted Winter Veggies

We love roasted veggies—the mix of tastes, the eye appeal of the colours, the aroma as they cook and the edges begin to slightly caramelize, and the ease of them cooking in the top of the oven above the meat dish already there. There's even a bonus: leftovers make a delicious cold lunch, topped with yogurt the next day. Don't forget to squeeze the soft garlic paste from the husks and smear a little over each bite.

Choose vegetables from the garden (or the store) in whatever amounts you desire to fill your biggest baking tray.

1 to 2 heads garlic, separated but not peeled
Acorn (or any other) squash, halved, de-seeded, and cut into ½ inch (1.3 cm) slices
Small white onions, peeled
Beets, parboiled, skins removed and cut into quarters or eighths to match the size of the onions
Carrots, parsnips and turnips, peeled and cut into pieces to match the size of the onions
Peppers, halved, de-seeded and quartered
1 Tbsp (15 mL) each of pesto, olive oil and balsamic vinegar, mixed
Several springs fresh rosemary, chopped
Salt and pepper

Preheat oven to 400F (205C) and grease a baking tray.

Place all the vegetable pieces in a large plastic bag.

Add the pesto mixture to the bag. Shake the bag and rub its contents between your hands so the pesto mixture covers all surfaces of the vegetables.

Turn the vegetables out onto the baking tray. Sprinkle with the chopped rosemary and season with salt and pepper.

Roast the vegetables in the oven for about 45 minutes, turning once halfway through. Cook until the vegetables are soft and their edges are caramelized.

The Pizza Garden Project

Teacher Julie Johnson was hoping to interest the Pender group of home-school learners, known as "Spring Leaves," in creating a garden. "What's your all-time favourite vegetable?" she asked.

Their answer was unanimous. "Pizza!"

Unfazed, Julie decided to turn this into a learning situation, and she and the children embarked on the "Pizza Garden Project."

The Spring Leaves dug a circular plot and planted wheat, tomatoes, squash and some herbs. They amended the soil with natural mulch, watched the crops grow, and charted progress. To their delight, by fall they were able to harvest organic Canadian Red Fife wheat by cutting the heads off with scissors borrowed from the kindergarten.

The children then followed the story of the Little Red Hen to do all the necessary jobs, threshing and winnowing by hand and complaining about the hard work in best living history style.

The wheat was left to dry; the tomatoes, pulped and frozen; and the squash harvested.

By mid-winter, the wheat was dry enough to grind by hand, and the children made the flour into dough, topped it with their homemade pizza sauce and roasted squash pulp. They invited their families to taste the Pizza Garden Pizza, and watched the slide show the children had made to record their efforts.

This innovative project was so successful it has resulted in a large school garden being planted beside the Pender Elementary School, and the Pizza Garden Project is now open to all the island's children. The resulting enthusiasm means the garden has already been extended. It now includes a stir-fry bed and a salad bed, and the group successfully raised money for a greenhouse. There is even talk of building a cob oven.

"It's amazing," said Julie, laughing. "Children will eat all kinds of veggies they've grown themselves, stuff they'd never choose from the grocery store."

"So what's your next project?" I asked.

She grinned wickedly. "Salt. We're distilling it from sea water."

I stared in surprise. "Why salt?"

"We're growing potatoes—for homemade potato chips!"

Above and bottom right: Pender kids tend and harvest their pizza garden.

Festive Brussels Sprouts with Kohlrabi and Whisky Glaze

Though Dave rolls his eyes and makes a routine protest when I broach one of his special single malts, a celebratory splash of Scotch whisky gives these sprouts a lovely smoky, mellow flavour, and the kohlrabi provides a contrasting crunch. If you don't grow sprouts, try to buy them still on the stalk and leave them outside propped up by the back door. They're an organic treat that stays fresh much longer outside than in the fridge.

Makes 8 to 10 servings

2 lbs (0.9 kg) Brussels sprouts
¼ cup (60 mL) butter
2 Tbsp (30 mL) Scotch whisky
Pinch sugar
1 large or 2 small kohlrabi, peeled and cut into ½ inch (1.3 cm) chunks
Pinch each salt and pepper
1 green onion, chopped, for garnish

Trim sprouts and cut an X in the base of each one. Halve large sprouts. Bring a large saucepan of salted water to a boil, and cook sprouts until tender-crisp, about 7 minutes. Drain.

In the same pan, melt butter over medium-high heat. Stir in whisky and sugar; cook on high while stirring for 30 seconds. Lower heat, return sprouts to pan and add kohlrabi and seasonings. Gently stir until everything is coated with the butter mixture and the kohlrabi is heated through.

Serve, garnished with the green onion, in a warmed dish.

Leave Your Root Vegetables in the Garden

After an abundant fall harvest, space in the pantry and the freezer is at a premium, and most of us do not have an old-fashioned root cellar. Therefore, it's a relief to learn you don't have to harvest everything at once. In our climate, some vegetables can be left in the ground till well after the first winter frost. Brussels sprout stalks are not harmed by cold weather, and carrots, parsnips and beets actually improve if left in the ground for a while. A snap of frost concentrates the sugars in the roots so they become sweeter. However, once the sugar content peaks, harvest these vegetables or they become woody.

The Not-So-Humble Mashed Potato

Opposite: Work up an appetite on the forested trail running through Bodega Ridge Provincial Park on Galiano.

There is no denying it: in winter, Canada's staple comfort food is the potato, and eating locally means we consume them regularly. The trick is to make the humble potato interesting. Mashed potato is a familiar dish that both adults and kids love, so let's give it a twist. Here are some suggestions to spice up this perennial favourite.

Prepare all versions using six large boiled potatoes.

Makes 6 servings

Apple and Cheese Mash

Mash boiled potatoes with:

> 1 cup (250 mL) homemade unsweetened apple sauce
> 1 cup (250 mL) grated local hard strong cheese
> 1 tsp (5 mL) curry powder
> A knob of butter
> Salt and pepper

Garlic, Parsley and Carrot Mash

Mash boiled potatoes with:

> 2 cups (475 mL) sliced soft-boiled carrots
> ½ cup (125 mL) thick yogurt
> 3 large cloves garlic, finely chopped
> ½ cup (125 mL) finely chopped parsley
> 2 Tbsp (30 mL) local walnut or hazelnut oil
> Salt and pepper

Smoked Salmon and Green Onion Mash

Mash boiled potatoes with:

> 6.35 oz (180 gr) can Salt Spring Fishery's smoked salmon, flaked (reserve liquid)
> 1 bunch green onions, finely sliced
> ½ cup (125 mL) *crème fraîche* (recipe page 62)
> 1–2 Tbsp (15–30 mL) reserved salmon liquid, or make up amount with melted butter
> Pepper

Why Toast Nuts and Seeds?

Toasting not only heightens the flavour of nuts and seeds by caramelizing some of the surface oils, but it keeps them crisp. When nuts and seeds are used raw in a recipe, they are insulated by the other ingredients, so this taste- and texture-improving step doesn't happen. So take the extra time and toast nuts and seeds before using them.

We find the easiest way is to toast nuts or seeds on the stovetop where you can see what's happening and avoid burning them. Use a small dry skillet over medium-low heat. Stir and shake constantly, until the nuts or seeds are fragrant and very lightly browned, about 3 to 5 minutes.

Turnip Soufflé

The turnip, so often underappreciated, earns new respect in this easy and delectable side dish. It's not really a soufflé, but rather a lovely light way to serve this nutritious, and cheap, root vegetable.

Makes 6 to 8 servings

2 lb (0.9 kg) turnips, or enough to make 6 cups diced turnip
1 tsp (5 mL) sugar
1/8 tsp (0.5 mL) nutmeg
Pinch pepper
2 eggs, slightly beaten
1/2 cup (125 mL) cream
1/4 cup (60 mL) soft bread crumbs
2 Tbsp (30 mL) toasted chopped nuts or sesame seeds
1 Tbsp (15 mL) chopped fresh parsley
1 Tbsp (15 mL) melted butter

Peel and dice turnip, place it in a large saucepan and cook in boiling water until tender, about 15 minutes. Drain turnip, return it to the pan and mash.

Preheat oven to 375F (190C).

In a small bowl, whisk together the sugar, nutmeg, pepper, eggs and cream.

Using the whisk, blend the egg mixture thoroughly with the turnip and turn mixture into a buttered casserole dish.

In a small bowl, toss together bread crumbs, nuts, parsley and melted butter. Sprinkle over turnip mixture.

Bake casserole for 50 to 60 minutes. Serve hot.

Our Daily Bread

A first stop for many people arriving on the Gulf Islands is the local bakery. Visitors and islanders alike join morning queues to pick up delights such as fragrant warm cinnamon buns, sourdough loaves and double chocolate brownies. Since most of the island bakeries include a café or deli in addition to the bakery counter, these places are highly conducive to lingering, enjoying a treat and catching up on local gossip.

Keeping an ear to the ground, however, will reveal other sources of our daily bread. Several islands are home to superb bread makers who don't operate from a storefront operation, but whose bread is available at the summer markets. These bakers enjoy incorporating seasonal local delicacies into their doughs, and there is always a rush when the first loaves containing the new basil, sun-dried tomatoes or chopped fresh figs appear at farmers' markets.

Several dedicated bakers work from their homes year-round, and with a little fast talking, new residents can join "the list" of regular customers who get private orders.

Bread making is a favourite winter comfort-food activity in many island homes, especially where wood-burning stoves ensure a warm place for the dough to rise. At our house, Dave is the regular bread maker. He takes time out from the computer to make a delicious variety of fragrant loaves using our bread machine. Handmade bread is my occasional winter indulgence for special occasions, such as crafting the three-tier Ukrainian kulich for our friends' Ukrainian Christmas celebration, our family's favourite hot cross buns or a fruit-stuffed plaited sweet bread for breakfast with guests. As the dough in the large towel-covered bowl rises on the hearth and the fragrance permeates the house, I feel the presence of my great-grandmother. She made bread out of necessity for her 15 children, and I gain great pleasure in carrying on her tradition in a small way.

We have such admiration for the island artisan bakers for whom bread making is a full-time passion; there are several on each of the islands, so seek them out.

Dana's Caramelized Onion, Potato and Rosemary Focaccia

"This dough is adapted from *The Italian Baker* by Carol Field," Dana explained. "My version makes a fairly thick focaccia, but if you like a thinner base, you can reduce the ingredients by about a third. I prefer to measure ingredients by weight as it's more accurate. Any number of toppings are possible. I have included the one I make most often for the Saturday market on Galiano. With the thick crust, a piece is just about right for lunch! If you're making focaccia as an appetizer or a side, you might want to make the thinner version."

This focaccia can be rewarmed but not refrigerated.

Makes a 10½ by 15½ inch (27 by 40 cm) sheet of focaccia

Topping

- 3 to 4 medium onions
- 1 Tbsp (15 mL) each butter and olive oil
- 4 to 6 medium potatoes, preferably French fingerlings
- Olive oil
- ½ cup (125 mL) grated Parmesan cheese
- 2 Tbsp (30 mL) chopped fresh rosemary (or more if you like)
- Coarse kosher salt (optional)

Peel the onions and slice cross-wise into ¼ inch (0.6 cm) slices.

Slowly sauté onions in the butter and olive oil until they begin to caramelize. Stir them often. Remove onions from pan before they become dark or crispy. (The cooking process will be completed in the oven, so if you cook the onions too dark, they will taste burnt and bitter by the time the focaccia is baked.) Reserve cooked onions.

Boil the potatoes until tender but still solid. Cool potatoes, and then slice them into ¼ inch (0.6 cm) slices. Reserve.

Gather together the rest of the topping ingredients and reserve.

Bread Dough

- 1¾ tsp (8.5 mL) active dry yeast; or 1 small cake fresh yeast
    (by weight: 0.6 ounces / 18 gr)
- 1¾ cups (430 mL) warm water
- 3 Tbsp (45 mL) olive oil, plus extra for topping
- About 5 cups (1.2 L) unbleached all-purpose flour (by weight: 24 ounces / 675 gr)
- 1½ Tbsp / 22.5 mL salt (by weight: ⅓ ounce / 10 gr)

Preheat the oven to 400F (205C). Lightly oil, or line with parchment paper, a 10½ by 15½ inch (27 by 40 cm) rimmed baking sheet.

Stir yeast into the water and let stand until creamy, about 10 minutes). Stir in the oil.

Using a stand mixer fitted with a dough hook, stir together the flour and salt. On low speed, mix in the yeast liquid until the dough comes together. On medium speed, continue mixing for another 3 minutes, or until the dough is velvety and elastic.

Place the dough in a lightly oiled bowl, cover with plastic wrap and let dough rise until doubled, about 1½ hours.

Roll the dough out to fit the baking sheet, patting and shaping the dough to reach the corners. Maintain as consistent a thickness as possible. Cover the pan with a damp towel and let dough rise for 30 minutes.

Dimple the dough with your fingertips to a depth of ½ inch (1.3 cm). Let dough rise again until doubled.

Brush the dough with some extra olive oil and apply the topping as follows:

Place the potato slices in even rows on the risen dough. Brush lightly with olive oil.

Sprinkle the partly caramelized onions evenly on top.

Sprinkle with cheese, rosemary and the coarse salt.

Bake focaccia for 20 to 25 minutes, or until the crust begins to brown.

Carefully slip the finished focaccia onto a cooling rack (cooling the focaccia in the pan will cause moisture to condense and make the bread soggy). Remove the parchment paper (if used). When the focaccia has cooled slightly, cut it into squares with scissors. Serve warm.

Slow Rising: Dana Weber's Raven Ridge Farm Bread

There is nothing slow about Dana Weber, other than his techniques for tasty loaves. Bread is his calling, and his drive to create the perfect loaf is palpable. "It's the long slow cold rising that makes the difference," he says, handing us the fragrant, crusty, chewy proof of his method. He was right. His bread has a big taste.

Once a baker, always a baker. Dana Weber, now of Raven Ridge Farm and Catering on Galiano island, had a previous life in the big city. He was the master baker behind the very successful Uprising Breads Bakery in Vancouver, one of the first commercial bakeries in the 1990s to bake only organic products containing no preservatives. This passion has continued. Now living full-time on Galiano, Dana and his partner, Eileen Beaudine, can be found every summer Saturday morning at Galiano's Saturday market, where they sell not only Dana's artisan loaves, but also a variety of wonderful organic vegetables grown on their land.

Dana bakes throughout the year for a list of loyal customers and arranges to meet them at various spots around the island to deliver their bread. We caught up with him one miserable rainy day in the parking lot of Daystar Market. Customers drove in with a flurry of mud spatters and huddled around the trunk of his car under dripping umbrellas while the bread orders changed hands, then drove back into the storm with cheery waves. In summer it's easier; islanders and visitors alike line up at the Raven Ridge market booth. Join in and you will be able to snag not only one of his loaves, such as a fig, anise and rosemary sourdough, but a lunchtime slice of Dana's fragrant focaccia, made with rosemary, caramelized onion and potato.

Salt Spring's Bread Lady: Heather Campbell

Known affectionately as "The Bread Lady" throughout Salt Spring, Heather Campbell sells her bread not only at the Saturday farmers' market at Ganges, but on some days from her traditional wood-burning bakery on Forest Road. You can also pick up loaves for a picnic at Salt Spring Vineyards or David Wood's Salt Spring Island Cheese Company shop.

Getting to her bakery is a trek, but worth the effort. Wend your way on Beaver Point Road towards Ruckle Park at the south end of Salt Spring Island and then turn right on Forest Road. It winds gradually uphill, becoming narrow and unpaved. Eventually you reach Heather's even narrower drive, so go slowly and be prepared to pull over if you meet another car coming down. (A steady stream of people may be picking up their bread.)

Heather is a prodigious baker. We visited on a Wednesday, when the bake was relatively light. Everything from several different kinds of loaves to focaccia, and both sweet and savoury buns, was available. On Fridays, to prepare for the Saturday market, Heather bakes a whopping 700 loaves!

She came to Salt Spring Island in 1990 for one year while her husband, Phillip studied at the University of Victoria. They never left. Now she is a dyed-in-the-wool islander who's created her own niche in Salt Spring's fabric through her love of artisan bread, and the fabulous wood-fired oven in which she bakes it.

In summer her bread-making routine starts the night before she starts baking. She fires up the oven at 10:00 p.m. and then lets it slowly burn through the night. Early in the morning, she rakes out the coals and ash and mops the oven floor. She prepares the dough for her organic hearth breads while the oven temperature cools from approximately 1,000F to 600F (538C to 325C). When the oven is ready, she bakes the focaccia and then moves on to the heavier breads, finishing with the fruitier ones. On an average day she bakes approximately 18 different varieties.

As many as possible of her organic ingredients are purchased locally from growers like Michael Ableman of Foxglove Farm. "I like to use seasonal ingredients such as peppers and tomatoes," said Heather. "They are wonderful roasted and incorporated in the dough."

Heather's bakery in the woods—Salt Spring Island Bread Company—is an unbelievably sophisticated operation. It's a careful marriage of old and new technologies, with tremendous respect for the tradition of artisan bread. The result is a high yield of loaves that taste as good as anything Grandma made.

Heather Campbell at work in her Salt Spring bakery. *Jan Mangan photos*

Pat's Five-Grain Soda Bread: The No-Time-for-Bread-Making Bread

Let's face it: in today's world not everyone has time for bread making, so here's a recipe especially for you. Our dear friend Pat Crossley gave us this tasty cottage bread recipe years ago. It's quick to make because it needs no rising time, yet it tastes delicious. Throw the dry ingredients into a bowl, mix in the wet, knead briefly and pop it in the oven. Bread making cannot get any easier than that—it's faster than driving down island to the store!

If you don't have a variety of flour on hand, just use all-purpose flour. No rolled oats? Use quick-cooking oats (not the instant kind). No buttermilk? Use ordinary milk and 1 tsp (5 mL) lemon juice, and you will get the same chemical reaction for raising the bread. All in all, this is a "never fail" recipe so very useful on these islands, where there is no handy corner store and unexpected visitors sometimes materialize off the ferry.

Makes 1 loaf

> 1 cup (250 mL) all-purpose flour
> ¾ cup (180 mL) each*:
>   whole-wheat flour
>   rye flour
>   graham flour
>   rolled oats
> 2 Tbsp (30 mL) sugar
> 1 Tbsp (15 mL) baking powder
> 1 tsp (5 mL) baking soda
> ½ tsp (2.5 mL) salt
> 1¾ cups (430 mL) plus 1 tsp (5 mL) buttermilk
> 3 Tbsp (45 mL) vegetable or olive oil

Preheat oven to 350F (175C). Grease a cookie sheet.

In a bowl, combine all dry ingredients.

Add the 1¾ cups (430 mL) buttermilk and oil and stir until dough becomes soft and sticky.

Knead dough on floured board until smooth (approximately 10 times).

Place dough on cookie sheet, form dough into a circle and pat down to a thickness of 2½ inches (6 cm).

Cut a cross on top of the dough and brush surface with remaining buttermilk.

Bake bread for 1 hour, or until it sounds hollow when tapped, or a toothpick inserted into the bread comes out clean.

*Alternatively, use 1 cup (250 mL) oats plus 3 cups (700 mL) of whatever flour you have on hand.

Power-Out Bread Baking

The bread's in the oven and the power has just gone out. No problem. It's probably winter, and the woodstove is going!

Place a wire rack on the top of the woodstove and your bread pan on the rack. Upend a large Dutch oven over the bread pan, and keep the fire stoked. The bread will cook in its makeshift oven. It might take a little longer than usual and not have quite as pretty a rounded top, but the bread will bake and be edible. Besides, you'll be eating by candlelight, so who's going to see its flaws? I guarantee you'll impress whomever you are dining with by your delicious ingenuity.

Raven Dark Coffee and Hazelnut Cake

All celebrations are improved by cake. A little extra bliss is imparted when pairing hazelnut from the island with Galiano Coffee Roasting Company's aromatic Raven Dark roast. Both add intense flavour to this light but moist cake, particularly when the hazelnuts are freshly harvested and at their peak.

This recipe requires a lot of beating, so use a stand-style electric mixer if possible. Toasting the fresh hazelnuts also adds to the flavour.

The cake will keep well in an airtight container on a cool dark shelf.

Makes 8 to 10 servings

Cake

    1 cup (250 mL) unsalted butter
    1 cup (250 mL) packed brown sugar
    4 eggs
    ¼ cup (60 mL) freshly brewed triple-strength Raven Dark coffee, cooled
    1 cup (250 mL) all-purpose flour
    1½ tsp (7.5 mL) baking powder
    ¼ tsp (1 mL) salt
    ⅓ cup (80 mL) chopped toasted local hazelnuts

Preheat the oven to 350F (175C). Line with parchment paper and grease two 8 inch (20 cm) cake tins.

In the bowl of an electric mixer, beat the butter and sugar together until pale and fluffy.

Beat in the eggs, one at a time; don't add the next until the one before is fully incorporated.

While mixer is still running, slowly pour in the coffee and beat well.

Reduce mixer speed. In a bowl, mix dry ingredients together. Fold into the batter, followed by the nuts (the batter will be runny).

Divide batter between the prepared cake pans. Level batter and make a slight dip in the middle to promote even rising.

Bake on the middle rack of the oven for 25 to 30 minutes, or until the cakes are golden and a pick inserted into the centre comes out clean.

Remove cakes from the oven. Cool on a wire rack for 10 minutes before removing from the pan and stripping away the parchment paper. Cool completely, right side up.

Buttercream and Toppings

½ cup (125 mL) unsalted butter
1 cup (250 mL) icing sugar
¼ cup (60 mL) freshly brewed triple-strength Raven Dark coffee
12 toasted hazelnuts
12 chocolate-coated coffee beans
Finely grated dark chocolate

In a bowl, beat butter and icing sugar together until pale and light.

Add the coffee and beat butter cream until ingredients are well combined.

When cakes are completely cool, trim tops to make the surface flat.

Place one cake, cut side down, on a pretty serving platter. Cover the top with half the butter cream.

Place the second cake on top, also cut side down. Cover with the remaining butter cream. Use the tines of a fork to make a decorative pattern in the butter cream, and place the hazelnuts and chocolate-coated coffee beans around the edge of the cake.

Sprinkle top with a little grated dark chocolate.

Pender children help plant hazel trees to increase food resources for the island.

"I Had a Little Nut Tree"—Pender's Nut Tree Project

Pender Island has several little nut trees and, unlike the trees in the traditional song, we hope they will bear a multitude of nuts. On February 28, 2012, eleven small hazel trees arrived on the island. An excited reception committee of children and adults, armed with wheelbarrows and shovels, greeted them, for planting these trees was a joint endeavour of the school and the community.

As a Pender Community Transition project, these young trees are hope for our future. It will take eight years of care for them to mature into the first of our community nut groves. But when they eventually fruit, it will be the core of a growing effort to help Pender towards a sustainable food plan for its residents in times of disaster. Nuts are an alternative and sustainable source of protein. This far-sighted initiative is part of a local effort to not only help residents in difficult times, but to bring food sources back under local control. These non-genetically modified trees will be tended using organic methods, and the school children will closely monitor their growth. Thus this project is educational, practical and full of dreams.

Winter Pear and Apricot Tart with Red Wine Chocolate Sauce

Winter pears are late-ripening pears that keep well through the winter and are superb to cook, staying firm and tasty. Two familiar varieties are Bosc and Bartlett, but others are found in our heritage orchards, so don't be scared to try them. Ask the farmers if you are not sure how to store or use them. For the chocolate sauce we like to use local chocolate, such as the Chocolate Cottage's Crow Bar.

Serve this sauce-drizzled tart either hot (allow to cool first for 10 minutes) or at room temperature.

Makes 8 servings

Tart

- 1 cup (250 mL) halved dried apricots
- ½ cup (125 mL) organic apple cider, home-pressed if possible
- 3 winter pears, peeled, cored and thinly sliced
- ¾ cup (180 mL) brown sugar
- 2 Tbsp (30 mL) all-purpose flour
- ¼ cup (60 mL) butter
- 1 unbaked pastry shell
- ⅓ cup (80 mL) buttermilk

Combine apricots and cider in a small saucepan. Bring to a boil, reduce heat, cover and simmer for 5 minutes. Set aside to cool.

Drain cooled apricots. Save cider for another use.

Preheat over to 375F (190C).

To prepare crumble topping, in a small bowl mix together brown sugar and flour with a fork. Rub in butter with fingertips until small crumbs form. Set crumble aside.

Arrange apricots and sliced pears evenly over the bottom of the prepared pie shell.

Drizzle with the buttermilk. Sprinkle the reserved crumble evenly over the top.

Bake for 45 minutes or until pears are tender and pastry is golden brown.

Sauce

- ½ cup (125 mL) Gulf Island red wine
- 1 cup (250 mL) chopped dark chocolate, such as Crow Bar
- ¼ cup (60 mL) light corn syrup

Prepare chocolate sauce while the pie is baking. Simmer the wine in a small pan over low to medium heat. Allow it to cook for about 8 minutes to reduce a little.

Turn the heat down, and add the chocolate and corn syrup to the wine. Whisk vigorously as the chocolate begins to melt, and then remove pan from heat and continue whisking until the sauce is well blended. Serve drizzled over slices of the tart.

The Chocolate Cottage

"Chocolate's healthy; it's a bean!" So announced our middle daughter as she offered me a square. Of course, she's correct—partly. Made from the bean of the tropical cacao plant, raw cocoa should be a health food. It contains antioxidants, vitamins and minerals, serotonin and a mild stimulant. Unfortunately, it's not very palatable unless sugar is added!

Many people have a love affair with chocolate, and Gulf Islanders are no exception. Obviously the cacao tree is not grown here, but chocolate is alive and well.

A craving for chocolate can be satisfied at almost all Gulf Island farmers' markets or at the multitude of winter or Christmas fairs. Homemade chocolate is a delightful craft to indulge in, and since moulds are now readily available in stores, several islanders are making seductive treats. However, a chocolatier on Salt Spring Island combines local ingredients with Belgian chocolate—and a touch of class.

Finding Colleen Bowen's delightfully named Chocolate Cottage, involves a trek up a little-travelled mountain road from Fulford Harbour. The fairytale exterior hides a small commercial kitchen that's the heart and soul of her Salish Sea Chocolate Company.

Colleen is a master chocolatier, having studied at Ecole Chocolat in Vancouver, and she produces a variety of hand-crafted chocolate bars made from high-quality Belgian chocolate. Sold as Crow Bars and Bear Bars, they stand out from the crowd not only for their silky taste, but also because of the visual impact of the stunning black and red labels designed by Haida artist Jim Hunt.

Both milk and dark bars are hand moulded and can be purchased plain or containing local hazelnuts, dried blueberries or dried cherries.

Colleen is branching out. She created a bar for Salt Spring's Sacred Mountain Lavender, with an imprint of lavender on top, and the day we visited she was rushing to finish an order for the Vancouver Aquarium, complete with a whale imprint, for one of their fundraising events.

Watch for Bear Bars and Crow Bars in island stores and fine food outlets on Vancouver Island. Other outlets include Salt Spring Vineyards, which serves pieces of the extra dark Bear Bar with its Merlot.

Colleen Bowen of the Chocolate Cottage mixes up another wonderful batch.

Wild Rosehip Jelly

The vitamin C content in rosehips is highest in when they have been touched by frost, so gather your rosehips in the winter, but don't leave it too late or the birds will beat you to them.

Before making the jelly, you will need to extract the juice from the rosehips. Use the juice in small batches. (Do not try to double the recipe.)

Makes four 8 ounce (250 mL) jars

Rosehip Juice
2 quarts (1.9 L) freshly picked rosehips
1½ quarts (1.4 L) water

Rinse the rosehips and use scissors to top and tail them.

Place the rosehips in a large pot. Add the water and bring to a boil, Reduce heat to a simmer, cover pot and leave to simmer gently for 1 hour or until rosehips are soft.

Mash or process the mixture into a rough purée.

Set up a jelly bag (or muslin-lined strainer) over a pot deep enough that the bottom of the bag won't touch the juice. Pour in the mixture and leave to strain for 24 hours. Do not squeeze the bag to hasten the process, as this will make your jelly cloudy.

Rosehip Jelly
3½ cups (0.8 L) sugar
1¾ cups (430 mL) rosehip juice
¼ cup (60 mL) lemon juice
1 pouch (85 mL) liquid pectin

Sterilize four 8 ounce (250 mL) jelly jars and and their lids, and prepare your canner following the manufacturer's instructions.

Combine sugar, rosehip juice and lemon juice in a large wide pot.

Bring mixture to a rolling boil that cannot be stirred down. Boil hard for 1 minute.

Follow pectin manufacturer's instructions for adding pectin.

When the jelly is ready, remove pan from heat, stir and skim the jelly for several minutes, and then pour into the prepared jars, leaving ¼ inch (0.6 cm) headspace.

Wipe the rims with a clean cloth, place sterilized lids on the jars and secure tops with the rings. Leave jars to cool. As they cool, you will hear pops as the lids seal.

Wipe and label the jars. Store any that haven't sealed in the fridge and eat first. Sealed jars can be stored on a dark shelf for a year.

Hastings House: Pastoral Elegance and Luxurious Food

Up a shady Salt Spring lane, marked by an unpretentious sign, is a waterside manor house. Built in 1939 to resemble Warren and Barbara Hastings' former residence, an 11th-century Sussex manor house, and surrounded by extensive grounds complete with a beautiful private view across Ganges Harbour, it was the much-loved home of the Hastings family for over 40 years. In 1981, after extensive renovations, the manor became the heart of the most prestigious hotel on the Southern Gulf Islands, and one of Canada's top hotels—Hastings House Country House Hotel.

This place is on our bucket list for that once-in-a-lifetime special celebration. Luxury is the key word here, from the bed linens, fresh flowers and tiptoe-quiet pastoral ambience, to an executive chef for whom a food and wine budget is not the primary consideration.

Fresh local food is of first importance to executive chef Marcel Krauer. Vegetables and herbs are picked from the hotel's organic garden, local farmers and fisher folk deliver daily to the kitchen and luxury items are flown in as needed (though the hotel is experimenting in growing its own truffles!).

The restaurant is open by reservation to the public in the evenings, and Salt Spring Island lamb and local Dungeness crab are guest favourites. (In fact, Hastings House staff currently invite hotel guests to join them in pulling up the crab traps and then teach guests how to clean, prepare and cook the crab before they sit down to a dinner of crab specialties Chef Krauer creates.)

Friendly manager Kelly McAree gave us free rein to use any Hastings House recipe from a large selection in the hotel's own cookbook, and there are many wonderful ones. But we feel the recipe we chose reflects the simple elegance, luxury and time commitment of Chef Krauer's approach to food. You see, while all Gulf Island restaurants serve ice cream, Hastings House makes its own.

Hastings House has its own kitchen garden.

Hastings House, on Salt Spring, overlooks Ganges Harbour.

Hastings House Vanilla Bean Ice Cream

So simple to make, so luxurious to eat!

Ice cream was once a rare Gulf Island treat beloved by pioneer children.

"We tried to make it," remembers Bunty England, one of Pender's Elders. "Dad had a cow so we had lots of cream. We tried freezing the cream in an icebox, but it wasn't successful. We didn't know anything about cranking it, or adding eggs."

"Ice wasn't easily available on the islands," explained Peter Campbell from the Pender Islands Museum. "There was no electricity, so no fridges and no way of freezing. Island children encouraged their parents to take an occasional trip to Victoria on the twice-weekly ferry *Princess Mary*. The boat's generator ran a freezer, and the children would buy ice cream from the purser."

This ice cream makes a wonderful island dessert when topped with Wild Rosehip Jelly (page 220).

> **1 cup (250 mL) whole milk**
> **1 cup (250 mL) whipping cream**
> **²/₃ cup (160 mL) sugar**
> **1 vanilla bean**
> **6 egg yolks**

Combine milk and cream in a saucepan and stir in the sugar. Split the vanilla bean in half. Scrape the seeds into the liquid and add the pod. Bring mixture to a gentle boil over medium heat.

In a large bowl, whisk the egg yolks until thick and creamy.

Gradually stir one-third of the heated milk mixture into the yolks to temper them, and then slowly return the mixture to the saucepan. Continue stirring over medium heat until the custard has thickened and coats the back of a spoon.

Strain custard through a fine-mesh sieve into a bowl to remove any small bits of egg and the vanilla bean and seeds.

Place the bowl in an ice water bath and leave to cool to room temperature.

Pour cooled custard into an ice-cream maker and freeze according to manufacturer's instructions. When ready, transfer to a covered container and store in the deep freeze until needed.

Note: Because homemade ice cream contains no artificial stabilizers, it melts very quickly, so plate and serve it as soon as you take it out of the freezer.

Island Potluck Gatherings

The potluck dinner is a regular and enormously appreciated aspect of island life. Spend enough time on one of the islands and before long you'll be invited to arrive on someone's doorstep with a casserole, salad or pie in hand.

One island resident summed it up: "For surprising, sharing, gourmandizing and celebrating anything—a new baby, a birthday, a wedding or funeral—the island potluck beats any four-star smorgasbord." Most islanders would agree.

Haggis Farm has been running a weekly potluck for years.

We entertain each other for dinner regularly, especially in the fall and winter, so it's become usual for dinner parties to be quasi potluck affairs. Upon receiving a phone invitation, most islanders immediately reply, "What can I bring?" The host and hostess provide the entrée and all the extras, one couple brings an appie, another brings dessert and everyone brings wine. This makes dinner parties remarkably stress free.

The longest-running regular potluck gathering we've come across is at Haggis Farm on Saturna Island. John Guy and Priscilla Ewbank have been hosting a Friday night potluck at Haggis Farm for over 30 years. We turned up with a dish and something to drink, and had the choice of participating in the optional wood-fired sauna or lounging around with the dogs. Guests helped set the long wooden table, and we chatted until everyone was through the sauna. Nearly 20 people sat down to dine on a wonderfully eclectic variety of local goodies, including nettle lasagna, a vegetarian chili, warm basil and olive bread and several incredible garden salads, followed by an indulgence of cakes, cookies and freshly picked strawberry tart. The wine and herbal tea flowed, and so did the stories. The party continued as everyone pitched in to wash dishes and clean up. This was serendipitous 100-yard feasting at its best—and long may the tradition last.

On Pender one of the most remarkable potlucks we've attended was a memorial feast at the community hall. When much-loved resident and Tsimpshian master carver Victor Reece died, islanders came together and put on a magnificent potluck/potlatch. It fed not only Victor's island friends and neighbours, but over 50 off-island relatives and friends who came to honour Victor and grieve with us.

Celebrating Winter

Our Christmas celebrations often mean the house is bulging and bouncing with family members, so we began a tradition of celebrating our wonderful island friendships on Winter Solstice, the longest night of the year.

We love Winter Solstice. It is significant to mark the peaking of darkness and to know each day ahead will now lengthen. We love acknowledging the warm companionship generated by good friends getting together. We count our many blessings by breaking bread and feasting, and sharing wonderful food with ones we love. On this special occasion, we are a little more formal; we begin by holding hands around the table and end with a traditional Celtic blessing.

We each bring a short poem, reading or song about winter, and a gift to swap. (There are two criteria for the gift giving: the value of each gift must be under $20, and the gift must be consumable—that is, food or drink—for none us need any more "stuff" in our lives). The result is that everyone goes home bearing some lovely local or homemade delicacy or bottle of wine.

Sometimes our party is a large island potluck, other times a small intimate dinner, depending on who's around at Winter Solstice. Last year we did something different. As a group we invited Pender chef Theresa Carle-Sanders to create and cook a locally sourced solstice dinner for us, so that we could include the recipes in this book. Here is the result.

We invite you to recreate our solstice feast. Spread the table with a beautiful cloth, light all the candles to symbolically dispel the dark, and share the following menu with your family or friends.

Chef Theresa Carle-Sanders

"I've been cooking my whole life. I wanted to be a chef right from the get-go. I enrolled in chef school at age 19, freaked out and decided I couldn't do it. In those days there were few women chefs, and though I knew I could cook, I wasn't sure I was strong enough to stand up to the men. I backed off and went travelling for three years. Came back, got married and followed my father's footsteps into business school." She laughed ruefully. "Got swept up in business until 2001.

"Then we left it all behind … just like that! Howard and I decided 'enough of this,' left Vancouver and came to live on the islands. Took us three to four years to figure out island living though. Eventually I went off on my own to a silent retreat in Maine. I sat on a hilltop for a week, meditating … and cooking came back.

"I rushed home the first week of August, found a course starting the following week at PICA [Pacific Institute of Culinary Arts], in Vancouver. Had to move back in with my mom for six months to take it.

"Turns out that I had previously met the chef instructor. You'll never believe this. He'd had a bistro in the seventies, when I was about eight. Dad had taken me there to experience a real restaurant and I ordered medium-rare steak.

"'You won't like it,' Dad said. 'It won't be cooked enough for you.'

"I kept insisting, and we argued. The waiter told the chef what was happening. He came out and said, 'If the little girl wants medium-rare, that's what she'll get.' I'd never forgotten him, and here he was again! I graduated top of three classes and was the medal winner of that year.

"Then I came back to Pender and started Island Vittles. The rest, as they say, is history!"

Celebrating Winter Solstice Menu for Eight

Created by Chef Theresa Carle-Sanders, Island Vittles, Pender Island

Hazelnut Bisque

Makes 8 servings

> 1 cup (250 mL) local hazelnuts, shelled
> 2 cups (475 mL) whipping cream
> 1 bay leaf
> 1 clove garlic
> 2 Tbsp (30 mL) butter
> 2 Tbsp (30 mL) olive oil
> 2 stalks celery, finely chopped
> 2 medium leeks, white and light green part only, finely chopped
> 1 medium carrot, finely chopped
> Salt and pepper
> ½ cup (125 mL) white wine
> 6 cups (1.4 L) chicken stock
> Sprig rosemary
> ¼ to ½ cup (60–125 mL) sherry

Preheat oven to 350F (175C). Toast the hazelnuts in the oven until very lightly golden, about 20 minutes.

Combine the toasted nuts, whipping cream, bay leaf and garlic in a medium saucepan and simmer over low heat for 30 minutes. Set aside.

In a large saucepan, heat butter and oil over medium heat. Add the celery, leek and carrot, and some salt and pepper. Sauté vegetables until translucent (do not let them colour), and then deglaze the pan with the white wine, reducing it until the pan is almost dry.

Add the reserved cream mixture, chicken stock and rosemary. Bring nearly to a boil, reduce the heat and simmer the soup for 30 minutes.

Discard the bay leaf and rosemary. Purée the soup until smooth in a blender or food processor.

Return soup to the pan, and heat gently over low heat. When hot, add the sherry to taste, adjust seasonings and serve.

Beef Wellington

Makes 8 servings

>   4–5 lb (1.8–2.3 kg) organic beef tenderloin
>   Salt and pepper
>   1 Tbsp (15 mL) vegetable oil
>   3 bunches chard
>   ½ oz (14 gr) dried wild mushrooms (porcini or morel)
>   3 anchovy fillets
>   1 head garlic
>   Zest of 1 lemon
>   Salt and pepper
>   ¼ cup (60 mL) Dijon mustard
>   1 package frozen puff pastry, defrosted
>   1 egg yolk, lightly beaten with 1 tsp (5 mL) water

Cut the beef into 2 equal pieces and season with salt and pepper. Heat the oil in a large, heavy frying pan over medium-high heat until almost smoking. Brown the beef well on all sides, and then remove it to a plate to cool.

Remove stems from the chard and blanch green leaves for 2 minutes in boiling salted water. Strain chard and shock it in an ice-water bath to stop the cooking process and keep the bright colour. Drain chard well, squeeze out all of the moisture and chop.

Soak the dried mushrooms in boiling water for 10 minutes. Drain and chop finely.

Finely chop the anchovies, garlic and the lemon zest.

In a large bowl, mix together the chard, mushrooms, anchovies, garlic and lemon zest. Season the mixture with salt and pepper.

Brush the pieces of beef heavily with the Dijon mustard.

Overlap 2 pieces of plastic wrap over a large chopping board. Spread half the chard mixture in a rectangle on the plastic wrap. Place 1 of the tenderloins on it and sprinkle some of the chard from the plastic wrap onto the top of the beef. Use the edges of the plastic wrap to draw the chard around the fillet, and then roll it into a sausage shape, twisting the ends of the plastic wrap to tighten it as much as possible. Repeat with the other piece of beef. Chill.

Roll half of the pastry into a rectangle almost half as long again as the beef. Remove the plastic wrap from the chard-covered fillet and place it in the centre of the pastry. Brush the edges of the pastry with the egg yolk mixture. Wrap the pastry around the beef, ensuring that the pastry overlaps by at least 1 inch (2.5 cm). Finish the ends as though you were wrapping a present, folding in the sides, and folding up the ends. Repeat with the second piece of beef.

Place the pastry-wrapped beef parcels seam side down on a greased cookie sheet. Glaze all over with more of the egg yolk mixture, and chill for at least 30 minutes, or up to 24 hrs.

Preheat the oven to 425F (220C).

Cook beef for 25 to 30 minutes for medium-rare, 35 to 40 minutes for medium. Allow to stand for 10 minutes before serving in thick slices.

Baked Golden Beets

Makes 8 servings

8 medium golden beets
1 fennel bulb
1 cup (250 mL) vegetable oil
½ cup (125 mL) red wine vinegar
½ cup (125 mL) white wine vinegar
Salt and pepper
2 sprigs thyme

Preheat oven to 425F (220C).

Trim and peel the beets. Cut each into 6 or 8 equally sized wedges.

Trim and core the fennel. Slice the bulb into ¼ inch (0.6 cm) wide wedges.

Arrange the beets and fennel in an ovenproof dish.

Whisk together the oil and vinegars. Pour mixture over the vegetables, season with salt and pepper and add the whole sprigs of thyme.

Cover dish with foil and bake beets until tender, about 45 minutes. Discard the thyme and serve beets hot with the beef.

Foxglove Farm grows an assortment of beets. *Jan Mangan photo*

Caramel Pound Cake with Brandied Apples

Makes 8 servings

Caramel

    1 cup (250 mL) sugar
    1 cup (250 mL) water

In a medium saucepan, stir the sugar together with ½ cup (125 mL) of the water over medium-high heat. Then boil, without stirring, until the caramel is a deep amber in colour, about 8 to 10 minutes.

Remove from the heat and stir in the remaining water. Be careful, as the caramel will bubble up vigorously.

Return caramel to the heat and boil until it has reduced to about 1 cup (250 mL). Set caramel aside to cool to room temperature.

Pound Cake

    ½ cup (125 mL) butter, at room temperature
    ½ cup (250 mL) sugar
    2 extra-large eggs, at room temperature
    1½ (350 mL) cups all-purpose flour
    ¼ tsp (1 mL) baking powder
    ¼ tsp (1 mL) baking soda
    ¼ tsp (1 mL) salt
    ½ cup (125 mL) buttermilk, at room temperature
    ¼ cup (60 mL) caramel
    ½ tsp (2.5 mL) vanilla extract

Preheat oven to 350F (175C). Grease and flour an 8½ by 4½ inch (21 by 10 cm) loaf pan. Line the bottom with parchment paper and grease and flour the paper.

Cream the butter and sugar with an electric mixer until light and fluffy, about 5 minutes. With the mixer on medium speed, beat in the eggs, 1 at a time.

In a large bowl, sift together the flour, baking powder, baking soda and salt.

In another bowl, combine the buttermilk, caramel and vanilla.

Add the flour and buttermilk mixtures alternately to the egg batter, beginning and ending with the flour mixture.

Pour the batter into the pan, smooth the top and bake for 45 minutes to 1 hour, until a toothpick inserted in the centre of the cake comes out clean.

Cool cake in the pan for 10 minutes, and then transfer it to a rack, strip off the parchment paper and allow cake to cool completely. Wrap well, and store in the refrigerator.

Brandied Apples

4 medium apples (King, Fuji or Granny Smith) peeled, cored and chopped into ½ inch
    (1.3 cm) pieces
¼ cup (60 mL) golden raisins
½ cup (125 mL) brandy
¼ cup (60 mL) butter
½ cup (125 mL) caramel
1 tsp (5 mL) ground cinnamon
Pinch salt

Combine the apples, raisins and brandy in a bowl. Toss well and set aside to soak for 1 hour. Strain the apples and raisins, reserving the brandy.

Melt the butter in a heavy skillet over medium heat until bubbling. Add the apples and raisins to the pan. Increase the heat to medium-high and cook for 5 minutes, stirring once or twice.

Add the brandy, and reduce until the pan is almost dry. Reduce the heat and continue to cook until the apples are tender, about 15 more minutes.

Add the caramel, cinnamon and salt, stir and remove pan from the heat.

When the apple mixture is cool, refrigerate until ready to serve.

Assembly

Gently reheat the brandied apples over low heat.

Slice the pound cake into 1 inch (2.5 cm) cubes and arrange in 8 bowls or martini glasses. Top with the warm brandied apples and their syrup. Serve with Hastings House Vanilla Bean Ice Cream (recipe page 231), or whipped cream.

Andrea's version of a traditional Celtic Blessing for Solstice

May the road rise up to meet you,

May the wind be always at your back,

May sunshine fall upon your face,

May silver never be your lack,

And may your fields be blessed by a soft and gentle rain,

And may your crops be plentiful,

Until we meet again.

Andrea and David
Pender Island, 2012

Appendices

How to get to British Columbia's Southern Gulf Islands

BC Ferries

Car and passenger ferry service is available from two main BC Ferry terminals. On the mainland the Tsawwassen terminal is located just south of Vancouver.

On Vancouver Island the terminal is at Swartz Bay near Sidney, north of Victoria.

Salt Spring Island also has other connections to Vancouver Island (Crofton).

During summer and peak holiday periods booking is advised between Tsawwassen and the islands, and schedules change seasonally.

Check for current service and booking information via the website

www.bcferries.com

Float Planes

The Southern Gulf Islands are regularly serviced by small floatplanes from Nanaimo, Vancouver and Victoria.

Harbour Air

1.800.665.0212
www.harbour-air.com

Seair
1.800.447.3247
contact@seairseaplanes.com
www.seairseaplanes.com

SaltSpringAir

1.877.537.9880

www.saltspringair.com

Boating

Boating around the Gulf Islands is delightful and there are many anchorages and marinas.

International vessels visiting these islands are required to check in with Canada Customs located at Poets Cove Resort, Bedwell Harbour, Pender Island, before proceeding to other destinations. Current information is available from the Canadian Border Services website

www.cbsa.gc.ca

Further Reading

If this regional food journey inspired you to visit the Southern Gulf Islands, we would encourage you to look for books by local writers and locally produced island cookbooks. All reflect their island community and are sold locally, and some are fundraisers for community projects. By acquiring them you not only peek further into island life, but you will be directly supporting the island community you are visiting.

About the Islands

Spalding, David A.E. *Enchanted Isles. The Southern Gulf Islands.* Madeira Park, BC: Harbour Publishing, 2007. (A general introduction which includes a list of key books on the islands.)

Regional Food (General)

Levinson, Elizabeth. *An Edible Journey. Exploring the Islands' Fine Foods, Farms and Vineyards.* Victoria: Touchwood Editions, 2009.

Richards, Gail & Kevin Snook. *From Farm to Feast. Recipes and Stories from Saltspring and the Southern Gulf Islands.* Vancouver: Polestar Book Publishers, 1998.

Regional Wine (General)

Hynes, Gary, ed., *Island Wineries of British Columbia.* Victoria: Touchwood Editions, 2011.

Schreiner, John. *BC Coastal Wine Tour Guide.* North Vancouver: Whitecap, 2011.

Galiano

Benger, Huguette. *La Bérengerie. A Taste of Galiano.* 2000.

Duanaan, Allison. *Galiano Island Soups.* Blackberry Patch Publishing, 2001.

Freir, Pam. *Laughing with my Mouth Full: Tales from a Gulf Island Kitchen.* Toronto: HarperCollins Canada, 2005.

Guin, Carol, co-ord., *Food Forever Galiano Cooks. Recipes with a dash of history from the community of Galiano Island.* Galiano Community Food Program, 2010.

Mayne

Cookbook Committee. *More Favorites From the Kitchens of Mayne Island.* St. Mary Magdalene Church, 2000.

O'Brian, Helen, co-ord., *Celebrating the Apple.* Mayne Island Farmers Market Applefest, 2009.

Pender

Hacking, Wendy, ed., *Pender Cooks!* Pender Island Fire Protection Society, 2010.

Kikuchi, Arthur. *Kikuchi Family Sustainable Cooking Recipes.* Kikuchi Family, 2011. www.filestube.com/ey35AzqHm3Ogjn2g3VLzfU/Kikuchi-Family-Sustainable-Cooking-Recipes-July-1st-2011.html

Montgomery, Georgina & Andrea Spalding. *The Pender Palate. Tastes and Flavours From our Favourite Island.* Winnipeg: Loon Books/Pender Island Play Group, 1992.

Salt Spring

Ableman, Michael. *Fields of Plenty. A Farmer's Journey in Search of Real Food and the People Who Grow It*. San Francisco: Chronicle Books, 2005.

Ableman. Michael. *From the Good Earth: A Celebration of Growing Food Around the World*. New York: Harry N Abrams Inc., 1993.

Ableman, Michael. *On Good Land: The Autobiography of an Urban Farmer*. San Francisco: Chronicle Books, 1998.

Brett, Brian. *Trauma Farm. A Rebel History of Rural Life*. Vancouver: Greystone Books, 2009.

Doust, Angelique. *Hastings House Country Estate*. Salt Spring Island, BC: Hastings House, 2006.

Gabriel, Maryanna. *Memento. A Coastal Recipe Treasure*. Salt Spring Island, BC: Magic Cottage Creations, 2009.

Gilkeson, Linda. 2011. *Backyard Bounty. The Complete Guide to Year-Round Organic Gardening in the Pacific Northwest*. Gabriola Island, BC: New Society Publishers, 2011.

Jason, Dan. *Salt Spring Seeds Cookbook*. Salt Spring Island, BC: Salt Spring Seeds, 1993.

Jason, Dan. *The Whole Organic Food Book: Safe, Healthy Harvest from Your Garden to your Plate*. Vancouver: Raincoast Books, 2002.

Polden, Rodney & Pamela Thornley. *Salt Spring Island Cooking. Vegetarian Recipes from the Salt Spring Centre*. Toronto: Macmillan Canada, 1993.

Sources

We have included all the contact information of agencies which have a significant mention in the text. All information was current at the time of publication but is subject to change. To avoid disappointment, contact the businesses before dropping by—hours vary, especially in the winter months.

General

Coastal Waters (PASCO Seafood Enterprises Inc.)
1.604.244.2342
info@pascoseafood.com
www.coastalwaters.ca

SeaChoice
1.604.685.7445 x26
info@seachoice.org
www.seachoice.org

Galiano

La Berengerie
Montague Road
Galiano Island, BC
V0N 1P0
1.250.539.5392
huguette@laberengerie.ca
www.laberengerie.ca

Figaro's Garden
1.604.253.1696
figaro@telus.net
www.figarosgarden.ca

Galiano Coffee Roasting Company
1.250.539.3389
www.galianocoffee.com

Galiano Community Food Program
galianofoodprograms@gmail.com
www.galianofoodprogram.ca

Galiano Inn
134 Madrona Drive
Galiano Island, BC
V0N 1P0
1.877.530.3939
spa@galianoinn.com
www.galianoinn.com

Hummingbird Pub
47 Sturdies Bay Road
Galiano Island, BC
V0N 1P0
1.250.539.5472
hummingbirdpub@telus.net
www.hummingbirdpub.com

Mayne

Christina's Garden
www.christinas-garden.blogspot.com

Deacon Vale Farm
1.250.539.5456
don@deaconvale.com
www.deaconvale.com

Farm Gate Store
568 Fernhill Road
Mayne Island, BC
V0N 2J0
1.250.539.3700
info@farmgatestore.com
www.farmgatestore.com

Springwater Lodge
400 Fernhill Road
Mayne Island, BC
V0N 2J0
1.250.539.5521
springwaterlodge@gulfislands.com
www.springwaterlodge.com

Pender

Browning Harbour Pub
4605 Oak Road
Pender Island, BC
V0N 2M0
1.250.629.3493
www.portbrowning.com

Carle-Sanders, Theresa
www.islandvittles.com

Hope Bay Farm
1.250.629.6934
info@hopebayfarm.com
www.masselinkdesign.com/wordpress/farm

Moonbeans Coffee Roaster
1.866.442.3267
banupender@gmail.com
www.moonbeanscoffee.com

Morning Bay Vineyard & Estate Winery
www.morningbay.ca

Morning Bay has closed down its operations on Pender Island but will continue to sell its wines through its website.

Outlander Kitchen
www.outlanderkitchen.com

Pender Community Transition
1.250.629.3825
info@pendercommunitytransition.ca
www.pendercommunitytransition.ca

Poets Cove Resort and Spa
9801 Spalding Road
Pender Island, BC
V0N 2M3
1.888.512.7638
reservations@poetscove.com
www.poetscove.com

Sea Star Estate Farm and Vineyards
6621 Harbour Hill Drive
Pender Island, BC
V0N 2M1

Salt Spring

Bruce's Kitchen
3106–115 Fulford-Ganges Road
Salt Spring Island, BC
1.250.931.3399
www.bruceskitchen.ca

Bullock Lake Farm
1.250.537.2633
www.bullocklakefarm.com

Duck Creek Farm
1.250.537.5220
duckcreek@telus.net
www.duckcreek.ca

The Fishery
151 Lower Ganges Road
Salt Spring Island, BC
V8K 2T2
1.250.537.2457
info@thefisheryseafoods.com
www.thefishery.ca

Foxglove Farm and the Centre for Arts, Ecology & Agriculture
1200 Mount Maxwell Road
Salt Spring Island, BC
V8K 2H7
1.250.931.5336
accommodations@foxglovefarmbc.ca
programs@foxglovefarmbc.ca
www.foxglovefarmbc.ca

Garry Oaks Winery
1880 Fulford-Ganges Road
Salt Spring Island, BC
V8K 2A5
1.250.653.4687
info@garryoakswine.com
www.garryoakswine.com

Gilkeson, Linda
www.lindagilkeson.ca

Gulf Islands Brewery
(See Salt Spring Island Ales)

Hastings House Country House Hotel
160 Upper Ganges Road
Salt Spring Island, BC
V8K 2S2
1.800.661.9255
info@hastingshouse.com
www.hastingshouse.com

Jason, Dan
1.250.537.5269
dan@saltspringseeds.com
www.saltspringseeds.com

Mistaken Identity Vineyards
164 Norton Road
Salt Spring Island, BC
V8K 2P5
1.877.918.2783
info@mistakenidentityvineyards.com
www.mistakenidentityvineyards.com

Monsoon Coast Trading Company
1.250.537.7535
andrea@monsooncoast.com
www.monsooncoast.com

Moonstruck Organic Cheese Inc.
1306 Beddis Road
Salt Spring Island, BC
V8K 2C9

1.250.537.4987
julia@moonstruckcheese.com
www.moonstruckcheese.com

Ometepe Coffee
Available on Salt Spring Island at:
NatureWorks organic grocery store (116 Lower Ganges Road)
Rendezvous French Patisserie (126 Ganges Road)
Saturday Market (April to October) in Centennial Park
www.ometepecoffee.blogspot.ca

Ruckle Farm
1.250.653.4071
rucklefarm@shaw.ca
www.ruckleheritagefarm.com

Sacred Mountain Lavender
401 Musgrave Road
Salt Spring Island, BC
V8K 1V5
1.250.653.2315
info@sacredmountainlavender.com
www.saltspringlavender.ca

Salish Sea Chocolate Company
1.250.653.0090
info@salishseachocolate.ca
www.salishseachocolate.ca

Salt Spring Centre of Yoga
355 Blackburn Road
Salt Spring Island, BC
V8K 2B8
1.250.537.2326
yoga@saltspringcentre.com
www.saltspringcentre.com

Salt Spring Coffee Company
109 McPhillips Ave.
Salt Spring Island, BC
V8K 2T6
1.250.537.0825
ganges@saltspringcoffee.com
www.saltspringcoffee.com

Salt Spring Exotic Mushrooms
1.250.537.9129
info@
saltspringexoticmushrooms.com
www.saltspringexoticmushrooms.com

Salt Spring Island Ales
270 Furness Road
Salt Spring Island, BC
1.866.353.2383
murray@gulfislandsbrewery.com
www.gulfislandsbrewery.com

Salt Spring Apple Festival
www.appleluscious.com

Salt Spring Island Bread Co.
251 Forest Ridge Road
Salt Spring Island, BC
V8K 1W4
1.250.653.4809
www.phillipvanhorndesign.com/bakery

Salt Spring Island Cheese Company
285 Reynolds Road
Salt Spring Island, BC
V8K 1Y2
1.250.653.2300
info@saltspringcheese.com
www.saltspringcheese.com

Salt Spring Seeds
(*See* Dan Jason)

Salt Spring Vineyards
151 Lee Road
Salt Spring Island, BC
V8K 2A5
1.250.653.9463
info@saltspringvineyards.com
www.saltspringvineyards.com

Saltspring Sunrise Premium Edibles
1.250.217.0000
info@saltspringsunrise.ca
www.saltspringsunrise.ca

Soya Nova Tofu Shop
1200 Beddis Road
Salt Spring Island, BC
V8K 2E5
soyanova@shaw.ca
www.facebook.com/pages/Soya-Nova-Tofu-Shop

Saturna

Breezy Bay Farm
1.250.539.5200
saturnaherbs@breezybay.ca
www.saturnaherbs.com

Saturna Island Family Estate Winery
PO Box 54, 8 Quarry Road
Saturna Island, BC
V0N 2Y0
1.877.918.3388
thebistro@saturnaislandvineyards.com
www.saturnavineyards.com

Saturna Lamb Barbeque
www.saturnalambbarbeque.com

Saturna Olive Consortium
Michael J. Pierce
1.250.539.3758
info@olivetrees.ca
www.olivetrees.ca

Where to Find Island Lamb

Saturna

Jacques Campbell
1.250.539.2470

Mayne

Farm Gate Store
568 Fernhill Road
Mayne Island, BC
V0N 2J0
1.250.539.3700
info@farmgatestore.com

Pender

Barbara Grimmer
MacDonald Farm Store
4415 Bedwell Harbour Road
Pender Island, BC
V0N 2M1
1.250.629.3817
firhill@gulfislands.com
www.firhillfarms.com
www.thefarmersstand.blogspot.ca

Martha McMahon
1.250.629.3964
penderislandfarm@shaw.ca

Diane McBain or Ann McMullen
Whalewych Farm
1.250.629.2077
southeymcbain@tenderling.com

Salt Spring

Mike and Marjorie Lane
Ruckle Farm
1.250.653.4071
rucklefarm@shaw.ca
www.ruckleheritagefarm.com

Darryl and Sheila Windsor
1.250.653.0080
rockfarm@telus.net
www.ssiwindsorfarms.weebly.com

Check the Salt Spring Organic
Farms Brochure for a full list of
other lamb, pork and beef farmers
on Salt Spring.

Index